THE COMPLETE GUIDE
TO MODERN MANAGEMENT
III

THE COMPLETE GUIDE
TO MODERN MANAGEMENT
III

Edited by
ROBERT HELLER

2000

First published in 1995 by Management Books 2000 Ltd
125A The Broadway, Didcot, Oxfordshire OX11 8AW
Tel. 01235-815544. Fax. 01235-817188

Printed and bound in Great Britain by The Eastern Press, Reading, Berks

British Library Cataloguing in Publication Data is available

ISBN 1-85251-182-6

CONTENTS

CONTENTS

CONTENTS

CONTENTS

FOREWORD

As if companies don't face enough difficult choices in their businesses, they confront an unprecedented embarrassment of promised riches in management itself. In recent years business process re-engineering (BPR), Total Quality Management (TQM), the virtual corporation, the learning organisation, time-based competition, continuous improvement (kaizen), core competencies, organisational architecture (OA), and so on have all come to the fore.

Many of them are examined or reflected in the following pages. As top managements grasp these concepts, so they seek to install them in their organisations. That can all too easily lead to the phenomenon known as the 'flavour-of-the-month': the latest 'programme', wished on the company by top management, that will be given some fancy name, involve people in fancy training, and then, after contributing negligible benefits to the business, fade gently away into memory, to be succeeded by the next whim.

In competitive times, nobody can afford this waste of effort. As the contributions to this annual make clear, there are many crucial, practical steps that must be taken by managements which want to win – and the path is clear. Wherever they start from, whatever brand they place on their product, all the gurus end up at the same destination. They all subscribe to the idea that corporate achievement rests on maximising the contribution of individuals, not by imposing controls, but by removing restraints.

What managers need continuously is faster performance of streamlined operations to higher quality standards, leading to greater customer satisfaction, achieved by people who use their own initiatives to realise those shared aspirations. But there is no perfect system that will produce perfect results, no panaceas – things will go wrong and require correction. Flavour-of-the-month, though, leads off with the gung-ho certainty that this programme, unlike its predecessors, will achieve the wonders required by the board.

Even the word 'programme' is suspect, because it suggests a one-off initiative that will one day be complete. Any management approach worth its keep will require many years of sustained effort. If 'programme' is one bad sign, though, another is a cast-iron guarantee of failure – top management's refusal to join in the party.

11

That must harm the collective performance of the team and the system. 'System' is another key word. Any of the approaches mentioned here, and others besides, are capable of producing sharp, even lasting improvements in aspects of performance But those improvements need to be integrated with all the other processes that constitute the business system. That is not the same as the company or the unit. It goes outside their boundaries to take in the customers at one end and the suppliers at the other.

Inside the boundaries, systems thinking takes in all departments and functions that relate to whatever is in hand. Most of the new approaches depend in common on multi-disciplinary, cross-functional team-working. And here the optional element disappears. This is not another flavour-of-the-month. Such self-managed teams are accounting for more and more activity within organisations, whether top managers like it or not.

By the same token, information technology is driving companies in the directions favoured by the gurus. The IT revolution and team-working are connected – literally connected, because the networked PC is linking managers and others in ways that rule out the old methods of working. One 1993 study of 75 networks found that, once the networks are used, a company's structure starts to change. Autonomous work teams, and also strategic alliances, lead to, and are fed by, the IT network.

To exploit the microprocessor revolution to the full, managements really do need all-inclusive, system-wide concepts that deliver quickening speed, rising efficiency, increasing effectiveness and happier people – customers, employees and suppliers. Which concept is adopted is less important than obeying the rules. First, aim high and system-wide, providing a strategic vision which will give process changes the required direction and leverage. Second, insist that all senior managers believe and participate in the chosen approach.

Third, seek and win large, revolutionary outcomes fast; but within, fourth, the context of a long-term commitment to evolutionary change. Some companies have been deeply involved in TQM for a decade or more: you need time to consolidate your advances. Many companies break all four rules – and thus waste the time, trouble and cost of their reforms. As one writer has noted, 're-engineering works best in organisations where employees really trust their managers, make many of their own decisions, believe they are paid for performance, operate well in teams, share information freely, and take risks'.

The cynical response is easy: if you have got all that, who needs gurus or their preachings? To that there is only one answer. To obtain these invaluable assets, which will be more and more decisive in the competitive wars, organisations are going to need all the help they can get. The chapters in the following pages show what help is available, what it will do for companies, and where to obtain it.

Robert Heller

LIST OF CONTRIBUTORS

James Adams
James R Adams Associates
36 King Street
London WC2E 8JS
Tel: 0171 836 5012
Fax: 0171 240 9460

Richard Agutter
KPMG Corporate Finance
1 Puddle Dock
London EC4V 3PD
Tel: 0171 236 8000
Fax: 0171 832 8276

Keith Alexander
Centre for Facilities
   Management
University of Strathclyde
Graham Hills Building
50 George Street
Glasgow G1 1QE
Tel: 0141 552 4400
Fax: 0141 552 7299

Ariane Berthoin Antal
IOC-Ashridge
International Business
   Park
74166 Archamps, France
Tel: 33 50 31 5600
Fax: 33 50 31 5606

Iain Arthur
Fleming Arthur Limited
35 St James Road
Tunbridge Wells
Kent TN1 2JY
Tel: 01892 539535
Fax: 01892 536535

Martin Ashford
Deloitte Touche
   Tohmatsu
Distribution and Logistics
Columbia Centre
Market Street
Bracknell RG12 1PA
Tel: 01344 54445
Fax: 01344 860723

Mike Beard
Taylor Woodrow
4 Dunraven Street
London W1Y 3FG
Tel: 0171 629 1201
Fax: 0171 495 4653

Peter Berners-Price
Spectrum
   Communications
16—18 Acton Park Estate
Stanley Gardens
The Vale
London W3 7QE
Tel: 0181 740 4444
Fax: 0181 749 5361

Simon Bettany
National Westminster
   Bank
10th Floor, Phase 1
Kings Cross House
200 Pentonville Road
London N1 9HL
Tel: 0171 714 3550
Fax: 0171 714 3611

Clare Birks
PA Consulting Group
123 Buckingham Palace
   Road
London SW1W 9SR
Tel: 0171 730 9000
Fax: 0171 333 5050

LIST OF CONTRIBUTORS

Denis Bourne
The Management
    Exchange
Whistlefield House
Overstone Park
Overstone
Northants NN6 0AP
Tel: 01604 494567
Fax: 01604 642633

Mark Brown
Innovation Centre Europe
Winton House
Alfriston
Polegate
East Sussex BN26 5UH
Tel: 01323 871117
Fax: 01323 871118

John Bruce
Symantec Europe
Sigmas Court
Market Street
Maidenhead
Berkshire SL6 8AD
Tel: 01628 592222
Fax: 01628 592393

Will Carling
Insights Limited
106 Dawes Road
London SW6 7EG
Tel: 0171 610 3161
Fax: 0171 610 3170

Keith Crichton
BP Oil UK
BP House
Breakspear
Hemel Hempstead
Tel: 01442 232323
Fax: 01442 224873

David Clarke
Compaq Computer
    Limited
Hotham House
1 Heron Square
Richmond
Surrey TW9 1EJ
Tel: 0181 332 3323
Fax: 0181 332 3353

Meryl Cumber
Meryl Cumber
    Communications
58 St Marks Road
London W10 6NN
Tel: 0181 964 9480
Fax: 0181 964 9477

Nicky Cutts
Barton Interim
    Management
Bere Barton
Bere Ferrers
Yelverton
Devon DL20 7JL
Tel: 01822 840220
Fax: 01822 841134

Michael de Kare Silver
The Kalchas Group
Summit House
70 Wilson Street
London EC2A 2DB
Tel: 0171 638 5060
Fax: 0171 638 5070

Guy Dresser
Business Intelligence
Forum House
1 Graham Road
Wimbledon
London SW19 3SW
Tel: 0181 544 1830
Fax: 0181 544 9020

David Etherington
NatWest Bank plc
135 Bishopsgate
London EC2M 2UR
Tel: 0171 375 5000
Fax: 0171 628 5716

David Evans
Grass Roots Group plc
Pennyroyal Court
Station Road
Tring
Herts HP23 5QZ
Tel: 01442-891125
Fax: 01442-825660

Michel Barjon, Philip
    Curra, Mike Freedman
    and Lynn Verdina
Kepner-Tregoe
13 Rue de la Porcelaine
CH 1260 Nyon, Geneva
Tel: 41 22 361 2131
Fax: 41 22 362 1281

Kepner-Tregoe Limited
13—15 Victoria Street
Windsor
Berkshire SL4 1HB
Tel: 01753 856 716
Fax: 01753 854 929

Nick Fryars
c/o PA Consulting Group
123 Buckingham Palace Rd
London SW1W 9SR
Tel: 0171 730 9000
Fax: 0171 333 5050

Paul Gardner
Apple Computer
6 Roundwood Avenue
Stockley Park
Uxbridge
Middlesex UB11 1BB
Tel: 0181 569 1199
Fax: 0181 569 2957

Peter Gardner-Hill
GHN
16 Hanover Square
London W1R 9AJ
Tel: 0171 493 5239
Fax: 0171 639 9245

Peter Goldsborough
Boston Consulting Group
Devonshire House
Mayfair Place
London W1X 5FH
Tel: 0171 753 5353
Fax: 0171 499 3660

Paul Hancock
International Factors
137 Regent Street
London W1R 7LD
Tel: 01273 321 211
Fax: 01273 207 651

Richard Hawksworth
Hyperion Software
Tofthall
Knutsford
Cheshire WA16 9PD
Tel: 011565 633 744
Fax: 011565 634 154

Jean Hilder
TMS Computer Authors
    Limited
Hambledon House
Catteshall Lane
Godalming
Surrey GU7 1JJ
Tel: 01483 414145
Fax: 01483 419717

Jonathon Hoare
TBWA
8 Crinan Street
Battle Bridge Basin
London N1 9UF
Tel: 0171 833 5544
Fax: 0171 833 8751

Max Kopjin
PA Benelux/PA
    Consulting Group
123 Buckingham Palace
    Road
London SW1W 9SR
Tel: 0171 730 9000
Fax: 0171 333 5050

David Laking
Peterborough Software
Thorpe Park
Peterborough PE3 6JY
Tel: 01733 316018
Fax: 01733 312347

Klaus Leciejewski
EIM Germany
Breinnerstrasse 43
8000 Munich 2, Germany
Tel: (49) 8959 3727
Fax: (49) 8955 04067

Executive Interim
    Management
Devonshire House
Mayfair Place
London W1X 5FH
Tel: 0171 629 2832
Fax: 0171 355 3437

Simon Majaro
18a Frognal Gardens
London NW3 6XA
Tel: 0171 435 8479

Phil Parry and Bernie
    Perraud
Ingersoll Engineers
Bourton Hall
Bourton-on-Dunsmore
Nr Rugby
Warwickshire CV23 9SD
Tel: 01926 427 088
Fax: 01926 623 450

David Perkins
Carlson Loyalty Marketing
Belgrave House
1 Greyfriars
Northampton NN1 2LQ
Tel: 01604 234 300
Fax: 01604 278 74

Glen Peters
Price Waterhouse
Southwark Towers
32 London Bridge Street
London SE1 9SY
Tel: 0171 939 3000
Fax: 0171 378 0647

Brian Plowman
Develin & Partners
211 Piccadilly
London W1V 9LE
Tel: 0171 917 9988
Fax: 0171 895 1357

Colin Pugh
William M Mercer
Telford House
14 Tothill Street
London SW1H 9NB
Tel: 0171 222 9121
Fax: 0171 222 6140

Alan Roach
Alcatel Data Networks
    Limited
Norton House
1 Stewart Road
Basingstoke
Hants RG24 8NF
Tel: 01256 692000
Fax: 01256 692003

Peter Robinson
Hitachi Data Systems
Sefton Park, Stoke Poges
Bucks SL2 4HB
Tel: 01753 618000
Fax: 01753 618543

LIST OF CONTRIBUTORS

Jan E Scheers
Price Waterhouse
Southwark Towers
32 London Bridge Street
London SE1 9SY
Tel: 0171 939 3000
Fax: 0171 378 0647

Waldemar Schmidt
ISS Europe
ISS House
44—50 Bath Road
Hounslow
Middlesex TW3 3EB
Tel: 0181 569 6080
Fax: 0181 569 6607

Michael Skok
European Software
   Publishing
36 King Street
Maidenhead
Berkshire SL7 1EF
Tel: 01628 23453
Fax: 01628 33220

Ben Smith
Novell
Novell House
London Road
Bracknell, Berkshire
Tel: 01344 724000
Fax: 01344 724001

John Stanley
IMD
Pantiles Chambers
85 High Street
Tunbridge Wells
Kent TN1 1YG
Tel: 01892 548933
Fax: 01892 547120

Colin Starr
Dun & Bradstreet
   Software
PO Box 273
Kings House, Bond Street
Bristol BS99 7AL
Tel: 01272 276866
Fax: 01272 214346

Gordon Stewart
PRTM
22 The Quadrant
Abingdon Science Park
Abingdon
Oxon OX14 3BR
Tel: 01235 555500
Fax: 01235 554835

Gary Sutton
Quadrant House
Kew Road
Richmond
Surrey TW9 1DJ
Tel: 0181 332 0062
Fax: 0181 332 0054

Dominic Swords
The European Innovation
   Project
Henley Management
   College
Greenlands
Henley-on-Thames
Oxfordshire RG9 3AU
Tel: 01491 571454
Fax: 01491 571635

Kathy Tilney
Tilney Lumsden Shane
5 Heathmans Road
London SW6 4TJ
Tel: 0171 731 6946
Fax: 0171 736 3356

Eric Walters
Schroder Ventures
20 Southampton Street
London WC2E 7QJ
Tel: 0171 632 1000
Fax: 0171 497 2174

Rod Whyte
IRI Software
Foundation Park
Roxborough Way
Maidenhead
Berkshire SL6 3UD
Tel: 01628 411000
Fax: 01628 411011

Michael York Palmer
Response Marketing
York House
St Judes Road
Englefield Green
Surrey TW20 0DH
Tel: 01784 430730
Fax: 01784 438820

Peter Zentner
Strategic Retail Identity
38 Woodland Gardens
London N10 3UA
Tel: 0181 883 0535
Fax: 0181 883 8025

THE STRATEGIC
IMPERATIVES

THE LOW-GROWTH CHALLENGE

Michael de Kare Silver

Low growth and low inflation are becoming recognised facts of economic life in the 1990s. Success in these challenging times seems to centre on focus and flexibility.

As the Western industrial economies slowly emerge out of recession, the view is taking hold that traditional lessons of economic development in a recovery no longer apply. Rather, companies will find themselves in a radically different economic environment. The West will be faced with lower growth, lower inflation and a higher plateau of unemployment than has traditionally been met post-recession. On a micro-level, this translates into over-capacity, increasingly ferocious – and global – competition, and continuous pressure on prices and costs.

Annual GDP growth rates in OECD member states are expected to hover around the 2—3 per cent rate for the rest of the decade, not enough to generate significant real expansion in most markets. Consumer inflation will cluster around the 2—4 per cent range, with producer price rises just below that. Only the emerging markets will enjoy a traditional macro-economic climate, with both GDP and inflation growth rates exceeding 4 per cent throughout the 1990s.

The low-growth, low-inflation scenario seems to have taken hold across a great variety of industries, including some that have long considered themselves immune to economic trends, such as health-care and pharma-ceuticals, or wines and spirits. For leading companies in their European and US core markets, low growth and low inflation appear to be increas-ingly inseparable facts of economic life, rather than a temporary blip. This will throw up new obstacles and set an entirely different framework for decision-making.

The negative impact of low or negative growth is self-evident, yet low inflation, although generally considered desirable, also poses new chal-lenges. On the one hand, firms operate in a more stable environment, with stable input prices, which facilitates long-range planning. On the other hand, firms will have to become more disciplined. As long as prices rose, profits and pay could increase in step, if not faster. As the role of price as the most stringent arbiter of the value of goods and services is reasserted, the market will no longer allow constant price escalation of either inputs or outputs.

More important, however, the new macro-economic environment of the 1990s can catalyse companies into rethinking every facet of their busi-ness with unprecedented rigour. Many firms, faced with the challenge of increasing profits after several years of recession, have made – or are in the process of making – individually tailored steps in this direction.

Cutting costs

Procter & Gamble, for example, has embarked upon a highly publicised programme to make significant inroads into the number of brands it supports. Perhaps less well-known are its plans to cut its overheads from 14.5 per cent of sales to 12 per cent within three years through a bottom-up re-engineering effort. Overheads and sales/marketing costs, however, are not the only focus. Numerous large multinationals using high levels of bought-in components are fundamentally reappraising supplier relations. While J Ignacio Lopez has captured headlines for his activities at GM and now VW, others are following a similar path. GE, for example, is looking at reducing supplier costs for its appliance division by 10 per cent annu-ally.

Cost cutting is not the only approach, though. The bold step of demerging ICI has provided greater focus and subsequent increases in profits and stock market value. Product value-added is another area of corporate attention. Goodyear, for example, has sold more than two million units of its premium tyre, Aquatred, in two years. Although the tyre is significantly more expensive than its predecessor, radical redesign has made it a success. In addition to featuring major points of differentiation, products are also developed quicker. Chrysler's new sub-compact car, the Neon, came to market within under three years of conception.

Our own client experience has also highlighted the way that many companies are tackling the low-growth, low-inflation challenge head on. One example is a retailer redesigning its processes to such a degree that 50 per cent of its cost base can be saved. Another, completely different example, is a domestically based textiles company that is using its relatively low cost of labour to sell into Continental Europe. Its success is such that sales to Europe will have moved from virtually zero two years ago to some 25 per cent of total sales in 1994—95.

The examples cited further confirm our belief that there is no one solution – even though it may be the vogue for self-styled gurus to highlight the Holy Grail of universal panaceas. The successful firms have responded to the specific challenges thrown down by their industry and their own company's condition. What we believe characterises the successful company of the 1990s is a state of mind that is prepared, first, to reappraise everything that goes on inside the organisation and, second, to challenge established views of how the company interacts with suppliers and customers.

Chief executives have responded to the task in a variety of ways. We have closely studied three cases which demonstrate that there is no easy formula for solving the problems posed by the low-growth, low-inflation 1990s. What they do emphasise, though, is the critical importance of grasping the nettle and challenging the way in which the business has been conducted.

The watershed for Ben Rosen, Compaq's chairman, came in 1991 when the PC company made its first quarterly loss. The immediate change of culture and personnel at the top, together with a major broadening of the product range and target customer base, paid rapid dividends. During 1991—93 sales doubled, while earnings per share doubled in the single year of 1993. All of this was achieved in market conditions which have almost halved gross margins from their previous level of 45 per cent.

In 1992, when Trevor Grice became CEO at Wace, the specialist printing and publishing group, the challenge also involved recovering from losses – £28.4 million before tax on £321 million of sales. Grice's impact was immediate and non-trivial. Debt fell by £13 million, and return on sales went from a negative 8.8 per cent in 1992 to 2.9 per cent in 1993; that year the share price trebled, making Wace one of the stock market's best performers.

The performance of John Robinson at Smith & Nephew, the medical to consumer products business, is impressive in a different way. The strategic picture for health-care companies makes it clear that good growth can only be obtained at the expense of other players. That demanded a wholesale redesign of the group's strategy and tactics, emphasising innovation, global marketing and cost-competitiveness. As a result, Smith & Nephew, by outgrowing the competition, has successfully overcome flat market conditions in the USA and Europe.

The trio offer fascinating insights for all companies facing the challenge of the 1990s. At Compaq, before the corporate upheaval, management followed the strategy of being a small player in a large pool, relying on premium prices to generate large sales and profits. Today, Rosen notes that high prices may look like the way to satisfy shareholders, but believes that the appearance is deceptive. 'You have to satisfy both customers and shareholders; the relationship is symbiotic, and you can serve both masters'.

Compaq's new tactics were to price aggressively from the start – and to reduce prices aggressively as volumes mounted. The plain result is to broaden the market, which 'is better for shareholders. High margins worked to their disadvantage'. Rosen argues that 'most things in life balance'; the new strategy is founded on achieving balance in every element of the business. The past strategy not only restricted market penetration, but unbalanced the production system, because fat prices and high margins encouraged fat costs.

The switch to DTC – designing to cost – 'is one of the ways in which we have achieved remarkable cost reductions'. Under the new system, new products have to hit targets, where before 'costs used to creep upwards' as undisciplined engineers added or altered features. There was a fear that DTC, aiming at lower prices, would equate with lower quality. The outcome was 'exactly inverse'. With more integrated designs and fewer components, the computers became more, not less reliable. The results are surely conclusive: Compaq is now producing at five times the 1991 rate in the same square footage with the same number of people.

Ten Commandments

To turn round Wace, Grice applied a coherent management philosophy all his own – 'developed', he says, 'over a period of time'. It reflects his business origins: not in general management, but as a chartered accountant. Experience showed him a particular way of using 'building blocks – fundamentals that apply to any business'. These have been translated into Ten Commandments, which Grice describes as 'a way of getting through to people in terms of the process of improvement'. The improvements will show through in higher margins: he regards their management as the must role of the managing director: 'everything fits into that goal eventually'.

The Commandments direct managers toward the goal. They link together three fundamental processes. First, they speed conversion back to cash (the main means of monitoring the units). Second, they balance the cash equation and improve the planning process. Third, they improve profitability through acting on the first two of the legs (only three) which support Grice's whole intelligently simplified strategic approach. That first pair of legs are (1) costing less and (2) charging more: the third is selling more. That is 'a separate issue, most important, but the other two must be in place – otherwise things are going to catch up and hit you'.

Standing on three sound legs, you can answer Grice's key question: 'How do we meaningfully build the business?' – or rather the several businesses. The group had 70 companies to start with, and there are no plans to amalgamate units: instead, Grice has started to create clusters, companies which have enough affinity and combined turnover to sustain a financial director. The latter's job is to ensure that Grice's processes are properly installed and are also underpinning growth. The strategy for that growth revolves round 'what we can safely achieve without risk' and something else of fundamental importance to growth: 'making sure that I get it'.

At Smith & Nephew, a number of conclusions led from the basic imperative of having to outpace the competition. Robinson explains that, first,

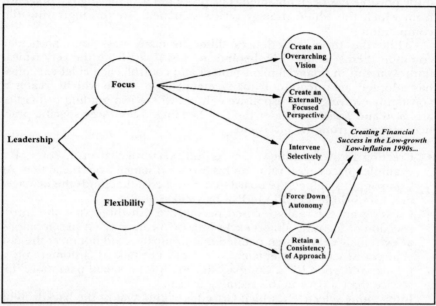

Meeting the challenge.

the group had to be genuinely international, which meant being large in the USA. Second, in key product areas it had to achieve sufficient size to support worldwide marketing programmes: that meant winning or sharing market leadership. Finally, Smith & Nephew had to be cost-competitive. With those three elements in place, the group could set about gaining share – which has clearly (and profitably) come to pass. In 1988—92, profits advanced by 32 per cent to £155 million as sales grew by 43 per cent to £858 million.

Robinson adds that sustaining this success depends on having products at least as good, preferably better, than the competition's; being regarded as a major player by the large buying groups which, in one form or another, increasingly dominate the medical supplies markets of the Western world; and selling and marketing of excellent quality. To this end, marketing programmes are no longer the sole responsibility of local managing directors. The new approach still seeks to maintain excellent country strengths, but marketing is global.

Smith & Nephew has established centres of excellence in the key areas (led by wound treatment, orthopaedic implants, and trauma and arthroscopy) to generate the marketing programmes, whose implementation for key products is obligatory. If centres of excellence are unhappy with compliance, they can report to Robinson: they have not done so yet. An annual centres-of-excellence review is designed to satisfy Robinson that all is going well. He is convinced that product growth that was not previously possible has been obtained. The proof lies in achieving the objective from which the whole strategy review stemmed: 'we're outgrowing the competition'.

While the three experiences differ in many ways, one particular common theme seems to lie behind success. Apart from the very typical improvements in financial management and control, each chief executive has adopted an uncommon management style – one which creates a constantly evolving and responsive culture, whose two guiding principles are *focus* and *flexibility*. Under the first heading, *focus*, three specific practices emerged from the interviews:

- Creating an overarching vision. As non-executive chairman, Rosen, for example, places great value on his further distance from the action. At Compaq, this helped the board to define a goal that binds the management – world leadership in PCs by 1996.
- Creating an externally focused perspective. All three view the introspection of focusing almost exclusively on a company's own operations as extremely risky. Rosen realised that Compaq could not meet the fast changes in its market efficiently if it did not talk to customers on a regular and open basis. Compaq, like many others, had paid more lipservice than service to this seeming truism.
- Intervening selectively, which Grice highlights against the backdrop of necessary management empowerment. Decisive action is vital on occasions – whether the issue is physically moving a long-established R&D centre (Smith & Nephew) or removing a CEO unwilling to change (Compaq). Readiness to challenge and dispense with sacred cows is perhaps the most critical, demanding requisite for success in a fast-evolving market-place.

Two further practices can be identified under the heading of *flexibility:*

- Forcing down autonomy. Given the need for flexibility and responsiveness, all three men view empowerment as a necessity, not a privilege, in a large global company. Robinson's annual centres-of-excellence review, for example, checks rather than determines strategy and its implementation.
- Retaining consistency of approach. Grice stresses how critical it is for evaluative criteria to be rigorously but consistently applied. In a complex company like Wace this is crucial for making meaningful assessments of the relative attractions of new investments or business. It also demonstrates even-handedness to the subsidiary managers.

Achieving sustainable financial success in these low-growth, low-inflation times is especially challenging. These three cases describe approaches and ideas that have been successfully adapted and implemented by leaders of very different styles and circumstances. Other companies will differ just as much in their situations and reactions. But the cases demonstrate one all-important general point: even in the low-growth, low-inflation 1990s, fast expansion in sales and profits can be won by appropriate strategies vigorously pursued.

Michael de Kare Silver is a partner of the Kalchas Group.

CREATIVE SEARCH FOR STRATEGY

Simon Majaro

The strategy of any business depends on its ability to satisfy customers. Creativity and innovation must become part of the firm's shared values in order to achieve success.

The search for a successful strategy is often hampered by the fact that top management is too close to the business. Clearly, the more involved executives are in fire-fighting activities and crisis management, the more the organisation needs a cohesive strategy. Hence, the strategy search concept. It involves an informal gathering of senior managers and decision-makers (usually no more than a dozen) from one organisation. Major strategic issues are ventilated and, whenever appropriate, creative techniques are used to help the participants to generate and evaluate viable routes that the company could pursue.

Participants are invited to appraise objectively the threats and opportunities that their organisation is facing and to recognise the company's strengths and weaknesses. The outcome of this analysis provides the starting-point for the development of successful corporate strategies.

One of the very surprising insights that I and my colleagues have gained from contact with top managers during such workshops is the fact that senior people do not always understand the meaning of creativity and what it can do for the firm. Nevertheless, the same people often cajole their subordinates to become more creative. The chief executive of a large

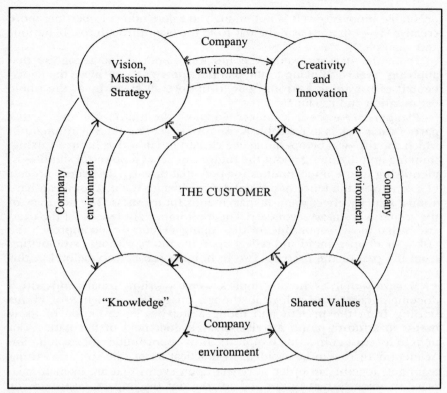

Figure 1. Satisfying the customer – the company's input: a holistic approach.
This model first appeared in an article written by the author for *European Management Journal*, June 1992

British-based multinational once expressed his attitude by saying: 'I pay people high salaries and the least I can expect from them is a modicum of creativity'. The problem is that different people ascribe different meanings to both creativity and innovation.

I define the two terms in a very simple and practical way: creativity is the thinking process which helps us to generate ideas; and innovation is the application of such ideas toward doing things better, cheaper, more aesthetically or more effectively, or both. An idea can be bizarre, outlandish, wild or even useless. On the other hand, an innovation must be useful, results-orientated, profitable or effective. Why waste time on crazy ideas? Because out of crazy ideas – the intermediate impossible – great ideas may emerge, if given a chance. History has shown that one needs many ideas to feed the innovation process. As many as 60 ideas are needed before a successful innovation emerges.

An organisation cannot, however, become more creative without a cue from the top. The sooner top management recognises its responsibility for stimulating the creative process in the firm, the sooner the firm may yield profitable innovations. It is not enough to cajole others to become more creative. The top must lead the way from the front through role-behaviour and example.

From the strategic vantage point, it is important to recognise that applying creative thinking to the planning process can achieve the added benefit of providing a strong spur to the overall creativity of the whole organisation and its climate.

Planners are essentially concerned about the future. This means that part of their task is to assemble a vision representing the environment in which the firm will be operating at a certain point in that future. Talking, thinking and dreaming about the future can act as a powerful stimulus to identifying future opportunities (or potential threats). The sheer process of gazing over the fence of present-day reality into the unknown can have a most salutary effect upon management's future vistas. The accuracy of the scenario is almost secondary. The most important feature of the exercise is that those responsible for developing a vision should approach the task with an open mind and reflect upon the future without extrapolating from the past or the present. Two techniques can be very helpful in this regard.

Scenario-writing. as the title implies, scenario-writing usually ends with a document describing a logical, though imaginary, sequence of events starting from the present and listing a step-by-step evolution of likely events to a future point. A well-conceived document of this nature can help to forecast events which offer the firm opportunities for exploitation or identify threats to be avoided. In practical terms, the scenario-writing team gets together in order to reflect upon events that are likely to take place in some distant future and to consider the impact, favourable or otherwise, which such events will have on the strategic direction of the firm. One disadvantage of this technique is that it is time-consuming and requires lengthy reflection and analysis before the appropriate document is available to the strategy search team.

Scenario-day-dreaming. This seeks to undertake the same task, but over a shorter period, and the visioning process takes place verbally. It is like a brainstorming session, but relates to the team's image of the world at a given date in the future, say, the year 2000. Each member of the visioning team is allocated a factor for exploration, such as economic trends, politics, ecology, mineral resources, and so on. Topics for reflection should be allocated in accordance with people's specific knowledge and/or expertise. During the exercise the participants must learn to catapult their thinking to a point in the future. They must talk about what is happening today in year 2000. The future tense must be avoided at all cost. A scribe records the main issues to emerge, and through an iterative process the vision is refined and the strategic implications for the company are explored in depth. Clearly, the more creative thinking is injected into the deliberations the better.

Once a vision has been assembled the team starts reflecting upon the most appropriate mission and supportive strategies. It is important to remember that the mission must reflect the firm's unique competence and strengths. It must relate to the firm's ability to excel in exploiting the opportunities that the vision has identified. In an attempt to identify creative options the following techniques are helpful:

- *The creative leap.* This method is based on agreeing collectively on what the perfect solution to the firm's aims may look like, and then working backwards with the view of identifying blockages and constraints to the attainment of such a perfect scenario. During a strategy search session this method can prove very fruitful in pointing the group in the right direction.
- *Metaphorical analogy.* The effort here is to explore creative solutions by attempting to draw parallels between the firm's circumstances and other spheres of endeavour, human or drawn from nature at large. Many exciting ideas can be derived from an open-minded comparison with what happens in other areas of the world.
- *Attribute-listing.* Where a specific product or service represents the firm's key success factor, this technique can help to enhance its quality even further. The group seeks to identify all the attributes that the product enjoys at the moment and then brainstorms about how to improve one or more of these features even further. The net result should yield a competitive advantage.

During the strategy search process the need to explore either new products or new markets often surfaces. A very useful technique for generating many ideas is *morphological analysis*. This technique originated in the complex world of astrophysics and rocket research and was the work of a Swiss astronomer by the name of Fritz Zwicky. In its simplest form, morphological analysis is nothing more than generating ideas by means of a matrix. So, for example, a matrix of two axes, with 10 items on each axis, produces 10 2 10 = 100 combinations. Make the matrix a three-dimensional cube, by adding another axis often items, and 100 2 10 = 1000 ideas.

Identifying and developing *shared values* is another important pillar upon which corporate excellence can be built. It is important for companies to articulate a set of values which reflect the firm's ethos and its well-accepted set of attitudes and code of behaviour. A set of shared values which is universally acted upon during the company's operations can provide the organisation as a whole a most powerful cutting edge. These shared values distinguish outstanding companies from the rest.

Clearly such values must be developed at the top and must be consistent with the firm's vision and mission. Moreover, their uniqueness and consistency can impart a significant competitive advantage, which is what the search for strategies is all about. Our favoured technique in this area is the metaphorical analogy already mentioned as a valuable tool in the strategy research sessions.

These search programmes were designed to help boards of directors or top strategists to explore a future direction for their respective organisa-

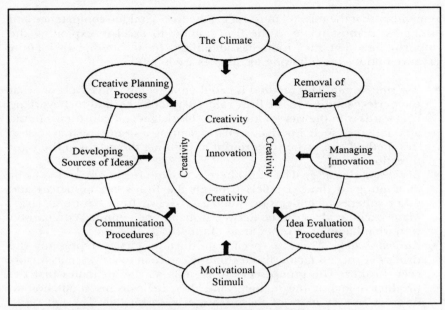

Figure 2. Creativity and innovation – an integrated approach.

tions. They have helped many companies to grapple with the need for change and, in some instances, to attain total renewal. In other instances, the process proved enjoyable but the outcome less clear-cut. Yet we discovered, almost by serendipity, a most significant result from all this work. The fact that the bosses were seen to play the creative-thinking game has had a most potent influence upon the organisation's creativity.

The news that top management was indulging in such techniques as brainstorming, scenario day-dreaming, metaphorical analogy, and so on seems to provide the most potent impetus for the rest of the organisation to behave in a creative manner. The desire to think and act creatively can easily infect the whole organisation. Indeed, what has started as a creative session at the top can easily become an all-pervasive bottom-up pressure of sustained effort at promulgating a more creative climate. In other words, the unexpected spin-off from a creative strategy search session can prove to have much wider developmental implications, though by association rather than by design.

The strategy search approach framework is based on a desire to go back to basics and look at the firm's environment in a practical and down-to-earth fashion. My basic proposition is that the success of any business depends on its ability to satisfy the customer. It is within this context that one needs to look at the various elements which can facilitate the process and help to make it more effective. Companies that fail to satisfy their customers are probably doomed. However, all this begs a number of important questions:

- Who is the customer and what exactly are his or her needs?
- Do our customers know what their needs are or do we have to know more about them than they know themselves?
- What kind of knowledge do we require to understand what would satisfy customers and their needs? Knowledge represents an added value in the firm's armoury. If one knows more about the customers' marketing and technological environments than the customers know themselves, a creative new relationship between suppliers and customers can be forged.
- Are you talking about today's customers or those of the future? Clearly looking at the whole issue from top management's viewpoint, it is the latter which is important. This is why you need a vision and mission which is anticipatory in character.
- Does your creativity help to satisfy the customers more effectively? This is a very significant question. In essence, it is only when creativity achieves a higher level of customer satisfaction that the customer acclaims the effort. Creativity per se is of limited value. On the other hand, rare is the customer who would not acknowledge with thanks the advent of 3M's Post-it notes or Glaxo's Zantac.

All these questions may help to grasp the implications of the strategy search model of creativity. It seeks to highlight the role that creativity and innovation can play in holistic system designed to satisfy customers and their needs. The four satellites, as shown in Figure 1 – vision, mission and strategy; creativity and innovation; shared values; and knowledge – are interrelated and represent the main tasks on which top management must concentrate with the aim of promulgating a successful, creative, marketing-orientated and proactive organisation. The four satellites must work in total harmony within the company's present and future environments. It is vital to recall that the main aim is to highlight the strategic context within which creative thinking can act as spur to longer-term excellence. Two important caveats must be stressed:

- The model described is only relevant in the context of firms that have adopted the marketing concept with its panoply of disciplines.
- The four elements shown as the satellites of the model must be viewed as an integrated assemblage. They interact, enrich and fructify each other. Creativity can enhance the firm's vision; a vision, in turn, can help a set of shared values to coalesce. Similarly the desire to acquire corporate knowledge can become part of the company's shared values and general philosophy. After all, in a world in which information technology is available to everybody, it would be foolhardy not to attempt to exploit such a facility to our strategic advantage.

In summary, in a marketing-orientated company, creativity and innovation can become part of the firm's shared values, thus providing the organisation with a cutting edge. When 3M talks about its so-called '25 per cent rule', it means inviting all managers to analyse their product portfolios and to ensure that, at all times, at least 25 per cent of the products under their control are less than five years old. The message is clear: you must invest time in creativity in order to innovate. This in turn becomes an integral part of the firm's shared values. Members of the organisation know what the firm expects of them. A firm that manages to slot creativity into such a holistic framework will be the winner of the 1990s. This can only happen at the instigation of top management – and it must start with the pursuit of a creative and visionary planning process.

Simon Majaro is a visiting professor of marketing strategy at the Cranfield School of Management.

CRITICAL FACTORS FOR SUCCESS

Phil Parry and Bernie Perraud

For any industry today, the critical success factors have to be understood so that companies can take needed action. Aerospace provides some global lessons.

Today, international civil aircraft manufacturing, a once-privileged club (at least for Europeans and Americans), is confronted by escalating customer pressures and intensifying global competition, notably from the Far East. It has, in effect, come of age and should now properly be treated like any other mature global industry.

Perhaps for the first time, it is exposed to the full competitive forces of cost, rapid response and minimal national differences. Doubtless there will be losers: Europe (especially in aerostructures) feels under particular threat and those suppliers in the lower tiers are at the greatest risk. These comments are not assertions. They are the headline findings of *Stacking Up to Compete,* the latest annual manufacturing survey from our consultancy, Ingersoll Engineers.

Its focus – the civil aircraft manufacturing business – is, for many economies, a critical sector. Worldwide sales for prime contractors and suppliers are estimated at $26 billion annually over the next 10—15 years. Facilitated by Ingersoll's international offices In the USA, the UK, France,

Germany, Italy and Australia, the survey was based on information from 98 chief and senior executives in 13 countries worldwide.

Including detailed analysis by region, by assemblers and by three tiers of suppliers (systems, sub-systems and piece parts), our survey set out, against a backdrop of staggered world recovery and declining defence budgets, to answer three questions:

- What are the critical factors for success in civil aerospace – both today and in five years' time?
- Are they common at all four levels of the supply chain; in other words, for final assemblers, major systems companies (for example, wings, engines), sub-systems suppliers and piece-part manufacturers?
- Most important, what actions are companies actually taking to ensure their survival and growth?

Each respondent was asked to look upwards to its customers; downward to its suppliers; and, in some of the most interesting commentary, across to its competitors. *Stacking Up*'s findings include:

- A striking similarity of perceptions worldwide, with all feeling under increased pressure from customers and competitors; all planning to demand more of their suppliers; and all believing that the top pressures today, and over the next five years, are cost and customer response
- A shift to a truly global market-place where the balance is expected to move in favour of new entrants, notably from the Far East, over the next five years
- Massively increased pressure on the supply chain, with companies in sub-systems (especially aerostructures) and piece parts particularly vulnerable over the same period
- However, little perceived threat from surplus defence capacity, except in aerostructures and marginally in systems.

Four years into the 'Peace Dividend', we are looking at an industry deprived of special protective factors and set for substantial remodelling. Indeed, our US and European Union respondents seem clear that their ability to protect future market share will vary with their success in building partnerships and commercial alliances. Newer players, meanwhile, are focused on building market share through price.

This stress on partnership by respondents is underscored by the fact that four of the six greatest anticipated increases in competitive pressures fall under this heading. They range across the board from finance (for example, product development risk-sharing) to technology (such as EDI – electronic data interchange). Similarly, customer pressure is expected to rise in 19 of 20 operational areas, with price alone (wishful thinking?) declining marginally, but scoring highest.

The next four highest customer pressure scores (rapid variant and new product development, lead-time reduction and lower aircraft operating

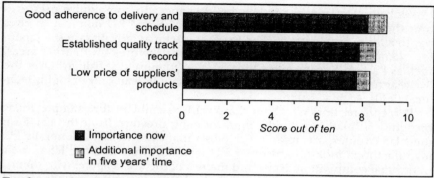

Top three requirements from suppliers.

costs) all hold ranking. However, technical sophistication tumbles from today's sixth to a forecast fifteenth. This again, in our view, confirms a mature industry perspective. So does the assemblers' forecast of declining demand for special custom features and variants. In short, our respondents foresee an increasingly integrated industry where, in effect, today's competitors jostle for position in a future, tightly knit, established supply network.

Clearly this jostling is likely to cause a fall-out and, by comparing companies' expectations of their customers' pressures against those they plan to put on suppliers, we conclude that this is most likely to happen in the lower tiers. The lower down they are, the less able companies feel to pass on pressures. In reaction, suppliers' 'to do' lists look beyond cost and response alone. They embrace market issues (such as risk-sharing and trade offsets); supply chain relationship issues (such as EDI and longer-term partnerships); and better technical support.

Perhaps not surprisingly, too, the further down the tiers, the stronger the drive toward partnership – both in terms of future risk-sharing and long-term sourcing. All three lower tiers, in fact, foresee step-change ahead. There are, however, considerable differences of degree between supply tiers. Assemblers, for example, already report the highest pressure scores (from recession-affected airline customers) and so expect least future increase. They focus on specific factors such as reduced aircraft operating costs and increased customer involvement in specifications.

The implications of this changing environment became clearer when we turned the analysis around and looked in detail at companies' expectations from their suppliers. Certainly general trends are confirmed. So low-cost and reliable delivery performance again lead the way. Closer working relationships and partnerships define the route ahead, while financial soundness stands high, as does an established reputation in aerospace. However, more specifically, major systems suppliers and piece-part manufacturers (notably in the UK) appear willing to look outside both the industry and the immediate region for new sources – a finding of considerable concern to the aerospace supply industry as a whole.

Globally, *Stacking Up* predicts rapid changes in competitive pressures over the next five years as today's reported US and EU dominance gives way to a more even pattern. The Far East is seen as moving fastest – Japan, for example, is expected to dominate in aerostructures – with other areas, such as Eastern Europe and China, also set to move up strongly. Over the five-year term, the West is expected to maintain its lead only in highly technical fields, such as systems.

Perceptions, however, differ sharply. EU assemblers, for example, today recognise a small but rapidly mushrooming pressure from the Far East: their US counterparts treat it as a substantial concern now. Generally EU manufacturers look toward other EU manufacturers and the USA, their traditional competition. Now (and the rest of the world agrees with them), they feel within sight of overhauling the US lead and are less concerned about other regions. US companies, by contrast, believe themselves well ahead, but take a more balanced view of global competition.

Treating the industry as a contest, the picture we get is of the USA setting the pace, with Europe chasing hard and the rest of the world focused, with some clarity, on what it takes to make an impact. As a result, when our respondents moved on from general perceptions to specific actions (completed, in hand, planned, and 'blue sky'), there are some marked differences of approach.

For example, to date, the USA has focused most effort on improving responsiveness – both in product development and manufacturing cycle times. It has also involved customers actively in specification development and has improved labour productivity sharply. In the future, it looks to streamlining processes, consolidating facilities and, above all and at all levels, building partnerships and alliances.

Europe, by contrast, has tackled costs – with inventory reduction particularly marked in the UK – as much as manufacturing cycle times, a possible reflection of capital scarcity. Only now is Europe moving to speed up product development cycles and to develop supplier partnerships. Formal alliance-building is positioned further ahead on the agenda. Elsewhere (again suggesting a Europe slightly behind in the industry's business cycle), its current priorities are workflow improvement issues, such as management systems and business processes.

Interestingly, when UK companies are unbundled from the European sample, they are found to be reporting, at one and the same time, the highest ratings for achievements to date and the greatest fears about future pressures. By and large, other countries stand further back in the industry's business cycle, with cost-reduction and funding the priorities, and price seen as the key competitive driver.

European perspective

The central conclusion to be drawn from our survey, then, is that civil aerospace is now a mature industry in which the critical factors are improving cost and customer response, as well as forging alliances to keep individual companies in the game. By extension, if to know equals to survive and prosper, then EU companies, having already apparently closed the gap on the USA, *might* reasonably congratulate themselves and settle back.

They should not. Both quantitatively, and qualitatively in extended comment, our survey points to an industry in which the competitive pressures are about to jump by an order of magnitude. At the same time, in the political dimension, the old cushioning special factors are being withdrawn one by one. It is in the UK that this process has gone furthest, and the fears of UK companies *should*, sensibly, awaken concerns across Europe as a whole.

Phil Parry is head of the aerospace group at Ingersoll Engineers UK.
Bernie Perraud is head of the aerospace group at Ingersoll Engineers France.

MANAGING ACROSS BORDERS

Michel Barjon, Philip Curra, Mike Freedman and Lynn Verdina

As business becomes more and more interdependent across frontiers, the need for common and effective cultures is growing.

What pointers for change can help a company to operate more effectively throughout its operations? Even a narrow geography, confined to one country, can lead to as much cultural diversity and therefore management difficulty as one spread across many countries. A Highland Scot is as different from a quintessential Cockney as a Japanese trader from an Italian, yet all four may work for the same company, and in the same office. The issue is how to ensure that each individual, in each company, reaches a state of optimum performance and satisfaction, while achieving common goals.

Jan Carlzon, former chief executive of SAS, points out that a corporate culture is created to harmonise with a company's commercial environment. 'When that environment changes, the culture usually has to change too if the company is to survive.' Kepner-Tregoe faces issues of diversity itself: an international management and consulting training company operating in more than 40 countries worldwide has its own experience of what clients require to manage cultural diversity.

Adopting a process approach to everything, we have developed a library of management tools, processes and concepts that are culture-free. They add up to a common language, style and approach for use in helping to achieve top management goals, regardless of the cultural origins of the parent company, individuals or subsidiaries. These rational processes have been applied at every level in organisations, in many nationalities, in 17 different languages, in each corporate function, as well as in every industry and government sector.

When adopted throughout an organisation, the processes provide a neutral and logical means of raising and resolving business issues. They not only gain acceptance when results are achieved, but also have the effect of team-building and providing clear focus on business activities. This avoids the normal type of task interference that comes from different habits and uniquely national approaches: time is saved and emotions are contained.

The programme for change as well as cohesion needs to centre around pragmatic methodologies that facilitate improved performance. These can be many and varied, but include such things as strategy formation, decision-making, problem-solving, project management, situation appraisal, performance system management, and so on. The applications of these methodologies are limitless. In recent years, however, they have been most frequently used to address such issues as quality and productivity improvements, cost management, results-based skill development and the management of change.

While their use helps in corporate unification, they are also a necessary (although not a sufficient) condition for effective performance. Detailed application may be more creative and elegant in one country, more analytical and straightforward in another, but they are recognisably the same processes.

The need for this common lexicon of management tools increases daily as companies become not only more international in scope and outlook, but also seek proactively to gain the benefits of cultural, ethnic and national diversity. In addition, the tools help to break down barriers and encourage management to look for similarities rather than differences between individuals. That approach is more constructive and positive, especially when significant change is needed.

It is a mistake to try to force-feed a corporate culture or values. A high degree of unforced commitment is really needed. It will be withheld unless management also provides the cement and tools with which to bind people together and to the organisation – management has got to 'walk the talk'.

Common performance system

Treating employees equitably and fairly is much easier if a common performance system is developed and implemented. Behaviours can be more accurately assessed alongside more tangible things such as business results. 'Behaviours' does not mean superficial indicators attached to national or cultural origins – like the alleged lateness of Italians or punctuality of the Swiss, the alleged creative genius of Latins versus the rationality of Anglo-Saxons. Far more important are behavioural characteristics that appear when individuals are confronting major problems, crises, decisions or situation assessments.

Using a common set of rational approaches to management issues enables management to capitalise on the unique capacities of the human brain and to overcome cultural, sociological and national differences to achieve focused cohesiveness and unity. These approaches, or processes, incorporate aspects of the logical common-sense ideas everybody uses to resolve concerns. Their strength lies in providing an efficient, systematic framework for gathering, organising and evaluating information. They build on the underlying principles of cause and effect to answer three key questions:

- Why did this happen? (Problem analysis)
- What course of action should be taken? (Decision analysis), and
- What trouble lies ahead and what can be done about it now? (Potential problem analysis).

Each process fulfils a clearly identified purpose. The choice of which to use depends on the question to be answered. In complex situations, more than one process may be needed over time. For example, when something has gone wrong, you need to find the cause (problem analysis). Once found, you can choose a corrective action that can be implemented quickly, inexpensively and with minimum personnel or material demands (decision analysis). With a choice made, you can protect its implementation by acting to forestall future problems, or at least limiting their effects (potential problem analysis).

Situation appraisal, decision analysis, potential problem analysis and problem analysis provide a common-sense approach for identifying and resolving concerns. The tools and techniques of each process are built on a fundamental framework.

Situation appraisal provides the start – a method for taking a complex or ill-defined situation and sorting it out. It does not find specific solutions. Its purpose is to clarify a concern that needs to be resolved by the other processes. It is a sensible way to approach any concern. Appraising the situation will help to manage difficult and complex issues that often defy resolution. Managers will make better use of their time – solving problems, making decisions and implementing plans – if they first use situation appraisal to:

- Recognise and clarify the concerns, considering both opportunities and threats in the list of concerns that deserve attention
- Systematically assign priority to ensure that the highest priority concerns receive the appropriate time and effort
- Determine the appropriate process for resolving the concerns: by iden-

tifying whether you have a problem to solve, a decision to make, or a plan to protect, you can make sure of using the most effective approach for information gathering and analysis
- Ensure that the analysis is undertaken in a thorough and efficient way by planning who will be involved in the resolution and what they will do.

Decision analysis. People sometimes approach decisions with minds made up. They already have a favourite alternative they want to choose. Their analysis of the facts, therefore, tends to be biased. Decision analysis helps shift your focus from alternatives to objectives, encouraging you to define carefully the decision to be made before jumping to conclusions. A more carefully reasoned decision, based on information and rational analysis, can be expected. The fundamental stages of decision analysis are:

- Clarify the purpose of the decision. State the basic goal and then set criteria that identify all the results you would like to achieve and the resources you are prepared to commit
- Evaluate a range of alternatives that might satisfy the stated objectives, and determine which alternative best fits the needs
- Assess the risks involved in choosing attractive alternatives
- Make a decision by balancing desired goals and identified risks.

Potential problem analysis. Everybody would like to guarantee success when implementing decisions and plans. Unfortunately, people usually experience problems. Potential problem analysis helps to anticipate the difficulties that might arise and determine what can be done about them. It identifies actions that can be taken to prevent problems from interfering with the successful implementation of the plan. It also identifies actions that will offer protection should the problems occur, despite all efforts. The end-result is an improved plan that can be monitored and implemented successfully. The key stages are:

- Identify future problems in areas critical to the success of the plan
- Identify likely causes of these future problems
- Take preventive action to remove the likely causes, reducing the probability that the problem will occur
- Plan contingent action to offer protection to the plan if the preventive action fails.

Problem analysis. When something does go wrong, people tend to focus on taking immediate action. But if the action taken does not make the problem go away, the efforts have been wasted. Often, you cannot take effective action unless you know the cause of the problem. Problem analysis is an efficient way to find the true cause of a problem before committing to a solution. Four stages follow in sequence:

41

- Describe the problem thoroughly by gathering specific information and organising it into a logical framework
- Identify possible causes of the problem, using knowledge and experience. If necessary, you can analyse the problem description to find other possible causes
- Evaluate the possible causes by testing them to see which best explains the facts of the problem
- Confirm the true cause by taking steps to verify questionable information about the most probable cause.

The Kepner-Tregoe processes are not a brand new way of thinking. Because they are systematic, thorough approaches to dealing with concerns, they help to gather and organise information effectively. Each process includes both a series of basic steps and additional techniques to manage complex concerns. The processes are inevitably a great help in managing complex businesses – and unifying complex cultures.

Michel Barjon, Philip Curra, Mike Freedman and Lynn Verdina all work for Kepner-Tregoe in Europe.

STRATEGIES FOR INNOVATION

Dominic F Swords

Growing uncertainty and the pace of change means that, for many businesses, innovation is becoming an increasingly important part of strategic development.

Innovation is the strategic response by organisations to anticipated change within their business environment. A European and worldwide trend toward deregulation has increased competitive pressures from new entrants in many industries previously dominated by a few global or domestically based giants. Patent legislation, especially in pharmaceuticals, is shortening the investment pay-back period on new products and may reduce the competitive advantage to be gained from undertaking basic research. Technological advances are increasingly accessible to many existing or new market players, with a reducing emphasis on scale economies. Added to these trends are social and demographic changes which have introduced new pressures on products, processes and the way in which people interact and manage at work.

'How' and 'where' of innovation

The strategic question for innovation is to identify the key forces for change exerted by the business environment and to discern the form of innovation that is most relevant to the needs of the sector. This tells the organisation the focus for its innovative strategies; it is the 'where' of innovation. Given the where, you can then plan for 'how' to implant higher levels of innovative activity into the organisation. These two elements of the where and the how of innovation are crucial to successful innovation strategies. The first sets the goals for innovation, the second the means.

The telecommunications industry in Europe and worldwide provides an example of a sector experiencing the whole gamut of pressures for innovation. Technology has been a major driver influencing the products and services available. The market-place has changed almost beyond recognition within a decade. Portable communications, faxes and multi-media are all facilities, now quickly becoming industry standards, that were only speculative possibilities in the recent past. Assisted by more accessible technologies and deregulation, new players have entered the market. Consumers, especially business users, have become alert to the possibilities of modern telecommunications and have exploited their potential for securing effectiveness and efficiency gains – exerting pressure on suppliers for value-for-money.

The strategies of existing and new players in the field have been striking. Previously dominant firms such as BT in the UK and France Telecom demonstrate the double-edged effect of dominance. While their experience in the industry has given them intimate knowledge of their customers, their established position – the legacy of previous investments, technologies and managerial structures – can cause problems as they attempt to shift strategic direction. The progress of BT has been impressive. Customer satisfaction levels and profitability have risen consistently in recent years (though not without setbacks). Investments in new technologies have been apparent, and a whole range of new business and residential services has been introduced. The integration of new business services through the telephone network in France has been under the direction of France Telecom. In the UK the market penetration of Mercury Communications in particular has been similarly striking.

BT's success

Innovation has been the reason for the success of these telecoms players. Within BT, technological and organisational innovation have run hand-in-hand. Since the late 1980s, BT's worldwide headcount has fallen substantially. Its structures have undergone several reorganisations. The aim has partially been to reduce the cost burden of over-staffing – the contemporary wisdom of downsizing and delayering. This itself requires innovations in working practices and in the assumptions people make about their roles. More fundamentally, the object has been to achieve a profile of people that matches the needs of their markets. Responsibilities have been devolved where possible. Lines of reporting have been reduced. A new culture of initiative and customer orientation has been developed and is still growing. Alongside this organisational push, technological developments have been focused and renewed. It is clear that competitive advantage will rest on striking the right balance between current applied research, producing relevant and cost-effective communications, and blue-sky speculative research that may lead to market-beating innovations from time to time.

Mercury Communication's success has been clearly associated with a keen focus on customer needs in particular market segments and making use of particular technologies. According to chief executive Mike Harris, speaking at an innovation conference at Henley, Mercury has consciously developed a relatively young workforce, led by a strong team whose members are keenly aware of market trends and developments, and are highly committed to the success of the business.

The lessons to learn from these two examples are that innovation needs to be defined broadly, and that the focus for innovation must resonate with an organisation's strategic business environment. While both UK players have positioned themselves differently, the one with an industry spread and the other with a niche focus, they have both been keen to identify key changes in the business environment and to think these through to their strategic implications. At the same time, they have sensitised the workforce to the strategic need for innovation in order to give meaning to the direction being followed. That task is perhaps more easily fulfiled in relatively small organisations than it is in market-dominating giants, but it has been an imperative for both companies.

Rover's innovative strategy

The case of Rover in the UK car industry illustrates and emphasises these points. From a poor position in the mid-1980s, the company has turned around its performance with a series of new launches in the 1990s and experienced sales growth throughout the early 1990s recession, when the rest of the European car industry experienced at best sluggish and, for most, declining sales. Rover's sustained improvement in performance has been based on innovations that were relevant to market trends and which influenced the whole organisation.

The turning-point can be traced back to the mid-1980s when Rover's strategy turned away from producing for the volume Europe market toward niche, up-market models in competition with established players such as BMW (now Rover's owner). Under the leadership of Sir Graham Day, and then George Simpson, the company moved gradually toward profitability by end-1993. Technology, investment and attention to design were all elements of the turnaround. So too was the development of innovative service elements that had meaning for customers who had grown accustomed to a relatively impersonal market delivering cars that were increasingly hard to differentiate.

The concept of 'vehicle birth certificates' was introduced. After the 'birth' when a vehicle is ordered, prospective owners are invited to visit the plant and view the vehicle through the next stages of production. More extensive customising options have been introduced. The work force is divided into work teams which enable operatives to become more involved and committed to the quality assurance process. Talking to people throughout this period has made it evident how much they understand and share the vision for the future of the business.

Research at Henley has been exploring the significance of innovation as a component of strategy and strategic planning. The findings amount to a subtle reorientation of the strategic process – a change which has a profound impact on organisations. The definition of innovation needs to be extended so that organisations are aware of the potential need for both established notions of innovation and contemporary softer forms. The strategic environment needs to be scanned and understood in terms of its impact as a source of innovative pressures. If the environment produces pressures for change, the organisational response is to innovate. Selectivity is important.

Clearly, good practice teaches that in broad terms companies need to provide new and better products or services that are cost-effective and relevant to customers' needs. At any one time, the specific needs of customers in different sectors will vary widely. The task of the strategist is to be deeply aware of currently emerging and likely patterns of change and interpret these for the organisation. Change is so frequent for many businesses, and so subtly differentiated between customer groups, that a simple nuance of understanding or quicker response time can explain the difference between a market coup and a failed project. Beyond the strategists, people in the organisation need to be aware and to understand the meaning of their organisation's strategy. This finding is an overwhelming comment by businesses, small, medium and large. It suggests that expecting people to work to internally defined goals without demonstration of their external meaning does not maximise commitment.

Best practice for many

The conclusions of research and the experience of innovation strategies are clear. The pace of change for many businesses in many industries means that innovation is becoming an increasingly important element of strategic development. Innovation is not necessarily an entirely new concept. Seen as technological development, it represents best practice for many. In a period of organisational stretch and growing uncertainty, the scope of innovation is widening and it is likely to become relevant to more and more businesses.

Innovation strategies represent a subtle reorientation of strategic thinking. Successful businesses in the future are likely to be those that see innovation in a broad sense – capable of being implanted across the organisation as needed. It is selective in its application, reflecting the needs of the strategic business environment and the internal capabilities of the organisation. An understanding of the innovatory forces present in an industry enables businesses both to set their strategic direction and also to communicate their intentions internally. This is important in ensuring that the full commitment of the workforce is harnessed. Those who manage innovation in the future are likely to be those who take hold of these insights and challenges and apply them consistently. In an environment of increasing uncertainty, this is perhaps one certainty that can be assured.

Dominic F Swords is director of studies for the part-time MBA at Henley Management College. Previous experience includes working for the economic intelligence division of the Bank of England.

USING EUROPE'S OPEN FRONTIERS

Martin Ashford and Kenneth Porter

The transport industry may still be adapting to open frontiers, but already there are several companies operating on a truly pan-European basis.

When a multinational supplier of consumer goods decided to centralise its stockholding and distribution operations for Europe at a single distribution centre in the Benelux region, this implied not simply a new warehouse, but total renewal of its existing nationally based transport deals and their replacement with a genuine pan-European transport contract. What was involved in achieving this? What obstacles had to be overcome? And what advantages were gained?

This blue-chip company has a policy of high quality and high service to support its retail customers. It supplies both small and large retailers, ranging from large national chains with their own central warehouses to specialist 'mom and pop' stores. Most products are supplied from the Far East. They have a short life-span and tend either to achieve runaway success or to stay obstinately on the shelf. In this situation, tight control of the supply chain is essential. Like many businesses, this one had until very recently maintained virtually autonomous subsidiaries in each national market-place in Europe. As well as marketing and selling, each was responsible for holding stock and arranging delivery to the retailers. The cost of delivery to customers varied substantially.

Following an extensive review of the company's logistics structure, we recommended the client to implement centralised storage and distribution of its products for the whole of Europe. The advantages included much tighter control over the supply chain, avoidance of the situation where France ran out of stock while Germany had too much, reduced incidence of unsold stocks having to be sold at discounts through parallel channels, and saving operational cost through implementation of the best storage and handling methods.

The detailed business case which supported these recommendations highlighted the savings to be achieved from these factors, but also, based on our modelling of the European transport operation, predicted an increase in transport costs caused by the greater distances involved in serving (say) Spain from Benelux, where the facility was to be located. Nevertheless, the overall result was predicted to be financially very attractive, and on this basis the client decided to go ahead.

At the time we made our strategic recommendations, we were confident that a suitable transport operation could be created to serve the whole of Europe from a single point. But we were far from convinced that the ideal solution was necessarily on offer from the transport industry. This indeed proved to be the case. The road transport industry in the European Union is highly fragmented. Deregulation, which has only come recently (and is still incomplete) in some countries, has led to fierce competition and downward pressures on prices. While a huge number of small operators eke out a precarious existence, major transport groups from a variety of backgrounds (parcel operators, freight forwarders, shipping lines and traditional truckers) are trying to build market share and extend their operations across the continent.

To build operating capability on a European scale calls for massive investment (whether in organic growth or acquisition of local businesses) just at the time when severe price-cutting has cut carriers' margins to the bone. Many have therefore sought to build alliances between themselves rather than trying to set up in all countries. There are at least three kinds of transport companies operating either on a truly pan-European footing or at least in several countries:

- Operators with a common identity in all countries and more or less standardised operating approaches. Examples might include UPS, Danzas and Nedlloyd, although the three are very different from each other
- Businesses that have invested in whole or part ownership of companies in other parts of Europe, while retaining the local brand identity of the acquisition. An example of this is the giant SCETA group from France
- Alliances of national carriers which retain their local identities but have agreed to work together and adopt some common systems. One such alliance, called TEAM, comprises Mory, DFDS, Schier Otten & Company, Sifteberti and Thyssen Haniel Logistic.

THE STRATEGIC IMPERATIVES

Our client had a strong preconception in favour of long-term contracts with just one or two carriers capable of offering a complete pan-European service. Knowing that the industry was still only gradually moving toward being able to offer this, we advised management that other approaches might have to be considered. To be entirely honest, though, we were not sure ourselves how the industry would respond to the invitation to tender that we began to prepare. One feature of this case which should be borne in mind is that the company needed operators capable of handling a lot of small deliveries (as small as just one or two cases), combined with a lesser number of large consignments, up to and including full loads. The need for parcel-type deliveries heavily influenced our selection of a long list of potential contractors.

More than 20 carriers, in part selected from those already working for the client in various countries, in part identified by us as potential pan-European carriers, were invited to attend an initial carrier-conference at which the company's plans were explained. Carriers were asked to submit a statement of their interest in bidding for the traffic. Just over half got as far as submitting a tender (a number of those invited to the briefing came together to submit joint bids, and a few dropped out).

Bid for power

The invitation to bid was accompanied by a detailed statement of the business profile. In this, we carved up Europe into a series of geographical regions, for each of which we summarised the volumes, delivery profile and other key data against which the carriers could build their price quotations. Clarity at this point is absolutely essential, whether the tender is national or international. Carriers clearly have a right both to be given clear information and to be treated fairly and equally when it comes to assessing their responses. Each bid was subjected to a detailed evaluation: all the carriers were seen by the client at this stage and given the chance to say their piece. From this process, half a dozen were selected for detailed negotiation, out of which four emerged as favourites.

Perhaps the hardest thing in judging tenders is the need to balance, as objectively as possible, both hard and soft factors. A variety of ranking criteria were devised to assist in this. But ultimately, whether or not the client feels happy about working with a given supplier is important and inevitably subjective. The hardest of hard factors is, of course, price. What emerged very clearly through the evaluation was that few carriers managed to be really credible or competitive across more than one or two countries. It has been said by others, but bears repeating, that the *pan-European transport market remains in its infancy*. So often we saw international carriers failing to offer competitive prices outside their home turf or simply not getting it together at all.

Two cases are perhaps worthy of mention to illustrate the problem. In the initial bids, two separate international alliances claimed to be linked to the same German local carrier: one of the two even insisted that it had an exclusive alliance with the German firm. This confusion was never resolved in a way that the client could consider satisfactory. The second case concerns one of Europe's biggest transport groups, which has parcels and other operations in all countries, but proved unable to tender for more than the Benelux and Germany. What use is size if you cannot manage it?

We were not surprised to have particular difficulties in the Italian market, where the fragmentation of the industry is particularly acute. Several of the major bidders failed to show credible strength in Italy. In this case the choice of a local specialist is almost unavoidable, but with preference for a carrier which can show that it is allied (and not just on paper) with a larger European group. Other factors, some harder than others, which were taken into account in assessing the bids included the systems capability of the tenderers, their ability to handle express shipments as well as normal ones, the extent of their depot coverage and simply the understanding which they showed of the client's needs.

The objective of having just one or two pan-European contractors was reassessed as the tenders were evaluated. Instead, for any given country or region, two carriers will be appointed, of which one will be given the lion's share of the business. These two will not be the same for all regions, although there will be a significant degree of overlap. Thus, to cover the whole of the EU, probably four or five carriers will be used (the final details had yet to be confirmed, at the time of writing). Over the next two years or so, as they demonstrate how they can perform, it is likely that one or two of them will eventually be eliminated. Certainly, the chosen few will have no grounds for complacency.

One of the factors that complicates the estimating of haulage costs is the degree of marginal pricing that goes on: if a carrier has an imbalance of traffic between two places, he will price at below full cost on the return leg. Despite this, the rates overall showed a close correlation to distance, particularly strong in the case of full loads. This is comforting from a modelling point of view: distance-based models may not be good predictors of cost for specific destinations, but they should be reasonably accurate in aggregate.

Cost-effective results

Our own modelling, for the original strategy, had predicted an overall increase of around 50 per cent in the haulage costs from the central warehouse to customers, compared to the current cost of transport within each country. This was expected to be balanced by some reduction in the costs of freight into the warehouse, thanks to its proximity to major Benelux ports. In aggregate, we expected transport costs to rise by some 10—15 per cent, well covered by the savings elsewhere (inventory costs, warehouse expenses, and so on).

In practice, the result has been better than predicted. The increase in transport costs to customers, caused by the extensive tendering and negotiating process, has been contained to a lower figure than had been feared, while the cost of inbound freight has been reduced further. In aggregate, the total freight bill will hardly change. This is a remarkable result, given that all parts of Europe are now to be serviced from a single location. It should enable our client to achieve cost leadership in logistics, combined with the other advantages of centralised stockholding. The transport industry may still be adapting to open frontiers, but the opportunity is there already for business to exploit them.

Martin Ashford and Kenneth Porter are members of the specialist logistics consultancy team of Touche Ross, the UK arm of Deloitte Touche Tohmatsu International.

THE CHALLENGE OF GLOBAL CHANGE

Ariane Berthoin Antal

As organisations try out new structures and strategies to meet the demands of the new world order, managers must cope with the changed global environment.

During the past five years restructuring within international organisations, especially at the level of business units, has been unprecedented. This phenomenon has been vigorously analysed and commented on. One startling, but little recognised element, is that the speed of the change process is far from uniform.

Research by IOC-Ashridge found that in financial systems, marketing and production, a significantly greater amount of restructuring across national borders is reported than in human resources. Only a quarter of respondents said that human resources had been restructured within the past five years against 59 per cent who had restructured business units; 56 per cent marketing; 45 per cent financial systems; and 34 per cent production. Given the crucial importance of human resource issues for international organisations this is, in many ways, a worrying trend. It is, perhaps, little wonder that human resource managers often now reveal that redefining their own role is a major item on their agendas.

Even though restructuring brings with it inevitable disruption and some degree of insecurity, the respondents – 181 managers working in most countries in Western Europe, as well as Scandinavia, North America, Africa, the Middle East, Australia, the Far East and South-East Asia – remain highly positive about the impact of restructuring on their work. Nearly half (46 per cent) claimed that international restructuring 'has facilitated my work' and a mere 6 per cent believe it has impeded their work. Nevertheless, it is striking that almost 30 per cent report no effect on their work.

Amid all the discussion about flatter organisations, the survey confirms that a high degree of de-layering has been carried out both at national and international levels. Interestingly, results suggest that there is much more national delayering than international. The reasons behind this require further analysis. It is also worth noting that there is no longer a universal pattern of delayering – there was some evidence of relayering. However, flatter organisations were, on the whole, regarded positively.

Clearly, the disappearance of layers of management in international organisations places even greater emphasis on high-quality communication. Interviews conducted by IOC-Ashridge in nearly 60 companies in 1992 indicated that a major area of concern among international managers is the need to promote sharing and learning across organisational and national boundaries. This was confirmed by the 1993 survey. The increased interdependence of activities in different corporate locations requires an open flow of information. Even so, companies find a number of barriers preventing employees in one part of the company from sharing knowledge with other departments or divisions.

We were eager to learn from the managers what techniques they found useful in sharing and learning across borders. By far the most important factor identified by the managers was frequent international travel. This raises some current problem areas. First, cost-saving measures often reduce travel budgets. This may have long-term consequences for cross-border communication. The reliance on frequent international travel also has the downside of placing a heavy burden on many managers and their families and private lives.

Expatriate assignments were also identified as an important means of encouraging sharing and learning – again, some companies have been trying to reduce costs in this area and will, therefore, have to develop alternatives. Previous work by IOC-Ashridge has examined some of the pitfalls of sending managers abroad. These include the neglect often experienced by managers when they return with their newly learned skills to an unchanging and unappreciative organisation.

The five rights of research

1. Get the market size and direction right.
2. Establish the company's right competitive position.
3. Pick the right target group on groups.
4. Use the right measures.
5. Ensure that you are surveying the right field.

International task forces

Some managers also regard international task forces as a useful medium for sharing. Similarly, managers who participate in in-house international development programmes appreciate the contact with colleagues from other countries. Some companies explicitly use such programmes to develop a more international culture and encourage the growth of informal networks.

There is evidence to show that companies are increasingly using internationally mixed groups, and that these often act as experiments in changing the organisation itself, encouraging greater understanding and co-operation between different parts of the organisation worldwide. Not all organisations actively promote sharing and learning across borders, though – 18 per cent of the respondents felt that the lack of action by their companies in this area was unfortunate.

Even so, the IOC-Ashridge research clearly shows a substantial growth in the international responsibilities of managers. Over the past three years, say 49 per cent of the managers, their international responsibilities had significantly increased, and 26 per cent believed they had somewhat increased. Only 7 per cent recorded a decrease. Given this, it is not surprising that many managers noted that they had increased their amount of international contact. Interestingly, although telecommunications media were almost universally used, travel and face-to-face contact were still an essential part of international contact – used by 73 per cent of the participants.

Mentoring and coaching

The faith in personal contact was also emphasised when the managers were questioned about their own development. Working in international project teams and assignments abroad of more than one year were identified as the most useful means of developing international management skills. The significant popularity and value of learning relationships with international mentors or coaches is an interesting element. We expect the use of such relationships (including peers and peer groups as well as mentors) to grow, particularly in the international sphere, as a means of providing coaching, support and challenges for managers – and opportunities for dialogue and reflection to help them make better sense of their experience.

Recognition of the usefulness of mentoring and coaching is, however, at an early stage. While 18 per cent identified international mentoring and coaching as useful, this is not reflected in the formal methods offered by organisations. Only 9 per cent of the managers worked for organisations with an organised mentoring or coaching system.

Though the demand for mentoring and coaching appears to remain unsatisfied, other development activities were already built into organisational development. While companies appear to be doing much to provide the kind of development opportunities their managers find most valuable, the identification of international potential still seems to be managed quite haphazardly. Serendipity and self-selection appear to be the dominant means by which managers become involved in international work.

Nearly half the respondents reported that their companies did not have formal systems for identifying people with international potential and many expressed concern that in the 1990s this was inappropriate. Only a small number of the organisations used more formal approaches, such as assessment centres, to identify those with international potential.

The continuing ad hoc approach to identifying international managers with high potential comes at a time when the managers and their organisations remain preoccupied with managing change. Respondents repeatedly summed up the challenges facing them as increasingly difficult market conditions; continuous change to meet ever-changing markets; a great rate of change in client companies; new technologies, a shorter product life-cycle; and increasing international competition.

Many of the changes reported by the managers focus on breaking down barriers within the organisation and on making it more efficient and responsive. Managers are certainly operating in a much tighter financial environment. Many, for example, reported a greater emphasis on cash control and cost reduction and containment – 'making the budget go further,' as one put it.

Increased responsibility and empowerment are often accompanied by a greater workload. The flattening of hierarchies heightens this effect. Typically, one manager said: 'Increased redundancies have made work much more demanding – we are doing the same with fewer people'. The increasingly tough demands of the 1990s working environment could be felt in the responses of other managers.

One reported that he was experiencing increasing responsibility and flexibility on one hand, and greater reporting discipline and integration on the other. Another summed up the change as increased paperwork, faster deadlines, more pressure, more responsibility and authority – less fun. This pressure is accompanied by increased complexity – or, as one manager phrased it, growing levels of ambiguity. Another observed that work is more diverse with many more issues on the go at any one time.

Even though the international element in the work of the managers had increased over the past three years, there was a conspicuous gap in their international perception. Relatively few cited cultural awareness as a key factor. It may be that some companies are still at a learning stage and have yet really to tackle this potential problem. Overall, however, managers registered a strong feeling of confidence that they were prepared to meet the challenges of change and internationalisation. A total of 71 per cent professed themselves to be well prepared.

Those who felt themselves inadequately prepared cited the same basic activities which they felt were necessary to enhance their readiness for international management. Most pointed to some kind of training or education as a possible solution. Language training was identified as the most valuable activity in this category.

While this research gives a fascinating insight into the attitudes and outlook of international managers, the field of organisational change and international management continues to generate many more areas which demand further research. In particular, this research raises four central issues:

- What is the relationship between organisational changes at the national and international level? Do companies tend to change both in tandem or is there really an important lag between the two?
- Considering the rapidly increasing need for international managers, how can they be identified more strategically and be developed more effectively?
- What are the key success factors for international teams as agents of organisational change?
- How can international corporations provide practical guidance for their managers that affords the necessary global vision and coherence while providing the local flexibility needed to respond to diverse cultures and markets?

Ariane Berthoin Antal is director of IOC-Ashridge.

THE TECHNIQUES OF ACHIEVEMENT

GETTING THE EDGE FROM RESEARCH

James R Adams

Companies can only get and keep that vital competitive edge by acquiring as much accurate information as possible on their competitive position, and acting on it wisely.

Success in business depends on providing customers with a product or service which they perceive to be better value for money than they can achieve from another supplier. It always has. The difference today is that customers are better educated about sources of supply, either through their own efforts, or through those of your competitors. In order to succeed, therefore, you have to know both how you and your competitors are perceived by customers and prospects, and who these people are.

Unless you are already seen as number one by all prospects, you will need to make changes in your product or service, or their perception of it, in order to make progress. If you are already seen in this way, you need to find out why all these prospects are not customers. For companies selling products and services to consumers (that is, members of the public), the use of market research is well-known and widely practised. For companies whose end-users are mostly other companies, this is less often the case. However, both types of business throw up large anomalies in their use (or lack of use) of research. For consumer studies to be useful to a company, they have to be used, and to be used, they have to be credible. To be credible, they have to be consistent with other reliable sources of information.

Internal sources, which are sometimes no more than company folklore, are usually seen to be the standard. If a market research study shows something which does not correspond with prior expectations, it may be rejected out of hand, instead of the prior source of information being reviewed. This in turn raises the double whammy often faced by researchers: if the study *doesn't* show anything not corresponding with prior expectations, what was the point of doing it? My favourite client once said 'The purpose of carrying out the study was to determine the truth. If we had already suspected what the truth was, that gives us confidence in our management. If we had not, it is very important for us to know now'. If only everyone was that enlightened!

Once, market research estimates for sales of a soft drinks manufacturer's major brand differed by one-third from management estimates; the research, not surprisingly, came under serious criticism. When we were called in to examine the situation, we found that the method which the company used to record its sales could well have produced results out by that much. The research estimate in this case had two valuable consequences: it gave management a clear view of its market, and uncovered a serious flaw in existing procedures.

The danger of historic perspectives is underlined by a recent case in the financial services area. This large company had an unbroken record of increasing sales and profits year by year ever since the past century. This record had persuaded management that all was well in their operation, and that no changes were needed (indeed, few had been made in the company's history). Only when it was pointed out that the company had been number two in the market at the turn of the century, and was now around sixtieth, were the internal figures put into perspective.

Most consumer-based companies realise that they need research, because they know that they have no direct way of getting feedback on their competitive situation. Wise managements will pay a lot of heed to their distributors – wholesalers or retailers or both – but this is no substitute for direct information. One reason is that it may be biased; the interests of distributor and manufacturer (or provider of a service) are unlikely to coincide completely. In most cases, there is a natural tendency to play back what will most benefit the distributor, which is not necessarily of most benefit to the originator.

Incorrect information?

In the second place, the information possessed by the distributor is quite likely to be imperfect. Even a retailer using EPOS, in possession of the most enormous volume of data about what products he has sold, where and when, at what price, with what promotion and in the presence of which competition, still knows nothing (from these data) about who has bought them, or why. True, markets are moving toward a situation in which many goods will be purchased with credit or debit cards, so that information about card-users can be allied to their purchases. So far this has not happened, and there would undoubtedly be cries from the Civil Liberties lobby if it did. However, even recording information of this kind is a very long way from the provision as usable management information to the suppliers of the goods. He will want to add together the information from at least six major outlets before having a reasonable guide to performance – and that is an information processing task of considerable severity.

For the business-to-business supplier, the danger of getting of touch is greater, simply because the company is manifestly in touch with its customers all day and every day, at all levels. The temptation to believe that no better information is available from research is therefore considerable. The fact is that all of this communication is biased, usually intentionally. The bias may be no more serious than that implied by the wish to have a peaceful life. Why complain if you can tolerate the situation? You can always change when a better offer is made. Brits, in particular, are notorious for this attitude: it is the largest single factor in the low international reputation of British catering.

More seriously, those charged with direct contact with customers, the sales-related executives, are likely (by their nature) to have serious career agendas of their own, and are likely to tell management what (they think) will best serve these agendas. Even if top management also has good contact with a wide range of customers (not an easy or common thing to do) they still have to rely on these customers to pick up and base on serious criticisms.

The great advantage of the professional researcher is the guarantee of anonymity given to the respondent. We recently had to stress this to the customer of a client for whom we were carrying out a satisfaction survey. When the customer was finally convinced of his anonymity, a horror story was produced. Our client would never have known about it by direct management contact; in consequence, the business would have been lost, and the fault possibly not remedied. Very few customers are reluctant to express opinions about their suppliers when this guarantee of confidentiality is given, since criticism is so clearly in their own interest. So, what positive steps should managements take to guarantee that research is providing them with the competitive edge they need to succeed?

- *Market size and direction.* It is fundamentally important to know where your market is going. Change is happening with ever-increasing speed, and there is no forecast that things are likely to slow down. Many areas have been completely by-passed by new developments, and companies have disappeared, not because they were doing what they were doing badly, but because the world moved away from them. Just think of manufacturers of steam engines, corsets, balances and butter coolers; all of them important at the opening of this century (although everyone should congratulate Price's Candles, a very old firm, which successfully changed its market from utilitarian to decorative, and has therefore survived with a new market). Then take the change from

63

valves to transistors, which eliminated one of the most expansionary industries of less than 50 years ago.

- *The company's competitive position.* This needs to be examined in a number of ways, as a matter of routine. Indeed, with many companies it already is; measures of customer satisfaction, which normally include measures of satisfaction with competitors also, account for a very significant proportion of market research expenditure in this country. It should be borne in mind that this type of study is no substitute for the first: manufacturers of electronic equipment did not stop buying Marconi valves because there was anything wrong with the company's products or service, or because someone else was providing better value valves. When commissioning customer satisfaction surveys the most important elements to bear in mind are (a) that the right target is being surveyed; (b) that the right measures are being applied and (c) that the right field is being covered. It should go without saying that the survey company must be run by members of the professional body, the Market Research Society.
- *The right target* may be less obvious than it seems. It is well known that most men's shirts are bought by women, which implies that both should be satisfied with the purchase. It is often more difficult to determine, for example, whether the most important person to satisfy in connection with a software package is the buyer or the user.
- *The right measures* will vary dramatically from one product or service group to another. In cars, to cite a classic, the advertising is of prime importance. For substances put into the mouth, no amount of clever advertising will overcome the gustatory experience. No company entering the field of measuring customer satisfaction for the first time should do so without extensive prior qualitative research, to determine what the parameters of the market-place really are.
- *The right field* is not always as obvious as it might appear, since to some extent all products and services compete for the available money with all others. It clearly may not be enough to show that your brand of conventional tea compares favourably with other brands, if your potential consumer is about to move to a herbal infusion. Similarly, there is questionable mileage in having what is perceived to be the best value in company car leasing schemes if changes in tax legislation remove the point of having company cars.

Only by obtaining the best possible information on your competitive standing, and acting on it, will you get and keep the vital competitive edge.

James R. Adams is chairman of James R Adams & Associates Limited

ADDING VALUE WITH IT

Max Kopijn

Improvement and renewal of business processes are vital to success in the current struggle for market share. IT, if managed correctly, can be supportive and add value to the business.

CEOs and financial managers increasingly ask what value IT adds to their enterprise. Although all managers in business need to know how well they are doing, surprisingly most of them have little or no idea. What is best practice in measuring IT performance, based on the needs of the dominant stakeholders in any business – owners (as represented by the CEO) and customers (as represented by the managers of the various customer departments)?

First, the IT department. Every company exists to create value for its stakeholders. So must the IT department within a company create value for its stakeholders. Two stakeholders' views of value delivered will be dominant in assessing the IT department's success: that of the CEO and his board and that of the managers of the customer departments. Typical forms of value for these groups are:

- Incremental wealth (a better investment than other uses of the same capital); this is the CEO's point of view
- The sense of getting a good deal (more than one paid for); this is the user department's point of view

The IT management process which must secure the delivery of the expected benefits to the main stakeholders is similar to any process which converts resources into outcomes. It can be shown as a closed loop system:

65

planning-implementation-monitoring-control- and so on. The aim of the process is to safeguard and drive up owner wealth through improved IT performance. The role of IT reporting is fundamental to this process.

Planning starts with owner's expectations. The only legitimate outcome from any business is a service or product which meets the customers' requirements and which they regard as value for money. All else contributes to waste. In the IT department as well the imperatives are therefore to improve performance in all aspects which impact on customers. These are the factors that drive up the value of the IT product or IT service to the customer:

- Delivery of services
- Cost of service, and
- Quality of service.

In this planning segment of the IT management process, the IT mission statement provides the link between expectations of the company as a whole (corporate) and the business planning process for IT itself. This is an enabling statement which should be developed within the framework of clearly defined corporate IT expectations. Expectations of performance and measures of value must be explicit, so that appropriate business outcomes can be identified at each level of IT management to drive up value as measured by corporate HQ.

The concept of value in the IT mission statement can be used to build a useful model around which monitoring activities can be designed. A value model identifies how much value is added top-down at each successive level of management. An example of such a model, which was developed as part of a project to introduce IT business performance monitoring for one of our clients, is shown in Figure 1.

The next level of the planning process is development of plans for the various sub-units of the IT department. These should ensure that the managers in charge of each one are accountable for the performance of their unit. The concept of accountability has been a key part of management theory since early this century. However, the focus has often been on the responsibility for administering *inputs*. This focus cannot provide the performance improvements necessary to provide a competitive edge. The focus must be one on accountability for *results*; in other words, accountability for effectiveness (actual outcome divided by planned outcome) and accountability for efficiency (outputs divided by inputs).

The success or otherwise of a business unit's or an organisation's performance can be monitored by identification of critical success factors. These are the four or five factors which are vital to unit or business success. They are usually monitored by setting and measuring key performance indicators. It follows that an external assessment is possible using key performance indicators which have been identified as the key influences which add value. Management performance at the business unit level can also be monitored by the identification of appropriate key performance

Level	Driver	CSF/KPI	Lever
Executive	Org profitability	Benefit of services	Level of investment
		Range of services	Insourcing/outsourcing
Manager of user depts		Value for money	Service received
Service agreement			
		Costs vs others	Sourcing of services
IT manager	Effectiveness of	Share of IT spend	Service policy defini-
tion			
	IT function	Comparative cost	Pricing policy
		Financial contribution	Resource levels
			Service level
IT operations mgr	Cost-effectiveness	Costs vs budget	Resource allocation
		Reliability	Methods/tools
			Training
			Staff
IT development mgr	Development speed	Time to in-service	Project scope
		Resource utilisation	Methods/tools
			Training
			Staff

Driver is what the stakeholder tries to maximise. *CSF* is the critical success factor. *Key performance indicator* (KPI) is how the stakeholder measures success. *Lever* is what the stakeholder is able to control.

Figure 1. Example of a value model.

indicators at each level.

The critical success factors and key performance indicators are closely related to the value drivers which increase value at each level of the value chain. The key performance indicators are in fact the measures of value added at each level. It should be obvious from the preceding paragraphs that these key performance indicators for IT cannot be set in isolation by the IT department's staff A project steering committee has to be formed, on which both the key IT customers and the key IT resource providers are represented. This committee is usually chaired by the financial director of the company and reports directly to senior line management. Key performance indicators do not stand alone. Often standards exist against which KPIs can be compared. These standards should be based on best industry practice for the particular indicator in each business unit.

The second element of the management process loop is implementation of the strategies and unit plans which support the corporate IT plan. The principal outcome which the IT management is expected to achieve is improved business performance and added value for its customers. The management challenge is to achieve these outcomes by motivating and leading the IT staff to meet customer requirements continuously, with the most efficient and effective use of capital, labour and materials, usually at the least cost.

The third element in the IT management process loop is to monitor activities. Management performance must be monitored against the business outcomes which have been identified as value drivers in the value chain. IT business performance monitoring (IT-BPM) is put in place to

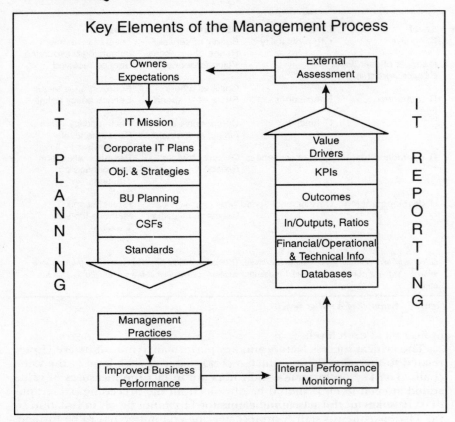

Figure 2.

provide information to managers at each level on the value drivers or key performance indicators. It is designed to enable managers to monitor, review and take corrective actions on those factors which are critical to their success.

The structure of IT-BPM is shown on the right-hand side of Figure 2. The information for monitoring and controlling the outcomes of the programme are the key performance indicators or value drivers shown at the top of the chart. These will measure the effectiveness of the corporate IT function in meeting its objectives. However, management will also need to know how efficiently the various units of the IT department are performing and, to measure this, ratios of outputs to inputs will be needed. The base data to drive the IT-BPM may come from the databases and operational systems already in place, as shown at the bottom right of the diagram. It is our experience however that, although most companies have an abundance of technical and financial data on their IT, only a small part of that is meaningful in a business sense. These systems may therefore need to be revised, or new systems may have to be created.

The final element in the IT management process loop is control. Management reports are the link between monitoring and corrective action. IT reporting that does not lead to corrective action by management will have no impact on IT business performance. The time and cost spent on data collection, measurement, systems development and computer capacity will be wasted if corrective action is not the final outcome of the IT reporting. The IT-BPM reporting formats are therefore designed to highlight priority issues which are affecting performance and to invite corrective action. The reports are designed to raise questions in the mind of the manager concerned; for example:

- Scorecard questions (how does actual performance compare with planned performance?)
- Attention-directing questions (what are the priority issues which should be the focus of management attention?), and
- Problem-solving questions (what is the best of several alternative ways to improve a result?).

Formats are used to illustrate the dynamics of the business in a cause and effect chain of outputs leading to the value driver for that level. Outputs and inputs are carefully matched. Reporting timescales are chosen to match the likely response times of each factor and the decision needs of each level of management. A mixture of financial, physical and technical data will be required for management reports. Graphical methods are used to show trends in key performance indicators and input/output sensitivities.

A return to the planning element completes the IT management process loop. Regular review sessions must be held to discuss each unit's performance against plan, and to agree priorities and a future action plan. These sessions must be action-oriented, not a witch-hunt to apportion blame for past mistakes. The prime purpose of the IT management process loop is to drive the business according to plan. Feedback is the control mechanism. Corrective action is the way to improved performance.

The management reports from IT reporting provide the basis for regular review of current issues and future direction by a manager and the management team at the next higher level. The action-oriented meetings provide the critical forum for communication between managers about real issues based on factual information about the business. They play an important role in team building and management development.

Max E Kopijn is a management consultant with P A Benelux.

TOTAL INNOVATION MANAGEMENT

Mark Brown

Total innovation is the process of putting ideas into action for increased profitability and performance. The question is, how do you achieve it? There are four simple stages.

Total innovation can be defined as 'putting ideas into action for increased profitability and performance'. It can apply equally to a product, a process or a procedure. What, therefore, falls under this umbrella? TQM, continuous improvement, customer care, cost management and other such quality-type initiatives are all focused attempts at total innovation. Some of them may have their own built-in 'glass ceiling'. Terms like continuous improvement suggest the principle of doing things better – that is, evolutionary changes – and may exclude much-needed revolutionary changes; that is, doing things differently.

The focus for various popular initiatives (some might say fads) will continue to change. However, the underlying need for tapping the intelligence of people throughout the organisation, and empowering them to translate that intelligence into action, will not change.

Four simple stages

So how do you achieve total innovation? A simple and practical way for thinking about generating ideas and putting them into action. is to think of four simple stages – goals, ideas, selection/control and action. Minds begin to tick once they are presented with a problem goal or an opportunity goal. Many individuals, unfortunately, only begin to think once they are presented with a problem: cloudy, overcast *grey* day.

Less often, people try and seek out an opportunity – *white* thinking – like white light, which is omnipresent, yet very difficult to see. Once a goal is suggested, you start to generate ideas, coded *blue* for blue sky thinking. You then start to select among the various ideas. *Red* thinking captures this selection/stop phase (red traffic lights), the time to stop, think through the implications, run your ideas up against various decision criteria. Lastly, minds and bodies act on those ideas: *green* for go. So you have a goal, which can be white or grey, blue ideas, red selection/control and green action.

Individuals may show some preference for different parts of the ideas into action process. For example, you may be drawn more to the blue/ideas phase, or the red/selection or the green/action phase of thinking. A strong, divergent blue thinker may see the more applied red convergent thinker as a barrier. The other way round, the red thinker may see the blue as unrealistic and pie in the sky. Blues and reds in their turn may see greens as impulsive and headstrong. Greens may feel that blues and reds waste interminable time in purgatorial meetings. Once you begin to reflect on the question of which colour is most important, you realise that they are all equally important. It is only together that these colours create the synergy for turning ideas into action. Together they can create total innovation. At the team level, the colours also have a major role. Many teams fail to differentiate between information-sharing meetings, on the one hand, and creative problem-solving meetings on the other. In creative meetings later, the teams can work more effectively by consciously distinguishing between, and moving through, the blue, red and green phases.

Organisational profiles

The full process is: GISA: goals, ideas, selection/control, action. But many organisations are stronger in one stage than in others. An ISA organisation is 'all dressed up with nowhere to go'. Here you have an organisation without vision, or at least without a vision that can be simply and effectively communicated. In contrast, in a GIA organisation 'every idea is foolhardily actioned'. This is a more dynamic profile perhaps, since there is a vision and there are ideas – and all these ideas are translated straight into action. This profile may suggest a younger organisation, perhaps an entre-preneurial start-up.

With GIS, 'the whole is less than some of the parts'. This is a disem-powered organisation which cannot take action. This profile is present in many large organisations. Though there are many talented individuals, the output from the whole is stunningly disappointing. When you probe beneath the skin of such an organisation, you usually find that managers feel they are powerless to change things.

Individuals say that, although they may have many good ideas, they feel incapable of translating them into action because of the company, the system, the boss, marketing, finance, and so on. In such a powerless environment, individuals point an accusing rigid digit at other departments, functions or simply at the organisation. A good indication of how disempowered people feel is the way in which they describe their organisation – as though there is some monolith that actually exists.

Clearly an organisation is no more than a legal figment. All that actually exists is a number of people and perhaps some technology. Sadly, the hierarchy and the culture of many organisations leave people feeling that the problem with getting ideas into action is they, them, the organisation. The fascinating question is: how can you change the culture so that, every time individuals point that accusing rigid digit away from themselves, they are spontaneously reminded that there are always three fingers pointing back at them, asking the question 'what can *you* do to make things happen?'

GSA means no ideas. This is the most common profile I find in organisations. The very spark that originally gave birth to the organisation has faded. Although it has a clear vision, excellent control and high-action orientation, the culture does not stimulate or reward creativity and innovation. Imagine a new, naive manager attending his or her first management meeting in such a red culture. They may fail to realise that the organisation reinforces the safer act of red critical thinking. The blue individual may hold forth with some new ideas only to find that the culture is a master at idea assassination. Different organisations have their own polite or impolite ways of 'yes...butting' ideas.

What will such a new blue thinker do following an onslaught of red critical thinking? There are just three choices: turn red, leave the organisation, or move sideways into human resources!

Ideas into action

So how do you organise to put ideas into action? I have had painful experiences in several organisations when encouraging individuals and teams to act in more creative and empowered ways. In these companies, as there was no top-down blessing for such an activity, I ultimately came to see such interventions as counter-cultural and largely unhelpful, both to the individuals involved (except perhaps personally) and to the organisations. For instance, a large leisure company invited me to help them do a blue trawl. The aim was to stimulate a wealth of business ideas focused around customer care and service.

We ran a range of structured creativity sessions, some helped by a new piece of creativity software entitled *Brian* that I and another client organisation had developed. Several months passed before the complaint came back that, although there was now a flood of ideas inside the organisation, managers were literally drowning in the sheer volume. We generated too many ideas and we had also failed to find sponsors, champions and homes for them. This is a problem inherent in many suggestion schemes.

A board may request the formation of a think-tank or new product development teams. In such cases, the goal to be tackled is defined fairly clearly by the board/top team and then passed to the blue/red team which has appropriate skills in a range of analytical techniques. The teams themselves may not act, but they may make suggestions or recommendations. Think-tanks have been created to find innovative solutions for a wide range of products and services from submarine design and repair through to new kinds of foods.

GISA model

Following the leisure company client's criticism that we had flooded the organisation with ideas, it invited us to create and help implement a mechanism to put the ideas into action. In this case, the mechanism was focused on the quality of customer care and service. We produced the GISA model, now the basic formula that has been implanted in other client organisations. Usually the board/top team decides on the legitimate focus. All natural work teams then generate their own problem and opportunity goals relevant to that focus.

Teams can use a range of blue creativity and red *thinking tools*. They then take their ideas through to action. Usually a strong emphasis is put on empowerment. When we first experimented with this approach, we had never heard of that word. Undoubtedly, however, the teams not only became excited about executing ideas, they began clearly to identify much more closely with their own organisation – 'we are the company'. Blue, red, green teams in various organisations have been developed for many different purposes:

- Customer care
- Improving communications
- Turning corporate values and vision into a way of life
- Stimulating quality and ingenuity
- Salvaging failing quality initiatives
- New product development.

Some initiatives have been far more successful than others. A critical factor is situational empowerment. Think of the following continuum:

- Total disempowerment/no-go areas
- Mainly disempowered/yes, then go areas
- Partially empowered/go, then inform areas
- Totally empowered/go areas.

No-go areas speak for themselves. In the same way that people are disempowered from driving on the wrong side of the road, there are certain rules which you must either keep or not violate. If you do violate these, especially if this mistake is repeated, you will be justifiably fired. 'Yes, then go' means that you are transgressing some basic principle or practice and therefore need clearance before you can proceed. 'Go then inform' describes the situation where it may be appropriate to let your manager know. Go areas are those for total empowerment.

If ideas-into-action teams are going to be successful they need to understand both as teams and as individuals what parts of their jobs fall into each of these four categories. They especially need to know which are the ideas that they can carry through straight into action. Their zone of control must be very clearly established. This is not to say that some teams won't operate outside those zones of control; for example, in the case of business process re-engineering. It is simply that the BPR teams will probably be making recommendations rather than acting directly on many of their ideas. Initiatives are much more likely to succeed if creativity and empowerment are clearly established within a framework. Without such a framework, you tend to encourage chaos.

Mark Brown is managing director of Innovation Centre Europe.

DIFFERENTIATING FOR CUSTOMERS

Brian Plowman

A differentiating customer proposition is not a set of management clichés about customer care; it is a framework that leads to real corporate transformation.

Today's excellent companies have mostly followed a well-trodden path: TQM, team building, re-engineering, and so forth. These approaches are rapidly becoming commodity items: at best, one can only hope to improve at little more rapidly than competitors. At worse, they are solutions in search of a problem.

We advocate a different starting point: the differentiating customer proposition (DCP). This is a transformational concept. It is not a set of management platitudes or clichés about customer care. It is a unified approach that forms the basis for a new approach to the management of external positioning and internal capability. The concept of a DCP is much more than good intentions and fine ideals. It represents a framework for the whole organisation, the values that drive it, and the belief that the organisation has in itself and what it seeks to achieve.

The threat and opportunity in business today is the new dimension of the discerning customer. For many sectors, customer service has become the serious contender for the position of major differentiator, even where the obvious choice has traditionally been through the intrinsic quality of the product. People have become educated to recognise that they are

75

customers and, as such, have become aware of their status when dealing with organisations which have remained steadfastly ignorant of their need to treat the service receiver as a customer.

The change in focus has been dramatic and the implications far reaching. Standards of acceptable service do not appear to be sector-specific. Customers have a basic set of standards that can be reset by any organisation and transferred as a need to other organisations. The implications for any business are that just to watch competitors in your own sector is to risk missing a change in customer needs or expectations that has been created by someone outside the industry.

Market segmentation

Most service businesses are still at the pure functional stage of market segmentation. Banks look at consumer groups by age, social class, salary, number of cheques written, and size of overdraft. Railways look at frequency of travel, fare paid, and destination point. It is this kind of analysis which leads to special savings accounts, budget fares, and so on. There is nothing mistaken with any of these 'slices', but they are functional slices which do not embrace a relevant, motivating customer psychology. These may lead to cost-effectiveness from the supplier's point of view, but are insensitive from that of consumer psychology.

A vast amount of effort has gone on into Customer Care or Putting People First programmes, and so on. The initial focus was aimed primarily at changing the behaviour of operators, shop assistants and other people in regular customer contact. While claiming some success, many of these programmes served only a superficial purpose, many ending by alienating both staff and customers.

Customer expectations were raised, but the processes failed to deliver consistently. Staff knew in their hearts what issues plagued the customers, but lacked the empowerment to influence the processes outside their control that would truly create customer care. The issues that staff cannot normally influence are interdisciplinary, or require high-level decisions, or are enmeshed in organisation politics, or are outside the comprehension of those in ultimate authority. Beware the company charter issued to customers and the exhortation of the vision statement issued to staff.

The heightened awareness of consumers, both in making value judgements and through societal trends, will mean a greater need for external orientation of businesses and faster response to emerging changes in attitudes, global issues and legislation. Similarly, there will be increased accountability to customers in terms of providing information, being accessible, dealing with complaints, and providing proper service. A company will need to encompass both the consumers' interest in the product or service itself, and the consumers' greater interest in the company as a whole. This trend will raise the leverage that corporate reputation exercises on influencing consumer choice.

Consumer uncertainty and changing trends create opportunities for new products and services which provide clear differentiation. What will not work in the future is special offer price discounting, reducing tangible quality to reduce prices, or cutting back on support values such as customer service. There will be a shift to purchasing value, where the criteria that make one product or service valuable will be different for another; but generically, value will need to represent real additional benefits to customers. It is in this area that positioning will impact on the company's capability; its own values, attitudes and beliefs, and the systems and processes that deliver the end quality to the customer.

When people first make contact with a company they are prospects. After a purchase they are customers. If nothing happens to upset them, they may become supporters. Up to this point, companies are vulnerable. Much cost and activity may be wasted if a prospect is not converted to becoming a customer. As a customer, and at any stage in that relationship, the way the company treats customers can drive them away into the hands of a competitor. Although customers may not find that things are better elsewhere, in the meantime they are lost. When the relationship with customers is only at the level of supporters, customers are still tempted away through competitor pricing or perceived better service.

The vital next step in the relationship is to make them advocates. These are customers who tell other members of the family, their friends, or other businesses, that the company is the best. Advocates stay, which is far cheaper than trying to replace customers who have left. The final step is for both parties to see each other as partners.

Both partners then win as both perceive and get value. For the supplier, the key is to add value to the customers' lives or businesses. This is something different from selling them products or providing a standard service. This is all about understanding, even predicting, a customer's real needs in an environment of total trust. This condition is very fragile and can be quickly eroded if the company falls back to its old ways.

Meeting the needs of external customers, and creating a relationship that bathes them in a warm glow, raises the issue of hygiene and motivating factors. Many examples exist where the distinction has not been recognised by the company, leading to unnecessary changes to process capability. Also, factors that motivate customers initially become industry standards over time and change to being hygiene factors. Again, not recognising the transition will have companies focusing their capability in the wrong directions.

Hygiene factors:

- Only need to be achieved
- Meeting them causes an absence of dissatisfaction
- Meeting them does not cause positive satisfaction
- Meeting them causes no contribution to differentiation
- Not meeting them causes a state of irritation, often beyond the supplier's comprehension.

THE TECHNIQUES OF ACHIEVEMENT

Motivating factors are very different:

- Exceeding them leads to customer delight
- Experiencing them leads to recommendation and advocacy
- Experiencing them can outweigh a degree of poor delivery on hygiene factors
- Not experiencing them is a lost opportunity to notice differentiation.

For hygiene factors, over-exceeding expectations will tend to increase customer expectations in areas that are not competitive differentiators. Costs go up without any appreciable increase in customer satisfaction.

Parts of processes that deliver hygiene factors are generally easy to measure. What gets measured gets done and becomes the key influence on behaviour. Setting numerical targets and performance-related pay schemes are the insidious barrier to delighting customers. They serve only to focus staff on the internal measures that satisfy management. Motivating factors delight with the unexpected. They tend to be cultural issues which arise from allowing staff the flexibility to use their judgment; the basis of trust and empowerment.

Vision statements

Many companies have a vision, often expressed as a simple phrase, which is intended to unite employees and point the way forward to a better world. But why is it that these simple statements generally fail to polarise the whole company into action, break down barriers, inspire, win commitment, improve performance, delight customers, or create growth?

Many vision or mission statements fail to meet this intent because they imply a clarity of management thinking, a sense of direction, and a commitment to action that do not exist in practice. They may also espouse values that are not part of normal management behaviour, and are therefore unrealistic. Too often vision statements are exhortations where the real need is to formulate a strategic plan that will take the business forward. We prefer to replace the word vision with the differentiating customer proposition (DCP).

The DCP is not a set of management platitudes or clichés about customer care or being the best. It is not a treatise of good intentions and fine ideals. In contrast, it is a framework that leads to genuine corporate transformation through recognising the crucial link between an organisation's positioning and its capability and making changes through a series of pragmatic steps.

Thinking holistically

In our experience, companies are so close to the workings of their own businesses that they can have difficulty in imagining how customers perceive the company. Real differentiation, customer retention and advocacy come from presenting customers with a proposition that goes beyond any found through a customer-needs survey. To some extent, there is an element of risk associated with innovation. However, a far greater risk comes from professing to the public a given level of service before the organisation has the capability to deliver it. This is the problem that has dogged charters and made victims of customers and staff alike.

From our experience, it is seldom possible for an organisation to make the transition to its DCP directly. The journey needs to be taken in two steps.

Step 1, involving everyone in improving current processes, involves the elimination and reduction of waste in current processes, and removing the barriers to cross-functional management of business processes that are ingrained in functional organisations. This step is also driven by the need to address failures to meet current customer aspirations; those failings found through the mechanism of a customer-needs survey or through acknowledging a move ahead in service by a competitor. The result of this stage is to improve short-term effectiveness so that the company can meet current customer needs.

A company's major asset is its people. The people manage and work in the processes and know when they are going right and when they are going wrong. The people may not know all the causes of their problems, but they will be spending time on dealing with the symptoms. Their time is valuable, they want to do a good job, but often the process defeats them. Through their involvement in improving the current processes, the organisation gains the spare capacity which enables it to reallocate resources and improve the relationship with customers. Through involvement, pride in workmanship, at all levels, is restored. Through involvement, commitment is gained and implementation of change accepted.

The primary objective of Step 1 is to examine all or part of a company's processes and to develop implementation plans to improve efficiency and effectiveness. In overall terms, the key drivers for change could be cutting costs while simultaneously improving quality and current customer service. Step 1 provides a burst of activity that brings out the major proposals for process improvements and uncovers many minor irritations caused by local process failures. Implementation of the proposals from Step 1 needs to be absorbed into the transition to a state of continuous improvement.

Step 2, delivering a differentiating customer proposition (DCP), involves changing the capability to meet the long-term positioning of the business. This requires both market research and innovation by senior management. The resulting positioning may demand significant change to internal capability, and therefore substantial redesign of the whole business in terms of processes, organisation, competences, technology and culture.

The DCP must lead to customer retention and customer advocacy, providing a total service where being a customer is to value the relationship. The relationship creates a delight factor that has a value to customers greater than the sum of the traditional constituent parts of the products and services. Building a partnership relationship is thus the challenge and will require a different way of treating the customer.

The DCP must include the dimension of accessibility; access determined by customers, convenient to them, locking out competitors. Traditionally, many companies talk of distribution or delivery channels. On closer inspection, these often turn out to be mechanisms put in place for the convenience of the business. In recognising this, companies will need to look at all the places where customers are and what they may need at any time. This knowledge will determine when and how the company will always be accessible to its customers. Meeting this challenge will be another building block in growing the business.

Structural changes

The DCP must encompass the internal framework of the entire business and all its processes; a lowest unit cost business that is also a real pleasure to work in. Conventional ways of operating and organising businesses are an impediment to making the proposition a reality for customers. It is clear that companies will have to shed many of the previous constraints that conventional structures impose on a business, put behind them feelings of functional parochialism and start again. Structural changes will be a key difference between a company and its competitors and will account for much of the success of making the DCP a reality.

Using a green-field approach to developing the organisational framework will be the way to overcome some of the old prejudices. The principle of lowest unit cost is established by rebuilding the organisation, starting from the customer interface, and then only including added-value activities aligned in processes with minimum hierarchy, with a management framework of help and facilitation.

The key is to think innovatively, with all employees being brought into exercising their minds on creating the overall propositions which may be valid to support the DCP. At this stage, they would only be ideas resulting from a burst of innovation. However, staff facing the customers, once they are released from the shackles of rules and mistrust that so often characterise the environment in which they have to work, are generally very good at knowing how to build all the components together.

Procedures put in place in the interests of standardisation and efficiency can confuse some customers and leave others feeling patronised. The implications will have a profound effect on the nature and degree of empowerment that staff can use to deliver the proposition.

In any programme of change much is heard about top-level commitment, and the need to review the business fundamentally. On hearing these words, why is it that staff treat them with cynicism and scepticism? They have heard it all before. Staff want to put their trust in the senior team. After all, just like the senior team, the staff want job security and to be able to take pride in what they do. Staff cannot make the business go in a new direction, but they are often driven to take the business in directions contrary to the long-term building of customer retention and advocacy. Despite their better judgement, the measures that drive their behaviour constantly leave them victims of lack of trust and short-term profit generation at the expense of customers.

Is there a choice?

The changes that need to take place can be limited to just tinkering with current processes to meet current customer needs. However, to make a real difference through to the end of the decade and beyond, companies have to become something different both in the proposition they offer customers and the way in which the processes deliver the proposition to customers. Maybe, nothing short of corporate transformation is the destination managements now have to contemplate.

But if, through complacency, managers are already confident that everything can stay as it is, they have a choice. They can do nothing, and only later discover that they are on a journey to obscurity.

Brian Plowman is a director of management consultants Develin & Partners. His book on the subject, High Value, Low Cost, *is published by Pitman Publishing.*

THE IT OF BETTER CUSTOMER CARE

Clare Birks

To succeed in Europe, many companies need radically to improve their standard of customer care. Along with better organisation and rationalising processes, IT is a key enabler.

The Single European Market opens up significant business opportunities (and threats!), containing more than 300 million people in 12 states and growing, with more than 60 per cent concentrated in a triangle in the north-west. The largest 50 companies in Europe command together 12 per cent of the total expenditure on goods and services. How can companies succeed in this competitive market? More and more are concluding that the quality of customer care will be the key.

In some industries, customer service and total quality programmes have been common currency for several years. These early programmes drew their inspiration from global competition in manufacturing, particularly in the motor industry, and the pressure has been double-edged, *to improve service at the same time as reducing cost*. The 'cost of quality' argument has been compelling – flexibility and responsiveness have been shown to cost a lot less than the traditional approach of maintaining buffer stocks and excess capacity. Improvements on a global scale have been possible. As Ford has found with its world car programme, however, breaking national barriers takes time and investment. Targeting Europe rather than the whole world makes transcending national boundaries no easier.

Where should you start in thinking radically about customer care? We use the word care to distinguish this concept from customer service simply because we see that the opportunities to add value to the customer (and hence gain advantage over competitors) arise well before the need for post-sales service, which is the traditional domain of customer service. We include in the definition marketing activities designed to find out how customers and prospective customers think and feel about products and services, and to inform them about what choices are available and what to take into account when choosing. We also cover sales activities, including the often-maligned order-processing function, along with billing, handling complaints, spares, after-sales service, training, hotlines and even (in some industries) product disposal and recycling.

Telecommunciations brings many innovative opportunities. The number of users of Internet is growing at a compound 10 per cent every month, and advances in market research and buying from home will clearly follow. Doctors working in remote areas can consult medical specialists through networks which offer images of the patient and the problem, remote discussion of shared X-ray images and video conferencing for the consultation process. Only a little way down the track are domestic fuel meters intelligent enough to provide information (both ways, to customer and to supplier) and other services, such as energy management. Voice systems are used in public access services such as telephone directory services and timetables.

The choices are wide. With a broad definition of customer care, it can be difficult to know where to start. In the early days of service improvement initiatives, many companies worked on the basis that they had to improve all aspects of service at the same time. The realisation dawned for one of PA's clients, a major European consumer goods manufacturer, some months into the programme, that this approach was rather a blunt instrument. Interviews with the retail outlets selling the company's products, carried out for other purposes, showed that the retailers and the final customer had strong views about quality of service, views which differed significantly from the premise on which the service improvement initiative was based.

Reliability

Not everyone put a high value on rapid delivery, for example. For some, it was much more important that delivery came reliably, when promised. The company had assumed that, when customers called out a service engineer, they would want the engineer there very quickly. It became clear that what customers wanted was to make rational choices for themselves about how much they were prepared to pay for an appropriate level of service – in some cases they would pay highly for an emergency response; in others they wanted the option of a cheaper, slower service. The company was able to refocus the initiative and related investment in systems to those aspects of service with the greatest impact from the customers' point of view.

83

Indeed, the impact of focusing on improving things that do not matter to customers can be negative. The emphasis placed by British Rail a few years ago on improvements in rolling stock were derided by passengers who would have much preferred to see the company concentrate on a more reliable service. The new rolling stock should, of course, improve reliability because of fewer breakdowns, and need less maintenance; but that was not how the case was presented to passengers. These examples show that there is a strong need for careful research and testing of customer care ideas before swinging into action. This is especially important where there may be national differences in perceived value. National differences show in a wide variety of ways – witness the French preoccupation with the health of their livers, and the marked differences in the acceptability of suppositories in medicine across Europe.

More choice

Perceptions change over time, too. Remember how much value was placed on the solid, heavy, high-quality engineering that carried many German and Swiss companies, including Siemens, Leica and Landis & Gyr into the forefront? Compare that with the current value placed on lightness, mobility and rapid upgrade to the next model. Perceptions about service will also change, almost certainly in the direction of the customer wanting more and more choice.

There is still significant scope for tailoring the care package, including product, service, routine maintenance, billing, payment and other options, to meet the individual requirements of customers. This can be costly in the first instance. That is why private banking is exclusive and why some choices are only available to commercial, rather than retail, customers. But usually over time, the special facilities available to companies (for example, itemised telecommunications bills) do filter down, courtesy of IT systems, to retail customers as well. Competitive pressures, resulting from deregulation, changes in tariffs or fundamental shifts in the economics of the industry speed up investment in IT to support customer care. What companies hope is that they can:

- Increase the speed of response
- Minimise the number of encounters with the company customers need in order to achieve their purpose (for example, it should take one phone call to fix a time for an engineer to visit and one visit to effect a repair)
- Maximise the value of each encounter – for example, when engineers visit to repair a fault, they can also carry out routine maintenance; or when customers call the telephone banking service, they can arrange for standing order, payment of bills, production of statements, and so on, all in the one call to one representative
- Provide a service closely tailored to customers' needs – for example, narrow delivery or appointment bands to reduce waiting

- Reduce cost by careful resourcing of both staff, spares and other materials. Only one in five calls by an engineer was successful in one telecommunications supplier until the process was redesigned and queueing theory was used to establish the optimum resourcing pattern.

The changes being put in place involve technology, process redesign, reorganisation, and changing the skill profile and the culture of the company. They are complex. However, as customer expectations are raised by the provision of better service in the market-place, every company must plan to keep making improvements. The company must make an informed judgement about whether to tackle service improvement on a Europe-wide basis or approach the task first within its home country. The latter route secures the core business and allows the organisation to learn from the experience before embarking on a geographically more ambitious programme. However, time may be of the essence in securing or growing market share in an overseas market; so it may be important to start where the problem is most acute. The essentials are to:

- Set appropriate targets for customer service, which will deliver the business results needed
- (Re)design customer processes to 'script' each encounter so that the company can ensure that maximum value is provided
- Define the new competencies required (for example, the role of backroom staff metamorphoses into telephone sales) by reskilling or recruitment
- Define a new organisation structure to manage the process, often cutting across existing organisational boundaries
- Put in place the appropriate IT support, which normally focuses round a shared database of customer information, and often round networks enabling a staff member or a customer to carry out a variety of tasks from remote locations.

The skills issue is a very real one. A back-office role confined to processing paperwork requires a markedly different set of skills from a telephone-based customer care service where strong communications and maybe sales skills are required. On some estimates, such a person can be asked to tackle any of up to 30 subjects and is expected to answer 90 per cent of the questions. The skills required derive from the way the customer care processes are designed and the performance targets set.

Some years ago, it was believed that, to make any headway, the company had to have a corporate customer database. However, many companies foundered on that rock, committing themselves to projects with ever-increasing forecast expenditure for little return. In retail banking, it was not unusual to find that a customer database project was planned to cost well over £200 million. But technology has moved on. There are now many more ways of developing interfaces and providing access to customer information.

IT support

This means that it is now possible to consider, first the designing of the various customer care processes (say, sales, complaints) in an integral way with the necessary IT support, perhaps provided by local systems. That gives the opportunity to tailor the process and the system to national or other customer preferences to meet local performance targets. From PA's work with more than 50 clients on customer care, it is apparent that each business must define and develop its own customer care initiative to obtain the best from the excellent market opportunities which the wider Europe unquestionably offers.

Clare Birks is a partner of the PA Consulting Group, in computers and telecommunications.

ADDING VALUE IN MANUFACTURING

Gordon Stewart

High value added or high EVA can give companies superior performance in terms of financial stability and operating costs. How does a company improve its added value?

The management concept of value added is making something of a comeback. Management focus areas in the past decade have included managing balance sheet debt, reducing the threat of unfriendly takeovers, and re-engineering business processes. As a result, there is a renewed emphasis on deploying capital to maximise shareholder value.

The idea of value added, normally meaning the difference between net product revenue and the cost of external purchases of materials and services, was first promoted and became popular as a measure of company performance in the 1970s, most particularly in the financial community. Expressed simply, this concept involves looking at the value added by a business in the process of converting materials bought in at one value to a product sold at another value. The difference in financial terms is referred to as value added, and gives a comparable measure of productivity across different companies within an industry or industry sector.

It has long been recognised that different industries exhibit different levels of value added. In a basic industry which converts raw materials into intermediate materials, and applies capital and labour to produce a finished product, there is typically a high level. Examples might be a steel

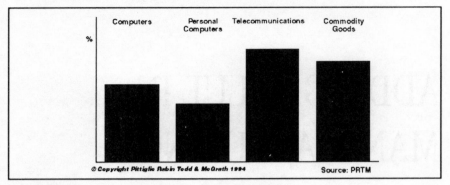

Value added as a percentage of revenue (industrial average).

foundry or primary chemicals manufacturing plant. In other industries such as computers, where a high percentage of the product is bought from other suppliers, value added as a percentage of total revenue may be lower.

The recent re-emergence of value added in management thinking is partly due to the application by economists and others of economic value added (EVA) in relation to the maximisation of shareholder value. EVA measures returns on the cash invested in a company as one of the costs of adding value, by determining first the true cost of capital, and then how much capital is locked up in the business.

The management looks not only at expenditure on raw material and other direct purchases, but also at the total financing cost of fixed assets, inventories and other elements of working capital in a business, to determine the real value added. This methodology says that, of two companies which are able to carry out the same conversion or value adding process, the one which uses less capital in the form of plant or machinery, or invests less in inventories and work in process, is the more efficient.

Pittiglio Rabin Todd & McGrath (PRTM) conducts an annual supply-chain performance benchmarking study, which generates a comprehensive set of fact-based performance measures. These measures have been developed in close co-operation with the study sponsors, who include some leading world-class technology-based companies, and can be used to describe accurately world-class supply-chain performance. These benchmarks are used by industry leaders to gain a broad supply-chain-process perspective, and to quantify their own performance improvement opportunities across the entire supply chain.

This study has measured value added across a number of technology industry sectors over the past three years. While it has confirmed that value added varies between industry sectors, the study has also shown that value added also differs markedly between best-in-class (top 20 per cent) and industry average companies within the same sector.

Our supply-chain performance benchmarking study also shows that, in addition to value added as a percentage of revenue, the figure per employee or per dollar of wages paid within the business also varies greatly between one company and another. So if high value added or high EVA is what gives companies superior performance in terms of financial stability and operating costs, how does a company go about looking at improving its added value?

Supply-chain performance

This question was put to PRTM by a client in the aggressive, tight-margin personal computer industry. There had been a dramatic increase in the volume of computers being built. But as volumes grew, because of higher level integration within components and sub-assemblies, the value of bought-in assemblies had risen in relation to the selling price of the computers. The incorporation of this new technology had reduced not only the financial value added, but also the number of people and amount of space required to build the same number of computers.

The plant had reached a position where, despite remaining very successful because of the increased volumes being produced, it nevertheless found itself with surplus space in its large modern manufacturing facility. The question which now had to be resolved was how (viewing this space as a capital cost) could the company best make use of and add value in that surplus space within its overall supply chain?

In looking at the role of the plant within the supply chain, PRTM sought to identify and evaluate alternative business opportunities, and develop a detailed evaluation of the best one or two. To do this, we first established a profile of the building, encompassing space, layout, access, construction parameters, permitted and prohibited uses, the cost to occupy and the date from which it was available.

We next developed a view of the plant's current and future roles in the client's supply chain and order fulfilment, in terms of key external suppliers and supply points, and its current ship-to role. We were then able to identify those key areas of value added in this supply chain which were not being carried out at the plant, and the extent of value added currently performed by external sources. Each of these external activities was evaluated in terms of what benefit would accrue to the client if it was located in the plant, and what would have to be done to bring that activity on site.

All the business opportunities which initially appeared to be feasible were examined within the scope of a 'synergistic model', which can best be conceptualised in a supply-chain sense as comprising activities upstream or downstream of the plant's product assembly operations. Upstream activities are those which happen before material comes into the plant. They include, for example, bare board manufacture, printed circuit board assembly, and the assembly of monitors and keyboards; in other words, the things which other companies undertake in supplying components to our client. We sought to determine what difference it would make to the value added through that plant if any of these activities were instead carried out by our client, or executed on a partnership basis with individual suppliers willing to co-locate their manufacturing within the plant on a joint-venture basis.

Downstream activities included the loading of country- or customer-specific software, integration of CD-ROM into the unit, country-specific keyboards and documentation, and anything which might be done specifically for one customer or to configure products for specific markets. For example, PCs that can be purchased in a retail store are typically a different configuration and carry different features from those which are supplied through business channels. PRTM examined whether this client could put more value added into the plant by carrying out some of these downstream activities on the same site, or perhaps by integrating them into the production process.

We defined the most desirable feasible alternative, or synergistic option as that which would, in extending or developing the plant's key processes, deliver the highest value added and also support a trend toward more flexible (mix and volume) manufacturing. A total of eight synergistic options were identified; a number were upstream activities, though some were downstream.

Each option was recharacterised with regard to its impact on the plant, in terms of reduced cost of product, reduced cost of carrying inventories, improved flexibility, improved customer satisfaction and therefore potential impact on revenue. Each option was assessed from the perspective of how it would impact the value added in the plant, either by improving the revenue line or reducing the cost line, or by reducing the cost of capital employed in the conversion process, primarily through reducing the inventory required to support the process.

Having characterised each of the eight synergistic options, and assessed their impact on the plant, we then assessed the attractiveness and degree of difficulty the plant faced in implementing them. This process took account of the characteristics of the plant, level of expertise or familiarity with the technologies involved, management capabilities, the proximity of suppliers or supply base, and the proximity of markets.

After making these assessments, PRTM then assigned a score for the attractiveness and degree of difficulty in implementation for each of the eight synergistic options. This we plotted on a matrix. The bottom left-hand corner of this matrix represented the least desired range. Any alternative which fell clearly within that area did not represent an economically viable option for the client, because it had low impact on value added and was difficult to implement. By contrast, anything which fell within the top right-hand corner was deemed to be highly attractive, because it had high expected value added and was relatively easy to implement.

Based upon this initial evaluation, which took four weeks to conduct, we were then able to identify three viable options very quickly for the client to evaluate in greater detail. Within another four weeks we had identified a clear strategy for one of those options. On the basis of the rational approach to the project, and rational elimination of options which had appeared to be alternatives for many months, corporate management was rapidly able to agree to the local plant's strategy in terms of enhancing value added through the plant, and confirmed funding for new investment. Implementation of that strategy is now under way, thus securing the plant's future within the overall worldwide supply chain of the corporation, and enhancing the plant's role in improving value added for the corporation.

Gordon Stewart is director of Pittiglio Rabin Todd & McGrath.

THE FUNCTIONS OF QUALITY

Garry Sutton

QFD systematically translates customer requirements into suitable company strategic requirements and actions, through a planning model and discipline known as the House of Quality.

Quality function deployment, or QFD, is a contemporary and powerful planning tool, pioneered in the Japanese ship-building industry, and popularised by Toyota. The tool has its roots in Japan, but its use is not restricted to Japanese companies. You can forget, from the outset, the notion of the mystique of Japanese culture providing the unique recipe for the success of yet another proven and powerful tool.

The only cultural ingredient essential to the successful application of QFD is an organisational culture which positions the customer as its primary point of focus; prizes and promotes the benefits of organisation integration; invests in, involves and believes in its people; has management stamina – a determination and belief in the quest for continuous improvement. Significant competitive advantage, the product of QFD, can be available to all.

There is no single, definitive description of the term quality function deployment. It can be summarised as: a process which systematically translates customer requirements into appropriate company strategic requirements and actions. The process extends throughout the total spectrum of a business activity, from research and development through engineering and manufacturing to marketing, sales, distribution and service. Think of QFD as the means of taking the voice of the customer into product development cycles, on to the factory floor and out into the market-place. It is not a discrete quality tool – it is, to repeat, a powerful and highly disciplined planning tool.

The primary objective of QFD is to fulfil the needs and requirements of the customer through a proactive and preventative, rather than reactive, approach to the development of products. This type of development approach seeks to fulfil and, indeed, anticipate customer requirements by focusing on rigorous planning and problem prevention in the product and process design stages. This results in fewer production problems and reduced resource requirements for fire-fighting production crises. The benefits of this approach can be illustrated using the quality lever. Assume that improvements made in production realise a payback relative to effort of one-to-one. If the same improvement were made in the process design, the payback would be in the region of 10:1, and improvement in product design would yield a return of 100:1. The payback improvement in process and product design is realised through the planned prevention of problems.

Clearly, the absolute values will be somewhat subjective, but the concept is indisputably correct. The focus on preventing problems at the earliest stages of product and process development is significantly more cost-effective than fixing product, process and customer satisfaction issues once the product is in the market-place.

Paradoxically, companies in the West typically acknowledge and reward fire-fighting efforts in production – the work of 'macho manufacturing man' – in inverse proportion to the implied benefits of the quality lever. Quite simply, in a traditional manufacturing environment chief executives and managing directors recognise and relate to the hard-working manufacturing and production directors, who labour until midnight on a Friday to meet the week's shipment commitment, or the supervisor who reschedules all jobs on the shop floor to meet a special order deadline.

In contrast, the considered approach of a design engineer working with a manufacturing engineer and production manager to predict and head off new product problems proactively is neither sufficiently visible or adequately rewarded. As a consequence, companies will need to realign management and organisational attitudes to acknowledge the value and true contribution of prevention being better than cure.

Identify customer requirements

The basic approach of QFD is one inherently pursued by manufacturing companies around the globe. It requires customer requirements to be identified and translated into production requirements. The fundamental problem with customer requirements, though, is that they are often vague:

'I want it to be easy to use'; 'I want it to feel good'; 'to last a long time'. Traditionally, this customer input will flow from the sales representative or marketing manager into the factory with no mechanism to convert the desire into manufacturing reality.

QFD is just such a mechanism. Translating the voice of the customer into product and service solutions is systematically achieved through a planning model and discipline known as the 'House of Quality'. So named because of its shape and format, this is arranged to progress systematically an initial customer requirement into the ultimate product and service solution. The QFD process works through the houses of quality to deliver consistently a necessary focus on listening to and acting in accordance with the voice of the customer. The house of quality contains:

- *What.* The list of customer requirements
- Potential design requirements needed to satisfy the customer requirements
- *Relationship matrix.* This matrix assesses how the design requirements will potentially impact the customer requirements. These inputs are highlighted by placing symbols at the intersection of the 'whats' and 'hows' which are related. Common symbols stand for: strong relationship; medium relationship; weak relationship
- *How much.* The fourth key element is units of measure or target values which represent how good you have to be to satisfy the customer. These target values are again a Japanese concept. They are used by companies to set performance goals for key characteristics or attributes. Target values often exceed exact customer specifications with the aim of delighting the customer and leap-frogging the competition
- *The correlation.* A triangular table – 'the roof of the house'
- *Matrix.* Establishes the correlation or impact of each 'how' item. Again symbols are used to illustrate the nature of the correlation: strong positive; positive; negative; strong negative
- *Competitive assessment.* A critical feature of the QFD process. Competitive assessments should be considered in two key areas. A competitive customer assessment, secured through interviews or surveys, will be used to assess relative performance versus the competition in relation to the 'whats' – the customer requirements. The second competitive assessment is a technical one in which the product attributes and characteristic target values are compared to the competition. This is typically obtained through product tear-downs
- *Importance rating.* This is the critical step in establishing the priorities on which the organisation will work. A rating is assigned to each 'what'. This is normally on a relative scale (1 to 5 or 5 to 10). The higher the number, the greater the importance to the customer. To satisfy the customer requirement, however, you must take action on the hows. To ensure that an organisation focuses on the correct priorities, importance ratings must be calculated for the latter.

To achieve this, weighting is assigned to the relationship symbols: strong 9; medium 3; weak 1. The weighting achieves a distinct variance between important and less important items, thus defining the priorities for action. The calculation is straightforward – for each 'how', the 'what' importance value is multiplied by the symbol weight. This produces a value for each relationship, and summing these values vertically defines the 'how' importance value. Once these values have been determined, managers can develop detailed programmes for implementing customer-focused improvements.

The mechanics of QFD described above are repeated in four critical phases as the process cascades down throughout all production and business processes. The process of transforming top-level customer requirements into product planning considerations is the first phase of QFD. Phase two is involved in converting product planning needs into identifying the parts required. Phase three examines required parts changes or modifications and assesses their impact on process needs. Phase four establishes the detailed production plans and manufacturing procedures which give operators a clear route map for delivering products, which meet or exceed the customers' requirements.

All of the following benefits have been consistently realised by those Japanese companies committed to the QFD process:

- Fewer and earlier product changes – through better and more timely definition of customer requirements
- Shorter development times, better planning, ability to freeze designs, focus on execution rather than replanning
- Involving suppliers as part of the team is a major opportunity for cycle-time compression
- Fewer start-up problems – through focusing efforts on problem prevention
- Lower start-up cost, with reduced subsequent process and material changes
- Warranty reduction – through a comprehensive understanding of how the 'hows' will interact
- Knowledge transfer – through the structured process and approach which demands the full participation of all functions
- Customer satisfaction – through a systematic, disciplined process dedicated to listening to the voice of the customer and providing product and service solutions.

To give an example of how customer satisfaction is successfully achieved: a global packaging company conducted widespread QFD interviews and discovered that inconsistencies in the length and diameter of its core product were generating considerable customer dissatisfaction. By focusing on this need – identified by the customer – the company was able to develop a solution through cross-functional teamwork. Following a rigorous training programme, statistical process controls were introduced on the key manufacturing lines, allowing employees to predict and produce a consistently high-quality product.

It is essential to appreciate that QFD is a demanding and detailed process – but one which, when properly applied, can yield significant competitive advantage for all companies. QFD can provide the path to excellence, but there are no shortcuts. It is a rigorous and detailed process that requires commitment and co-operation throughout the production cycle.

QFD is not a quick-fix or a flavour of the month or a new buzz-word invented by the consultancy profession. It is a tough, detailed and demanding process. There can be no management on-off switch if companies are going to make it work for them. Dedication and sustained commitment are the essential management hallmarks of successfully implemented QFD.

Garry Sutton is group technical manager for Peter Chadwick Limited, a European implementation consultancy.

BENCHMARKS FOR INVESTOR VALUE

Glen Peters

Low economic growth rates mean that many companies are focusing on customer retention to help maximise their shareholder value. Benchmarking has a crucial role to play.

In 1993 Price Waterhouse conducted a review of customer management that identified customer retention as one of the major business challenges of the 1990s. The logic behind this conclusion is straightforward. In the mature OECD economies, economic growth is likely to be sluggish at around 2 per cent for the foreseeable future – so most companies cannot realistically expect to make much impact from organic growth.

With low GDP rates, the best way to improve the revenue line is not to rely on new markets and new customers, but to get smarter at retaining customers. The obvious way to improve customer retention, apart from cutting prices and therefore profit margins, is to improve customer service. This will improve sales growth, maintain margins and, ultimately, build shareholder value.

True? Yes. Most companies lose 20—30 per cent of their customers every year. They therefore have to work that much harder to replace lost customers and to grow market share. If only they were able to reduce the rate at which customers left them, they would automatically see an increase in sales. The accepted wisdom is that improving customer retention by 2 per cent has the same impact on profitability as a 10 per cent reduction in overheads. It is as powerful as that.

Simple? No. While companies have found it relatively easy to identify best practice on many significant customer service parameters, they have found it much more difficult, even where they have identified their own shortfalls, to close the gap. In recognition of the growing importance of customer service, and in response to requests from its clients, Price Waterhouse in 1994 began a pan-European customer service bench-marking study which has uncovered some interesting facts. The study grew out of a forum held for 200 of its clients to discuss the problems that they faced in retaining customers. One of the conclusions that the clients reached was that benchmarking had a crucial role to play in identifying strategies to reduce customer attrition rates.

However, fewer than 10 per cent of the companies felt that they understood benchmarking or that they were able to do it effectively. They therefore asked Price Waterhouse to facilitate benchmarking aimed at improving customer retention. It is possible to define benchmarking as: a management process by which companies compare themselves with the brightest and the best in other organisations, even outside their own sector. Many companies have approached benchmarking in precisely that way, looking at the results of best practice either within or outside their own sectors, putting numbers to key parameters, and calculating how they themselves measure up to best practice companies.

For example, company X identifies that the number of sales calls per person a day in a best practice company is 10 and calculates that it is only achieving five; clearly, it should consider why it only manages five. Company Y finds that best practice in terms of number of telephone rings before the operator answers is between 1.5 and 2 and that it can only manage 6; clearly, it needs to consider if a faster response would improve its business. This kind of benchmarking, known as statistical or transactional benchmarking, has its uses, but many companies fail to appreciate that it is only part of the picture. While it helps to quantify weaknesses, it gives no information on the action needed to correct them.

When Price Waterhouse began to set up its Pan-European Service Excellence Benchmarking Study, the firm went back to about 30 of the companies that had attended the customer retention forum and found that they were using only statistical benchmarking techniques. Though they were generating comparative data, the techniques were not giving them any information on how they should set about improving their performance. What the companies wanted the firm to do was to play a role in what is called process benchmarking and strategic benchmarking.

Process benchmarking

Process benchmarking is the second of three benchmarking levels, of which statistical benchmarking is the most basic. While statistical techniques aim to draw quantitative comparisons between companies, process benchmarking aims to identify the processes that best-practice companies employ. Then the knowledge gained can be applied to improve, say, understanding customers; order fulfilment; or accounting for income.

For example, say that a particular airline is identified as being the best-practice company when it comes to understanding customers – that is, it knows what its customers want and is able to react very quickly. Process benchmarking would involve looking at how the airline goes about understanding its customers, looking at its use of third-party research, looking at how it uses its cabin crews, its sales teams, its reservation teams, and then backing that up with numerical data – such as the number of new products and services produced.

The highest of the three levels is called strategic benchmarking. It is about the strategy of an organisation. In the case of John Lewis, it is summed up by the phrase 'never knowingly undersold'. In the case of Midland, the phrase 'the listening bank' makes it clear that the strategy of this organisation is about listening to customers. In the case of General Electric, the company's strategy is summed up by two numbers 'ten-fifteen' – the company aims to turn its inventory 10 times a year and to realise 15 per cent return on sales.

The other part of strategy is clearly culture, people. What sort of culture does an organisation have? Is it a culture where the customer is number one or is it a company where the buyer is number one? Is it the chief financial officer who has the greatest credibility? Is it a very control-driven culture? Benchmarking, by capturing not just numbers, but processes, strategies and cultures, gives businesses clues to things that they ought to consider doing. However, the business has to be sure that it understands itself before going off to look at other companies.

A mistake that many people make is to look at others before they have started to look at themselves. There is a phrase in benchmarking, 'industrial tourism', which describes the practice of flying off to the USA to see 10 companies in two weeks. People who do that come back saying 'That was really great'. My reply to that is 'Well, what did you gain? How do you apply it to your business?' A lot of people wasted a lot of effort in the early period of benchmarking by going off without having done a thorough analysis of themselves.

Anyone who wants to start benchmarking should start by asking themselves questions. Do I know how I go about understanding customers? Do I know what my inventory levels are? Do I know what my lead-times are? Research by Price Waterhouse has shown that fewer than 15 per cent of companies have a good understanding of their cost structure, their lead-times, or their customer attrition rate.

One of the most interesting aspects of advanced benchmarking techniques is that companies can use them to look at how companies outside their own sectors approach particular problems. In fact, companies looking for real step-change are more likely to find an answer outside their own sector than within it.

There is a well-documented story about Domino Pizzas going to a hospital emergency ward to see how it was able to react very quickly to emergencies and coming up with the idea of the three-minute pizza. Another example is South West Airlines which went to the Indianapolis car race to look at how the mechanics turned around high performance cars in seconds. They asked themselves, 'if it takes us 55 minutes to turn a plane around and these teams can do their cars in six or seven seconds, what are they doing that we are not?'

What we have done at Price Waterhouse is to introduce to some of our clients a concept we call parallel learning. This involves benchmarking competencies. For example, one of the competencies that people in front-line sales need to have is consistency of role. If you are seeing 10 clients in a day, you need to be as alert and responsive for your clients at 7:30pm, when you are on your last meeting, as you are in the morning. Our approach was to study actors, who need a high consistency of role in treading the boards night after night, to see how they approach that problem. The techniques that actors use have been since been taught to managers in companies such as BT.

In setting up the Pan-European Service Excellence Benchmarking Study, the first step for Price Waterhouse was to identify five processes that needed to be benchmarked:

- How companies go about understanding customers needs
- How companies go about managing customer relationships
- How companies go about empowering their own people
- How companies go about managing dissatisfaction
- How companies go about measuring customer satisfaction.

Each company participating in the study is interviewed by a team of Price Waterhouse consultants who carry out a diagnostic, and then prepare a detailed report giving the company a score against the best-practice framework, comparisons with other participant companies, and a breakdown of best practices identified in each of the five key customer processes.

What is interesting is the discovery that 95 per cent of a company's effort in benchmarking goes into setting the thing up: finding out who to contact in the target organisation, working out the model to use for benchmarking, and how to go about it. The actual interview review is less than 5 per cent. So we are saving companies 95 per cent of that effort. By last autumn, 45 major plc companies were participating in the study. And though at present the study is pan-European, Price Waterhouse intends to promulgate it worldwide.

As an example of what participation can mean to a company, one of the organisations involved, a mobile phone provider, found that it had a customer attrition rate of 30 per cent. With this attrition rate, and a payback of between 18 months and two years on the expense of setting up new customers, you can imagine what the cost of non-retention was. Through benchmarking, Price Waterhouse showed the company that it could quickly reduce attrition by 5 per cent, which would boost shareholder value by about £650 million and improve profitability by around 65 per cent.

Since the beginning of the year, Price Waterhouse has taken benchmarking several steps further with the announcement of its Value Builder initiative. The Pan-European Service Excellence Benchmarking Study focused on only one of seven key value drivers identified in the Rappaport model for assessing a company's shareholder value: the percentage increase in sales year-on-year. The Value Builder initiative extends the use of benchmarking to all seven value drivers, giving companies an unprecedented opportunity to increase cash flow and thereby maximise shareholder value.

Glen Peters is a partner with Price Waterhouse.

MAKING MONEY WORK

INTEGRATING THE APPLICATIONS

Nick Fryars

Integrated application packages offer radical new possibilities to achieve rapid business transformation. But business management, not the IT department, must drive the project.

In this era of increasingly rapid and continuous change, many companies are seeking ways to deliver higher levels of customer service at lower cost. As in previous decades, many of these are looking to information technology (IT) for some of the means to do so. However, a major hindrance to the effective use of IT is often the inflexibility of the information systems on which current business depends. Integrated applications packages, a recent development in software technology which is now maturing, offer radical new possibilities to break out of this deadlock and achieve rapid business transformation. What problems do such packages address? How do they do so? What benefits do they offer? What costs and timescales are involved? Which factors influence the successful use of these packages?

Corporate information systems with their roots in the 1970s and early 1980s were typically built-up piecemeal with, for instance, one system supporting order-processing, a second handling general ledger, another credit control, and so forth. Each of these systems was developed to automate a specific business function and had its own database. Initially, this meant that islands of automation were created, with communication between business functions largely by means of paper or word of mouth.

Each island had its own administrative staff entering data relevant to that department into their computer application; often this data was gathered from paper produced by other departments' computer applications, with small, but significant, differences in grouping and format.

The same data might thus occur in several different systems, names and addresses of customers being an obvious example. Disadvantages of such duplication include the possibility that the two systems may disagree on, say, the address of a customer (the service department may have noted an address change that the sales department had missed). Such problems led to the interconnection of the systems originally developed as islands. This usually meant writing extra software to transfer data between islands and to translate the representation used by one system into that used by another.

Network of disparate systems

Copying of data by administrative staff, with the attendant risk of introducing errors, was then substantially reduced, but the cost-savings were frequently more than outweighed by the IT costs involved in developing and supporting the extra software. As interconnection was also often done in a piecemeal fashion, management overview information was not readily available from any system; this in turn led to the development of separate management information systems, with feeds from a patchwork of business information systems. Managing data integrity across a network of disparate systems became a key IT function in many large companies.

Some companies attempted to unify support of several business functions in one system – for instance, order processing and billing. However, such systems were usually biased toward one particular business function and did not support others well; they also often took so long to develop that they were obsolete before they entered service. Whichever route was taken, the sheer volume of software in use within an enterprise typically led to spiralling IT cost, much of it in the area of system maintenance. Moreover, the organisation could no longer perform its function without the supporting information systems, and these had become so large, complex and difficult to change that they were a serious impediment to organisational flexibility.

Integrated applications packages such as SAP's R/2 or R/3, SSA's BPCS and Baan's Triton represent the first wave of a serious attempt by the IT industry to address this problem, creating a number of new possibilities for business while doing so. The basic premise behind these packages is that there is only a limited number of ways in which most major business functions can be organised. Such packages aim to contain all recognised approaches to organising business functions, as well as to support the buyer in selecting and configuring the specific functionality he wishes for his organisation.

The organisation of any given company can thus be represented as the result of a finite series of choices out of standard ways to organise business functions. Choices are offered in terms of business objects such as orders, invoices and stack levels; there is also a considerable emphasis on business processes and the way in which business objects flow through the organisation in question. The use of a single central database which may be physically distributed across several machines and locations, but functions as one database, substantially reduces data integrity problems and minimises the data management work involved; in addition, it makes available valuable management information which was previously too difficult or expensive to obtain. An example might be a comparison of price/performance ratios and return on investment of different types of production equipment, taking into account such factors as volume produced, availability, depreciation and actual maintenance costs.

The first products in this area appeared about 10 years ago, but were then comparatively crude and often primarily focused on production planning. As often occurs with such new technologies, time was needed for these products to mature. (The now-popular operating system Unix took 13 years from its initial appearance to gain wide market acceptance.) Although the maturing process for integrated packages is not yet complete, the use of Windows and graphical user interfaces (GUIs), as well as moves to open systems standards, has vastly enhanced the ease of implementation and use of these products. The benefits which can be achieved by employing them are considerable. Specific examples include:

- Explicit support of cross-functional business processes, giving better visibility and control with these results: more informed decision-making; a more proactive and competitive business; better service to customers.
- Elimination of much administrative work – all data are entered only once, thus obviating all forms of copying with these implications: immediate cost savings; fewer possibilities for introducing errors; reduced overall cost of quality.
- Better overall control of stocks, leading to: less capital tied up; greater flexibility (less need to shift old stock).
- Downsizing or elimination of the IT application development and maintenance function.

At a more general level, these packages offer far greater flexibility in supporting changes in business processes than traditional systems. Such changes do not come free; considerable reconfiguration and data migration may be necessary, and all major changes cost time, effort and money, whatever their nature. The major difference compared to traditional systems is that in many cases the package will already contain the functionality required to support the new business processes; the core of the work involved is making this functionality available to provide the support needed. This reduces greatly the lead-time needed to develop software to support a new situation.

The organisation can thus react far more quickly to changed market circumstances by redeploying itself as needed, with substantial changes often possible within a few months. The implications for competitiveness hardly need to be stated. However, it must be constantly borne in mind that these benefits do not accrue immediately when the package is purchased and installed. Real returns are only achieved by setting clear and realistic goals, defining an approach to reach them and applying professional project management to do so.

Substantial differences

There are three major areas in which projects involving packages of this type differ from traditional automation projects: (1) the opportunities for business transformation involved, and thus the scope and scale of the project; (2) the type of development work involved; (3) the roles of IT and user personnel in the project.

Integrated software packages offer hitherto unprecedented opportunities for the effective support and management of cross-functional business processes, the most obvious of which is the sales chain or opportunity-to-cash process found in any business venture. However, supplying the possibilities is not enough; the project scope needs to involve redefining the business processes supported as well as implementing these redefined processes in such a way that the potential benefits are actually realised.

The development work required is very different from the traditional approach. Little or no programming in the traditional sense is required. Instead, a large number of decisions need to be taken. A typical recent project for a manufacturing enterprise operating in several countries involved approximately 3600 separate decisions. These decisions relate to how business functions will work, how they will interact with one another, and what parameters (such as reordering levels for various stock types) will be appropriate. The result is, in effect, a detailed redefinition of the business processes involved, in terms derived from the concepts embodied in the package.

Given the emphasis on redefining the business and the lack of development work involved, the role of the IT department in a project of this type is limited to supplying the infrastructure required and taking care of any interfaces with existing systems that may be needed. Most of the design work to be done relates to how the business will work in the new situation, and this can only be done by the management and staff of the business functions involved, who will also play a major role in starting live operation and rolling the new system out across the organisation. In essence, this puts users in the driving seat of the project, a position which most will find unfamiliar, if not uncomfortable. To run a project of this nature successfully, users will require three sorts of skills:

- Skills in designing business processes; some managers will very likely have these, others may need (external) consultancy assistance
- Skills in relating the business world to the concepts embodied in the

specific package involved; this will always involve some external consultancy from the package supplier or consultants with specific expertise in the package in question
- Skills in structuring and executing the change process itself, which should be run as a multidisciplinary project and take account of the idiosyncrasies of both the business and the package in question. Again, professional help may be required here, since running such projects is not routine practice within most companies.

The costs and timescales involved depend on many factors, including the scope of the project in terms of business processes to be supported and the size of the organisation involved. A project with significant impact on business processes will typically involve a purchase cost for the software package of £500 000 to £1 million, though higher figures are not unusual. The cost of the package itself typically accounts for 15—30 per cent of the total out-of-pocket project cost, giving a typical cost range of £1.5 million to well in excess of £5 million for an ambitious programme.

A tangible major factor in project cost is often the hardware required. Various recent product offerings make extensive use of the so-called client-server concept, partly because of its associations with popular tendencies toward decentralisation and downsizing. In such an arrangement, information relating to the business is stored centrally on one or more so-called server machines. Client machines, usually PC-type workstations, call up this data as required, perform any necessary manipulations and present it to the user in an appropriate fashion. Often, a heavy processing burden is placed on the workstation, implying that a powerful and thus relatively expensive PC will have to be bought.

In addition, this workstation will in many cases require a large and thus expensive screen to allow presentation of all relevant information to the user, as well as a high-speed data link to ensure acceptable system response times. The number of workstations will usually run into tens and possibly hundreds. The use of PCs should thus not mislead the buyer into believing he is buying cheap hardware; experience has shown that overall infrastructure cost for a client-server-oriented system may well approach (though not exceed) that of a mainframe system.

A significant cost whose value is often very difficult to measure is the time which company personnel, including management, will need to invest in the project. Their driving seat role implies a major commitment in terms of time and effort for the duration of the project. Ideally, some key people should be freed from their normal tasks for the duration of the project. Because the only appropriate people for such roles are often those already playing a major part in keeping the business on its toes, this is often a difficult issue. However, it should not be avoided by allotting large portions of this work to the IT department.

Integrated applications packages allow far more functionality to be made available to users within a given time frame than is possible with traditional approaches to system development. Exceptions to this statement can be found, but they usually involve very specific situations such as a large and rapidly growing high-value market and a very large company which can afford to invest exceptionally large sums of money in a short time to achieve the results which are required.

However, introduction of such a package needs careful preparation and a substantial configuration effort. A first-time user introducing a system with substantial functionality should expect to spend one to two years on the project. You must also bear in mind the fact that early adopters spent more (and some far more).

Clear view

Many of the benefits listed above are not realisable without a clear view of how business processes should work in the new situation. For each major business process, a clear view is needed of how it is to work, what its relationship is with other business processes, and how the package is to support the process concerned. Benefits which will result from the new situation need to be clearly identified during this exercise, and their realisation must be explicitly managed. This requires managing the project in a well-structured fashion; less development work does *not* imply less project management. Not appointing a capable project manager is the surest way to kill any project, and especially one at the sharp edge of implementing technology in business.

A manager contemplating the introduction of an integrated package in a large company with many existing information systems will almost certainly be confronted with decisions relating to system and project scope. An integrated package will usually replace several existing systems, but not necessarily all. Choosing the right places to draw the line is an important success factor, and requires careful analysis of the benefits, costs, risks and implementation difficulties of various scenarios. A migration plan involving the introduction of a package in several stages can be of great value here.

The youth of integrated packages means that all those involved, including the suppliers of such packages, have some way to go up the learning curve. Most leading packages are still under development, with major new releases occurring twice to three times a year. This has two important consequences:

- *Lead-time.* Project plans should allow for taking on new software releases as and when they become available. Depending on the stage reached in the project, up to three weeks may be needed to migrate to the new release. (Not migrating is usually an impractical option.)
- *Scarcity of expertise.* Expert knowledge in new areas of a given package is often somewhere between scarce and non-existent, with even the supplier being able to give only limited guidance. The name of the game here is finding the technical consultant who is furthest up the learning curve. If he or she does not exist, you should be prepared to

grow your own (and make sure somebody does not head-hunt them the moment you turn your back).

The final point to note is that a hands-on role for business management is absolutely essential. Nearly all projects involving an integrated applications package are not about implementing the package, but about remodelling the business. The history of these packages is littered with examples of companies who thought they could work wonders by getting the IT department to put the package in. None of them succeeded. Major, in-depth involvement of the right business managers is the single most important key success factor.

Nick Fryars has almost 20 years' experience in applying IT to solve business problems, and in the course of years has worked in a wide range of industry sectors.

THE FINANCIAL BUSINESS BUYER

Eric Walters

Selling to a financial buyer is an attractive way of divesting a business unit. Competitors are not involved, few parties take part so confidentiality is greater, and the deal process is faster.

A strategy to focus on core activities and to dispose of non-core or poor performing businesses has become the norm rather than the exception. Stock market thinking has turned against broadly based conglomerates. Head office management time is too valuable to spend dealing with businesses which do not fit into the long-term corporate strategy. While flotation or a trade sale are options, never discount the option of selling to the existing management.

The parent selling a subsidiary should feel that it has received a fair price for the business, without jeopardising the future of the business as an independent company. A financial buyer such as Schroder Ventures contributes experience, resources and flexibility to create these conditions. The management team are unlikely to have the experience or the financial resources to make an outright purchase. Financial buyers provide equity finance, which will not increase the level of debt, and can also help a business to fund rationalisation or finance acquisitions following divestment. We have experienced business managers in our team with good industry knowledge and contacts. Financial and operating expertise can be devoted to developing a business plan with the management. This plan will form the basis of a realistic purchase price.

The business that a vendor wishes to sell may need new management structures and separate accounting systems to be able to stand alone. This requires practical assistance. An experienced buy-out specialist will recognise the requirements and be able to assess in-house capabilities. Often the most useful catalyst is to introduce an experienced businessman to complete or head up a team. It takes resources and a willingness to take risks in order to be comfortable with a turnaround or complicated business situation. The venture capitalist able to take the long view may be willing to take on packages of businesses that others are not interested in. Loss-making troubled subsidiaries that may be unsaleable to a trade buyer who demands returns in the short term may represent an opportunity for a venture capitalist willing to wait for a return on investment.

All-important flexibility

Flexibility in structuring a transaction can be critical, however. A business can be bought outright, a joint venture with the vendor can be formed, or an earn-out arrangement can be set up. Long-term supply contracts or other contractual commitments may be important to the vendor, and the deal can be structured to take account of this. A competing trade buyer may not have this flexibility. The flexibility of dealing with a venture capital buyer can make the difference between a grudging sale and a fair deal. As noted, the vendor may wish to continue trading in the future with the business being sold. More fundamentally, vendors can retain an equity stake to share in any upside value created under the new ownership. With the right partner, a venture capital investment can be the key to maximising the value of the shareholding.

In the UK the majority of larger buy-outs are divestments of subsidiaries or divisions from corporate parents. In Continental Europe most buy-outs are purchases from private or family owners. The former owner often remains a minority shareholder with a continuing management role in the business. This is especially true in Italy, where there are a large number of family-owned companies offering a single product or service, principally for the local market. Synergies can often be obtained by bringing together under a single holding company a number of such companies which are selling into the same broad market sector, adding professional management and adopting a co-ordinated marketing approach.

This group-building strategy has created what is now easily the largest logistics business in Italy. Schroder Ventures' Italian Fund has purchased a succession of businesses to create a group providing logistics services to a number of leading companies. The business has 27 constituent companies, whose activities range from the warehousing and distribution of Olivetti products and Fiat components to the logistics of book distribution. In all, Schroder Ventures has completed almost 300 management buy-out and buy-in transactions over the past 10 years.

Although the buy-outs are diverse in terms of size, business sector and stage of development, we adopt the same investment philosophy throughout these worldwide operations: investments are only made where there is a local on-the-ground team totally familiar with the local business environment and plugged into local networks of entrepreneurs, intermediaries and banks. We seek to take majority stakes in companies, with a presence on the board and to work closely with management to help companies achieve their full potential. A high percentage of partners have industrial experience at a senior level and are therefore well placed to provide strategic advice. Involvement in day-to-day management is not sought.

While each local team operates principally within a single country, the international network offers significant benefits to vendors with cross-border operations, enabling the execution of complex international buy-outs. An example of this is the recent buy-out of Kassbohrer Gelandefahrzeuge GmbH, the off-road vehicle division of Kassbohrer, the German automotive group. The deal involved funds from Germany, the UK and Italy.

Kassbohrer is the world's leading manufacturer of snow-grooming vehicles, sold under the Pisten Bully name and also a leading manufacturer of Setra brand buses. Expansion in the 1980s was met by significant recession in many of the markets served by the bus side of the business. It was under this threat that management and family shareholders appointed an investment bank to advise on the divestment of the Pisten Bully division, which would enable the company to focus upon the rescue of its core bus business.

A buy-out by the senior management of Pisten Bully, led by Erwin Wieland and backed by Schroder Ventures, was proposed. Against bids from a number of trade and other financial buyers, we won the mandate to proceed down the path of due diligence on an exclusive basis. The Kassbohrer Group's difficulties were public knowledge. During the selling process it became evident that the Group could not placate the 30-odd banks in its banking syndicate, to which it owed somewhere near to DM700 million. In early 1994 the Group was forced to return to its lenders for additional funds. These were provided on the basis that the family shareholders ceded control. They did, and potential buyers for the Setra bus division emerged. In late July 1994 Mercedes-Benz agreed to take over the Group. It therefore became necessary for Mercedes to approve all the agreements entered into for the sale of Pisten Bully.

The diligence process was not lengthy, but it was thorough. Pisten Bully has operations in Austria, North America, Italy, France and Switzerland, in addition to the main facility in Ulm. Arthur Andersen in Germany, appointed to perform in-depth financial due diligence, called upon its offices in other countries to investigate the financial position of local sales operations. An in-depth investigation of the market-place and Pisten Bully's position within it needed to be carried out as well. This aspect of the diligence exercise was performed by speaking with customers, suppliers and ski industry experts. With offices in nine countries around the world, our own operation is able to bring resources to bear quickly to facilitate international due diligence investigations.

Future growth and profitability

Teams were dispatched to all major Pisten Bully facilities, where venture capital personnel speaking the local language tested the division's projections of future growth and profitability. Pisten Bully's dominant position in the worldwide market for snow grooming equipment was confirmed and shown to be enviable, as was its reputation for reliability and service. The combined international office networks of both venture capitalists and reporting accountants enabled a large quantity of work across a number of regions to be accomplished in a short period of time.

Pisten Bully had never stood entirely alone within the Kassbohrer Group, so the division's historic profitability had to be confirmed. The business shared administration as well as production facilities, and the quantification of the stand-alone costs associated with the future Pisten Bully business was key to the confirmation of the price. In addition, a number of continuing relationships with the group were necessary until a full separation could be achieved. These needed to be contractually agreed. It was also necessary to plan the physical separation of Pisten Bully Division from its parent. This would involve the removal and reinstallation of production lines from existing facilities. External consultants worked with management to plan a smooth and efficient move. The consultants were useful both in terms of their specific skills and the back-up that they provided to management during the peak sales season.

As the buy-out of Kassbohrer shows, selling to a financial buyer can be an attractive way of divesting a business unit. Competitors are not involved, and as few parties participate, confidentiality is enhanced. The deal process is generally faster than other options (such as trade sale or flotation). The new owners are strongly committed to the future success of the business and the selling price has to be competitive.

There is no standard leveraged buy-out process, but deals typically follow a similar pattern. Corporations considering the sale of a business unit may contact a financial buyer directly or through an intermediary. A complete business plan is not necessary. Vendors can simply provide a brief description of the business, its products and markets, a historical financial summary and future projections.

Based on this preliminary information and possibly a phone call or meeting, we will provide a response within days, indicating a level of interest and a possible valuation range. Initial terms of agreement with the vendor are usually reached within a matter of weeks. The process then follows several parallel paths: due diligence, the arrangement of finance, and standard negotiations. Due diligence incorporates a review of the management team, financial position and projections, operations, market position, and legal and environmental issues.

MAKING MONEY WORK

All this information is kept confidential. Simultaneously, Schroder Ventures will arrange the financing (debt and equity) and negotiate terms with vendors and management. Although each situation is unique, the whole process can be completed within two to three months. As companies consider divestment possibilities, they should therefore keep a sale to a financial buyer firmly in mind. It can be quick, confidential, and prove both financially and strategically attractive.

Eric Walters is a partner at Schroder Ventures.

MAKING THE MOST OF DERIVATIVES

David Etherington

Derivatives are a valuable financial tool, but CEOs should control their use to harness the power of these instruments and to avoid the dangers of over-leveraging.

Derivatives are so called because the product exists with respect to, or is derived from, its underlying asset in the cash market. The basic idea is that companies using commodities, deposit and loan instruments or foreign exchange can take out a hedge by entering into a contract to protect themselves from sudden changes in commodity prices, interest rates or currency rates – which, in the case of option-based derivatives, involves the payment of a premium. For instance, if a corporate buys a basic currency option to hedge an underlying currency exposure, and adverse changes occur, it is spared the loss. If not, all it has lost is the premium; but, in so doing, it has managed a potential market risk. On the other side is the trader, who writes derivative contracts, pockets the premium if all goes well, but stands a potentially large loss if the market swings the wrong way.

Cause for concern?

The debate over the value of derivatives as a financial tool in managing a corporate's business was heightened in 1994 because of the catalogue of financial trading losses reported in the media. The recent global spate of financial losses related to derivative trading – that is, taking derivative positions without an underlying exposure – has prompted regulators to worry that the huge growth in options, futures, swaps and other derivatives is threatening the stability of the world's financial system. The furore has also seen banks accused of force-feeding client companies with inappropriate products. This has served to exacerbate the panic waves flowing through the world's regulatory bodies. Because derivatives bind banks and others together in a global web of deals, regulators fear that trouble in one market or country could instantly spread to others. Often invoked, yet poorly defined, this systemic risk lies in the danger that the failure of one firm will cause others to default in droves, forcing governments to intervene to prevent a system-wide collapse.

A bill put before the US Congress would end federally backed deposit insurance for banks trading derivatives on their own account. The fear is that a bank might suddenly default on an interbank derivative obligation, which in turn might start a domino effect on the world's banking network. One reason for US wariness is that legislators want to improve on a mixed record of anticipating financial disasters. They failed to foresee either the savings and loan debacle or the collapse of the junk bond market in the late 1980s. The derivative market is a prime candidate for concern, since it is relatively young, global and very large: one much-quoted guess is $14—16 trillion for the supposed notional value of outstanding derivative contracts. Moreover, to outsiders, futures and options – let alone swaps and collars – sound suspiciously complex. This impression is reinforced by the mathematical jargon that permeates the business, and the product terminology such as knock-ins and knock-outs, ratchet swaps, up and in options, and collared floaters.

If derivatives were such a suspect financial tool, though, the market would not have mushroomed to its present size. It is driven by many customers who have had numerous satisfactory and remunerative experiences when using derivative instruments. The range of end-users suggests that the growth of derivatives will continue to be rapid. The fact is that huge global markets have evolved because derivative instruments make good financial sense to a large and diverse group of users. Regrettably, bad experiences make better headlines. But, by hedging tomorrow's transactions at today's prices, while a company may not increase the profit it makes, it can certainly eliminate much of the risk involved in making that money.

Powerful tool

Derivative instruments have allowed numerous corporates and investors to raise money at more competitive rates than they could have achieved with vanilla securities (that is, straightforward or basic ones) in their domestic markets. These instruments have allowed managers to tailor their liability portfolios to reflect changing interest rate environments, generating hundreds of millions of dollars worth of savings. Derivatives have also helped companies to protect and boost returns on their short- and medium-term cash balances, as well as creating sources of cheap funding that would not otherwise have existed. The evolution of the derivative markets has been very much customer-driven.

In an environment in which corporates in all sectors are realising that the key to enhancing long-term shareholder value is globalisation, many corporate users understand that derivatives are a powerful tool in their armoury. When used properly, they can mitigate the adverse effects of the inevitable exposure to foreign exchange and interest rates that expanding companies face. In addition, an effective and proactive risk management programme that includes derivative instruments can boost a corporate's earnings stability and thereby further enhance shareholder value.

Many of the recent problems with derivatives have tended to arise less from anything inherent in the instruments themselves and more from a basic failure of management and errors of judgment. Many of the corporates that got into trouble did so as a result of defects in the types of internal controls and systems needed to manage their derivative and other capital exposures. In addition, many US and foreign corporate treasury departments are targeted as profit centres and have used derivative instruments to make money. This raises two issues.

Speculate or hedge?

First is the difference between a corporate that uses derivatives to speculate, as distinct from hedging. To hedge is to take out a position that offsets an existing exposure. To speculate is to take out a position that either increases that exposure or is not matched by any underlying exposure at all. Moreover, even if the hedge is matched by a position in the underlying exposure, it is speculative to put on and take off hedges that are not justified by market movements or the underlying exposure. The vast proportion of derivative contracts transacted by corporates with banks in Europe and elsewhere are to hedge an underlying exposure. The purpose of a hedge is not to make money; rather it is to reduce risks and provide certainty, with the corporate weighing up the potential cost of the hedge and the certainty it provides against the cost of, say, interest rates moving adversely. In the context of corporate hedging activity, derivatives can hardly be regarded as high-stakes gambling.

Second, there is a significant difference between derivatives and the cash markets. That is the relative ease with which certain derivative positions can create leveraged exposures which are speculative simply by virtue of their size. For instance, a futures investor might put $100 000 down on a contract committing him to buy $1 million worth of bonds in a given period of time. The investor stands to make 10 times the profit, or 10 times the loss, that he might make by buying $1 million worth of bonds outright and holding them for a given period. Last year, US companies and mutual funds could easily buy derivative products that were leveraged as much as 50 times.

119

More recently, the leveraged swap, or floater with a 'kicker', has been the source of much scrutiny, because the corporate buyer assumes a higher risk profile by taking a view on future interest rate movements. The leveraged swap or floater is an interest rate swap which has an interest rate option embedded in the swap and has been sold by the corporate to the bank in return for an upfront cash premium. Such derivative-linked swaps, while rare, are pegged to a complex formula that reflects a company's or investor's view that interest rates may rise or fall. This formula is used to determine the spread to the London Interbank Offered Rate (Libor), or kicker, that the corporate will pay after the first reset period for the remainder of the swap. Problems can arise when a corporate takes an aggressive view of interest rates which proves to be wrong.

The saving relative to Libor is reduced if interest rates rise by the change in the value of the kicker. Simply put, the saving relative to Libor is represented by the option premium that the bank is willing to pay to the corporate involved in return for acquiring the option. The premium paid for this leveraged bet is a mixture of volatility in the interest rate market, the leverage expressed by the kicker, the structure of interest rates, and the life of the option. Over the past two or three years, the markets have been a one-way bet for corporates – interest rates have been stable or falling. However, in a scenario where this type of instrument is being used to achieve aggressive funding targets, the risk exposure of the corporate is dramatically increased if the market environment changes, and interest rates start to climb. In short, the company bears the market risk of an unfavourable change in the value of the financial instrument underlying the option.

The fact remains that derivatives offer a company a powerful financial risk management tool. The point, as with so many things in life, is that these instruments need to be understood, the upside and downside risks quantified, and then used sensibly. To manage and control derivatives, the company must first establish a policy for their use and link them to internal management controls. A worthwhile starting-point here is to check on how rigorous the company's policy and procedures for the execution of derivative products are in relation to the granting of supplier and customer credit terms, or even to placing deposits with a bank. The level of derivative exposure assumed by a corporate at any given time is for the board to determine. The objective must be to eliminate the possibility of hidden surprises because the policy on their use is vague or, if well-articulated, poorly communicated and not supported by internal management controls.

Well-defined corporate policy

If a corporate is to harness the power of derivatives to manage commodities, interest rates and currency exposures, it needs to have a defined policy on their use. At the centre of that policy should be an unequivocal statement on the type of derivative instrument the company is prepared to enter into and the magnitude of leverage and downside risk, if any, that it is willing to tolerate. In particular, the corporate needs to set objectives and articulate whether or not it is merely going to hedge underlying exposures or speculate, using derivative contracts to generate income. The board also needs to check that the parameters it sets as a maximum aggregate downside risk exposure for its Treasury operation cannot be unconsciously circumvented by the use of leveraged derivative positions to roll up further potential loss exposure. This scenario is quite feasible if the company is trading derivative contracts as distinct from hedging underlying interest and currency rate exposures.

In addition, it is worthwhile reviewing how other goals of the company impact upon the potential use of derivative products. For example, if the goal is to reduce the cost of capital – in other words, run with aggressive funding targets in any given market scenario – then the board must view holistically the additional risks which the business incurs by using financial instruments such as derivatives to achieve those goals. This process will help to align and balance the linkages between various objectives put before the Treasury management team from an aggregate corporate risk and reward perspective.

Second, the company must impose discipline over the way derivative instruments are executed and monitored. As with most products, it is difficult to prevent the business being exposed to outright employee fraud. It is possible, however, to develop guidelines to control punting by Treasury staff (at its worst an individual trader acting alone); or watching the market change and not reacting to the events taking place; or (perhaps the worst strategy of all) doubling exposure if, say, the currency markets have turned against you, in the hope that the market will correct itself and enable the loss to be recovered.

The corporate history books are full of companies that have tried to ride out losses by deferring them, or have increased their exposures in an attempt to win back what they have lost. In both cases, the motivation is a blind hope that the financial markets will move in their favour, so that there will be no need to report a major financial loss to senior executives or the stakeholders.

When buying derivative contracts, there are several things that could be done to improve the management process:

- *Quantify the worst case risk scenario at the outset.* The upside to using derivatives is easy to explain, but the risk assumptions are equally important to quantify. For the more complicated derivative products, most banks are able to provide computer discs with the leverage and supporting sensitivity analysis to enable due diligence to be undertaken. Even so, most market commentators agree that the worst case scenario (in other words, the magnitude of the financial loss at risk) can be determined using a pocket calculator. The complexity of many of these derivative products is a mathematical smoke-screen. The maximum loss needs to be determined, based on a 'what if' analysis of potential market circumstances.

121

- *Develop exposure management principles.* Watching an exposure go from bad to worse is not good management. When entering a complicated derivative contract, especially where the corporate has taken the decision to carry a speculative or trading component, it is prudent to set out the conditions and circumstances which would require corporate corrective action or termination if markets suddenly move in an unforeseen way – in other words, setting out the parameters of the exit strategy. In this regard, most banks are able to provide on-going sensitivity analysis of a corporate's derivative trades as well as mark-to-market evaluation reports. (Mark-to-market is the process of daily adjustment of an account or investment to reflect actual market value as opposed to historic accounting value.)
- *Regular review reports to the board.* Many multinationals already have a process of regularly reviewing at board level the risk profiles of derivative contracts. To prevent surprises, the board needs to be told regularly which derivatives contracts are under water or are about to flip into being a liability, together with the recommended course of action.
- *Authority to execute.* The company should give thought to the process for entering into various types of derivative contracts – that is, the checks and balances which exist in relation to the sole authority to commit the business along with the deal size/risk parameters capable of being signed off and by whom.
- *Internal* Treasury management procedures. Internal procedures need to exist and be policed to ensure that company guidelines in respect of derivative contracts purchased and sold are not breached. To this end, internal/external auditors should be required to report on the effectiveness of and adherence to company guidelines on a regular basis. To ensure adherence to laid-down guidelines on derivatives, it is worth considering linking employee annual appraisals, salary increments or bonuses to the quality of Treasury risk management practices and procedures – experience bears out the old adage, 'what gets rewarded gets done'.
- *Work with an acknowledged market-maker.* A lot of the requisite information technology is used by the market-makers, and this should be regularly tapped for strategic advice on derivative positions. No leading derivative house or bank has a crystal ball, but they can interpret latest market events, structure and customise innovative derivative-linked financial solutions to the corporate's needs and then provide a continuous reasoned and professional view on changing market conditions in respect of deals.
- *External reporting in respect of derivative exposures.* It is perhaps true that the recent switch to mark-to-market reporting from accrual reporting in the USA has shown many firms' derivative positions to be under water. However, the method of reporting derivative exposures is not consistent across the globe. Therefore, CEOs need to guard against dysfunctional behaviour in Treasury management as a result of shifts in derivative accounting practices. The point to remember is that

accounting methodologies have positive and negative implications; for example, mark-to-market introduces a high level of corporate earnings volatility which does not just apply to derivative contract exposures.

In conclusion, derivatives are a powerful tool in managing any business. With the benefit of a well-defined corporate policy for derivative exposure, which is firmly linked to internal management controls and related management processes, CEOs and boards are well placed to use derivatives to manage their businesses, and ultimately the bottom line, proactively.

David Etherington is head of corporate business development with the department of International Trade and Banking Services at NatWest Bank plc.

EUROPE'S CROSS-BORDER BUYS

Richard Agutter

The first half of 1994 saw a real pick-up in cross-border mergers and acquisitions; but many companies are still nervous about investing, and want to see further economic recovery.

The international economic recovery, which started in the USA in 1993 and is now apparent in the UK and other European countries, will no doubt stimulate domestic and cross-border mergers and acquisition activity in Europe. Although such activity fell in the second half of 1993, as compared to the first six months, there is optimism that M&A deals will increase thanks to this economic upsurge. In fact, the first half of 1994 saw something of a recovery in Europe, with cross-border mergers and acquisitions on the rise both in deal numbers and values.

However, many companies may still be nervous about investing before they see further recovery in European economies: and some may still be refocusing or rethinking their growth strategies. There is inevitably going to be some time-lag between the recovery of the international economy and increased M&A activity. Table 1 is a European league table of purchasing and selling countries, compiled by KPMG, based on figures for the first half of 1994.

The UK accounted for around half of all the corporate acquisitions made in the European Union in the first half of 1994 – an indicator of the fact that the UK is emerging more rapidly from the recession. There

European Union	Purchasing countries 1st half year 1994			Selling countries 1st half year 1994	
	No	$m		No	$m
UK	207	8 749	UK	125	4 363
France	84	3 596	Germany	129	2 474
Germany	78	2 163	Italy	42	1 410
Netherlands	69	641	Spain	28	1 240
Ireland	25	352	Netherlands	36	1 013
Italy	18	310	Belgium	19	476
Denmark	36	176	Denmark	36	125
Portugal	2	27	France	91	111
Belgium	8	19	Ireland	4	10
Luxembourg	5	0	Portugal	3	0
Spain	3	0	Greece	2	0
Greece	0	0	Luxembourg	1	0
Total EC	535	16 033		516	11 222
Rest of Europe					
Switzerland	48	10 622	Sweden	27	1 388
Sweden	23	757	Other	1	354
Finland	15	83	Switzerland	28	318
Norway	9	452	Norway	11	196
Austria	8	0	Austria	10	147
			Russia	10	56
			Poland	9	51
			Romania	1	21
			Hungary	7	15
			Bulgaria	2	5
			Finland	12	0
Total rest of Europe	103	11 914		118	2 551
Total Europe	638	27 947		634	13 773

Table 1. Cross-border M&A activity: outright acquisitions.

has also been a consistent rise in the number of German acquisitions, both in terms of deal values and deal numbers: although at the same time there has been a marked increase in sales by German businesses. This latter trend probably reflects the shock of the recession in Germany. Many German businesses refocused their businesses and divested non-core activities, but there has been an increase in sales by firms in financial difficulties. France has shown a fairly consistent trend over the past three half-years in terms of deal numbers, although total values showed a marked increase in the second half of 1993 and the first half of 1994.

In the rest of Europe, the most consistent and marked growth has been in Switzerland, where both deal numbers and deal values have increased. Part of this growth reflects Roche Holding's $5.3 billion acquisition of

Syntex, the chemical/pharmaceutical group, and Sandoz's $3.7 billion buy of Gerber (food and drink). But KPMG experts in Switzerland note that generally the past 12 months have been very active.

No clear trends are evident from the statistics on the other countries. In Eastern Europe, the full statistics on outright acquisitions, joint ventures and minority holdings reveal that Poland and Hungary still have the highest levels of activity, but that the growth of M&A in Eastern Europe may have slowed somewhat. Certainly, businesses are giving themselves the time to learn the lessons of the early pioneers.

The overall picture, though, is that the coming into being of the European Single Market at the beginning of 1993 has not, as many financial advisers had hoped, triggered a wave of M&A activity in Europe. While it is clear that there was a pick-up in cross-border activity in the first half of 1994, as always one must be cautious about drawing any firm conclusions. In the short to medium term, assuming there is no serious downturn in the economic climate, three factors are likely to foster increased deal activity in Europe. The first is ongoing privatisation. Second, industry deregulation will have a continuing effect. Third, industry consolidations along American lines will occur in sectors such as banking and financial services, and food and drink.

Acquisitions in Europe do offer exciting opportunities. But the fear of the unknown can often be an unnecessary barrier to companies pursuing them. The problems which companies often encounter when considering European acquisitions are many, and integrated international accounting firms with their European networks are well placed to provide advice on many of these issues:

- *Information.* Lack of publicly available information concerning private companies can make it difficult to appraise a number of likely targets
- *Valuations.* In an unfamiliar market, knowing how much to offer for a company without overpaying can be a particular problem. Specialist local knowledge will be important
- *Financial information.* European variations in accounting treatment, style and approach can have dramatic impacts on companies' accounts from country to country and make interpretation difficult. Awareness of these differences is vital to a thorough appraisal of any targets
- *Culture and language.* This might now seem irrelevant in modern Europe but it is essential that in negotiations all parties have a clear understanding of the other parties' position. Misunderstandings often lead to failure. Differences in negotiating style also have their impact. No doubt national differences had their part to play in the failure of the Alcazar project to merge four European airlines and the collapse of the proposed tie-up between Sweden's Volvo and France's Renault
- *Friendly deals.* In Europe, mergers are more usually constructed in the sense of true agreement rather than in the way more common in the USA, where one party is seen to defeat the other. Emphasis on the friendlier attitude when making European acquisitions will be an

important factor in completing successful deals. Those companies that are only interested in 100 per cent control will have fewer available opportunities and lesser ultimate chances of success

- *Regulatory issues.* Consideration of any domestic regulation which might prevent an acquisition needs early attention
- *Integration of the business.* This can often be a significant additional expense, both in cash terms and in wasted management time.

Management styles do differ between countries in Europe, and this must be taken into account. Thought needs to be given at the outset as to whether the cultures of the businesses are so different that the acquisition is never likely to integrate successfully. In that event, of course, the would-be buyer would be extremely unwise to proceed.

Richard Agutter is a partner of KMPG Corporate Finance.

PERFORMANCE'S NEW MEASURES

Guy Dresser

Non-financial measures of performance such as product quality, customer satisfaction and employee motivation are proving to be more accurate than traditional financial indicators.

The practice of forecasting future corporate performance on the basis of a series of financial indicators alone has had its day. Purely financial measures of performance lack predictive power. By their very nature, all they can reveal is where the company has been, not where it is going, nor what key changes are taking place in the customer base, markets or technology. Rapidly changing business circumstances require new means of predicting the direction of markets, innovations in technology and customer demands.

Financial data on their own will not provide management with the full picture, but a range of other measures will point to the underlying trends in a business. The real bottom line is that there is little correlation between profit performance of a business at any given point in time and what its performance is likely to be in the future. But there is a strong correlation between the underlying structure of a business, as measured by non-financial performance indicators, and its future performance.

Customer satisfaction, employee motivation, product quality and business processes are just a handful of the additional measures of corporate performance that need to be tracked. These, more than basic financial

128

indicators alone, will provide a meaningful picture of the underlying trends within the business. With the combination of financial and non-financial measures of performance at its disposal, senior management should be well placed to predict, and pre-empt, market developments and to direct the business accordingly.

The debate over non-financial performance measurement has been given added impetus by the decline in fortunes of companies which, just 5—10 years ago, were market and world leaders. IBM is one case in point. On assuming office, the corporation's CEO, Louis V Gerstner, said that customer satisfaction and employee morale were among the most important priorities for IBM today. Yet for most companies, the process of understanding, defining and implementing non-financial measures can be contentious, time-consuming – even tedious. Often many of the companies which have undertaken this process have done so only after the onset of a crisis, usually occasioned by a serious loss of market share. Subsequently, most have been highly impressed by the new focus which non-financial measures bring to their activities.

Inaccurate reflections

The main issue with traditional corporate performance measurement today is that it is both an incomplete and an inaccurate reflection of reality. Worse, many corporate managers believe that their company's systems both reward the wrong achievements and encourage the pursuit of the wrong goals. In particular, measures persist in reflecting the needs of a manufacturing-based economy, where corporate requirements arise out of the relationship between man and machine, rather than between customer and supplier. Today's economy is much more service-based, meaning that the most important assets in a business are its experienced customers and employees. Measures should therefore focus on these two groups at least.

For example, proper two-way communication with employees is vital. Once the initial input from staff has helped management to identify those areas which require improvement, the company can begin to empower staff at all levels to attend to them. At British Airways, the manager for market-place performance, Roger Davies, says that customers are 'the ultimate reality check; they let us know if we are getting things right or not'. Unfortunately research shows that many managers are not asking either customers or employees how to secure their loyalty. Consequently, managers' understanding of customer and employee requirements and motivations is, at best, limited and, at worst, wrong.

Besides being outdated reflections of corporate health, existing financial indicators lack predictive power and are too summary in nature. It is the *underlying* reasons for the figures, rather than the figures alone, which must be analysed to give a meaningful picture of the business. Benchmarking against competitors or other external operational indicators provides further clues for those seeking competitive advantage. Yet many company managers still only compare their current results with those from previous years, rather than seeking some external, competitive indicator against which to benchmark. Comparison with previous years' figures can provide only a partial picture of how the business shapes up and, in any case, fails to take account of major changes within the business itself by not comparing like with like.

To maximise its benchmarking activity, 3M seeks information on 'best practice' leaders. Peter Lewis, head of the company's customer satisfaction initiative, says that 'We may ask the client overall who is his best supplier. It may turn out to be someone we don't compete with. That information then provides us with a potential benchmarking partner'. Measuring the wrong indicator, though, will reinforce wrong behaviours within a company on the 'what gets measured, gets managed' principle. So if quarterly figures are the key business measures – as in many cases they are – this can result in the whole business being treated like a cash cow, with no focus on creating value in the longer term.

Performance measures

The decision to review the performance measurement system is not one to be taken lightly. There is also no clearly defined point, though, at which companies realise that a new framework of performance measures must be implemented. Indeed, one of the difficulties lies in persuading managers of the need to undertake the long, complex task of formulating new measures when their company appears to be performing adequately. In many respects, these managers would be right. Research by Business Intelligence has shown that the least effective starting-point for a performance measurement review is when a company has both the time and resources to study the situation carefully and methodically.

Without the conviction that is generated by crisis, such reviews will not receive the priority that they require. The most significant crises arise from the emergence of new competitors, changing customer demands, new regulatory environments, new ownership, the impact of new technology, or even outright financial disaster. There are plenty of examples of companies that have been forced by either a single one of these factors, or a combination, to develop the serious intent required for proper overhaul of performance measures.

Xerox faced a crisis in the mid-1980s under the onslaught of new entrants to the photocopier market. A radical overhaul in management philosophy, objectives and performance measures led to the emergence of customer service as the most important internal indicator of performance. At 3M, too, a shake-up of performance measures came about when it realised that it could no longer afford the lost investment on unsuccessful products. Margins had shrunk over a 10-year period. Now products had to satisfy customers first time – in increasingly competitive markets, the repercussions on business of a substantial market failure have become too costly to bear. Consequently, customer requirements became a major driver of product innovation, and the 3M answer to the question of developing a high-performance business emerged: 'First ask the customer what he wants and the way he wants it, and then give it to him just that way. All the time'.

New performance measures must usually be developed in conjunction with a full strategic review of the firm's activities, values and objectives. Those companies which have undertaken total quality or re-engineering initiatives therefore have a useful head-start. While customer satisfaction measures are the most important non-financial indicators that can be devised, defining the satisfied customer is not easy; nor is using the available data. There is also a close link between employee and customer satisfaction, since a motivated employee is likely to provide better service to the customer; new performance measures should thus track this relationship as well.

Most companies focus on qualitative benefits, such as improved planning, more reliable data, better internal communications, more motivated staff and faster response times. However, in many instances, the process of performance review sheds a new and harsh light on the real drivers of value in a company. Hence the review can trigger profound changes to products, market strategies, organisational structure, human resource policies and the information architecture of a business.

The nature of the review varies significantly between companies. Business Intelligence's research found the explanation: companies were also likely to be involved in one or more much broader management initiatives. The latter could also have a major impact on the process of performance measurement review – examples being total quality, change management, IT review, or process re-engineering.

At Rank Xerox, for example, the emphasis on quality led to developing a balanced scorecard consisting of three non-financial measures and one financial: customer service, employee satisfaction, return on assets, and market share. Change management is also a powerful context for reforming performance measurement, since the main thrust of change is to challenge existing corporate cultures. Here performance measurement is a powerful level.

IT reviews

IT reviews, too, can frequently result in a performance measurement exercise. This is because the exercise highlights classic management confusion over strategic goals and their relative priority. Often management will recognise that the difficulty with the outcome of an IT review lies, not with the existing systems technology, but with its strategic focus. This leads to initiating a performance measurement review, followed by a systems development phase designed to enable the company to measure performance more closely.

In essence, a new performance measurement system focusing on non-financial indicators can improve processes, satisfy customers and enable staff at all levels both to understand the company's new strategy and culture, and to work together to implement it. The significance of a performance measurement review cannot be understated – in the future, performance will be used increasingly as a tool for decision-making and systems for measuring that performance will no longer function. They will go to the heart of the business and its improvement.

Guy Dresser is reports editor at Business Intelligence, which published the business management report Performance Measurement: The New Agenda, price £395 (£445 overseas). For further information, telephone 0181-544 1830.

THE BUSINESS OF THE BENEFITS

Colin Pugh

Are employers in danger of losing control of their benefit plans? This is not just a question of plan design or human resources; there are major financial considerations too.

As with other aspects of its operation, a company needs both a strategy and a structure to be able to control its benefit plans. It needs to know where it is going in regard to the operation of its benefit programmes, and it needs a structure in order to establish and maintain control. The first basic step is simply to understand the pitfalls of not being in control, and to realise the rapidly increasing number of obstacles being placed in the path of an employer trying to manage benefits plans in an effective manner.

Benefit plans in this context encompass all company-sponsored programmes addressing retirement, death, disability and hospital/medical. The main focus next will be on retirement income. Pension plans are the most expensive element of the package and attract the greatest amount of attention from employees, legislators and others. Employer-sponsored defined-benefit pension plans dominate in Austria, Belgium, Germany, Ireland, Luxembourg, The Netherlands, Norway, Portugal, Switzerland, the UK and possibly Spain. These are the European countries where pension plans will demand the greatest attention. Defined contribution plans are far more common in Denmark, and are gaining

133

popularity in other countries. Multi-employer plans and equivalent, quasi-social security arrangements are dominant in Finland, France, Greece, Italy and Sweden.

Employers in most countries are not required by any law to establish a full package of pension and other benefit plans. However, if a company decided some years ago to establish such plans, it realised that certain regulations would have to be followed in order for the company and its employees to obtain tax deductibility for their contributions. This was readily understandable, and employers designed and financed their plans in accordance with these fiscal requirements. The problems arose much later, with a plethora of legislation from other branches of government. Some of this legislation created significant extra costs for the employer, often with retroactive implications. Employers were bewildered, and justifiably became concerned that they were losing control of their benefit plans.

Common traps

What problems do employers now face? What are the common traps? How can management control be increased? It first needs to be re-emphasised that proper management of company benefit plans is not just confined to matters of plan design; in other words, the determination of the levels of benefits to be provided to employees and their beneficiaries, and the conditions under which such benefits will be paid. Proper management also includes effective control over the financing of the promised benefits: the insurance contract, pension fund, internal financing or other approach to delivering the promised benefits.

Attention needs to be paid to the financing of every benefit plan, but funding of the company's pension plan is clearly the most important consideration in many European countries. It is also the aspect that attracts the greatest attention from employees and legislators, not to mention auditors and analysts. Pension plan funding is a fine balancing act between underfunding, where the assets are insufficient to cover the accruing obligations, and overfunding. Both are unattractive in the longer term, although the problems of being overfunded are less well understood.

The Swiss are supposed to have invented the concept of the three pillars of retirement income protection, in which the state, the employer and the individual are all responsible in their different ways for such retirement income protection. The concept has been adopted in many other countries and has generally worked very well. So, what is going wrong? The answer stems from the inability of most governments to fulfil their part of the bargain. The benefits cannot be financed by the existing social security taxes, and most countries are finding it impossible to increase the levels of such taxes. The social security benefits themselves must therefore be reduced. Belgium and Italy are among the countries that are currently expressing concern.

The three pillars will be realigned, but how? Some governments expect individuals (the third pillar) to assume more of the responsibility, and are introducing new tax incentives for personal retirement planning. Other governments are ambivalent. Most employees simply expect their employers to solve the problem. Will your company be stuck in the middle? In the absence of a proactive approach, employers will inevitably be caught in a trap.

European employers are being bombarded with government legislation, from various branches of their own national governments and from Brussels. It is difficult to argue against the basic thrust of some of the legislation, such as the removal of sex discrimination, but other legislative developments can make employers wonder why they implemented benefit plans in the first place.

Faster vesting, and therefore higher benefit, on termination of service is a logical evolution, but its application to accrued benefits means an overnight increase in company costs; Belgium and Switzerland are the latest countries to introduce very fast vesting requirements. Increasing pensions- in-payment to retired employees, and adjustments to deferred pensions of former employees, are also laudable objectives, but legislative imposition of such indexation as an additional and unplanned cost to the employer is difficult to defend. The Netherlands and the UK have complicated legislation in this regard. Then there is the latest Swiss legislation, giving employees the right to buy additional past service benefits for periods of time before even being with the company; the legislation is designed in such a manner as to impose significant additional .

New legislation

The retrospective application of much of the new legislation is its most disturbing aspect. Future benefits can often be modified to control the company's future cost exposure, but application of new legislation to old benefit accruals is simply a matter of changing the rules after the game has started.

However, all is not lost. Although the above constraints are real, there are still many important options to be considered by an employer when reacting to legislative developments. The process needs to be carefully managed. It is important to avoid the temptation to stack the new requirements blindly on top of existing benefits. This happens all too frequently. The end-result is an uncontrolled escalation of costs.

Financing is basically giving substance to the employer's obligation. It involves establishing and maintaining an arrangement for delivering the promised benefits. The choices are generally between a pension fund, insurance contracts or direct payment of the plan benefits by the company. The last option almost always involves the establishment of book reserves on the company's balance sheet. Not all of these basic financing vehicles are allowed or are tax-effective in a single country. It should also be noted that countries currently permitting some form of pay-as-you-go or book reserve arrangement are starting to push for external prefunding; examples are France and Spain.

Funding a pension plan is not simply a case of throwing company money at the pension fund or blindly accepting the advice of the fund's actuary. Funding needs to be very carefully managed. Most European pension plans have become very well funded during the past decade, and the time has come for plan sponsors (employers) to sit back and review their strategies. There are no universal definitions of underfunded and overfunded in this context, but there are some general concepts. If the assets are insufficient to cover the plan termination liabilities, then the plan is clearly underfunded. Is this necessarily a problem?

If there is no chance of the pension plan being wound up in the foreseeable future, and the employer has a sound funding strategy for the future, then the answer is No. However, most governments have decided this particular issue. Plan assets must either equal or exceed the plan termination liabilities, or any shortfall must be quickly rectified. At the other extreme, the plan is clearly overfunded if the assets exceed a realistic estimate of the present value of accrued benefits; including, where applicable, an allowance for the effect of future salary increases on such accrued benefits. This important measure of the accrued liabilities has become widely known as the Projected Benefit Obligation (PBO), which was the term introduced by the US accounting profession in the mid-1980s while developing its pension accounting standards.

This is where the debate really begins. When the assets exceeded the PBO, the resultant funding excess was traditionally viewed in a positive light. Although the pension fund did not currently need the money, governments still allowed corporate tax deductibility of further company contributions. The funding excesses provided a comfortable cushion against future funding requirements, but they became dangerously labelled as surpluses. New laws or regulations were then introduced governing the ownership and application of pension plan surpluses. Although supposedly designed to protect employees, these new requirements have become so onerous in most European countries that they effectively invite employers to take actions to avoid any such overfunding in the future.

Even before the most recent legislation, employers were already discovering that they had substantially lost control of the extra money they had cautiously set aside in their pension funds; money which was excess to the pension plan's requirements and was now needed to help keep the company going. In most European countries, excess plan assets cannot be withdrawn from either a terminated or a continuing pension fund. Even trying to stop company contributions can be tortuous process, and it is often only a slow and partial solution to addressing an overfunded position. Sometimes. even before the company is able to take corrective action, the funding excess has to be spent to enhance the benefits for current and former employees.

New funding strategies

As a result of all these considerations, employers are designing and implementing new funding strategies for their pension plans. Earlier strategies, even if they existed, are being radically overhauled. Company contributions are being appropriately adjusted in order to establish and maintain assets at a level less than the PBO, but still greater than the termination liabilities.

The good news is that EU legislation and a generally more sophisticated market-place have created new opportunities for more effective financing. Human resource and finance people must work together on these issues, and establish an increasing level of control. The rewards will justify the effort.

Colin Pugh heads the office of William M Mercer International SA in Brussels.

THE AVAILABILITY OF FINANCE

Simon Bettany

Banks want to back viable businesses and work in partnership with borrowers. They are ready to consider balanced plans and will price loans to win the best business.

Before looking at the availability of finance it is worth considering the lessons which have emerged from the recession for both bankers and borrowers, and reminding ourselves how hard an impact the recession has had on the UK economy Receiverships grew from around 1500 in 1989 to a peak of 5750 in 1991, before falling back to just over 3000 in 1993. Over the same period, unemployment rose by over 1 million to around 2.9 million. Additionally both commercial and residential property values have dropped sharply — the fall in commercial values being close to 40 per cent.

Not surprisingly, given this background, the Big Four clearing banks saw a four-fold increase in provisions for bad debt from 1989 to 1992 (excluding Third World debt).

Both banks and potential borrowers can learn valuable lessons from more general experiences during the recession. By building on these lessons, both sides will be better placed to ensure the future availability of debt. On a macro level, the following are some of the issues:

- It is easy to justify a business case using statistics. You simply pick the

138

ones that fit the conclusion you want and ignore the rest; even if you consider them all you have to make a judgment – which is not always easy to get right.

- It is not only corporates and their bankers who have difficulty in interpreting economic data; professional economists also have difficulty – their opinions often differ, and many of their forecasts are incorrect; so take advice from more than one source and always consider the opposite point of view.

- Do not underestimate competitive threats – a very important point. Businesses must react to what competitors are doing as well as anticipating their strategies. Doing this can be much harder when recession contracts the overall market.

Recession has also taught that internal company pressures can be great. Pressures to achieve targets, in whatever form, within an organisation are heavy and increasing. While targeting is fine, it must be focused on the right areas and regularly reviewed. Focusing exclusively on the wrong areas, such as market share, sales volumes and short-term profitability, without fully evaluating the consequences, has caused significant damage to many companies. There can also be a tendency for companies to focus on short-term profits growth by dressing up their accounts through creative accounting, instead of addressing core problems.

But what should borrowers and lenders focus on when looking at the future? Greater prudence is needed. I see a lot of business plans in my job. Almost without exception, they show companies increasing sales, gaining market share, raising margins, increasing profitability. It is not possible for every company to do this. As a banker, I would much rather see a business plan that is realistic or slightly conservative than one which is over-optimistic.

More planning and regular updating of plans is also needed – both in terms of longer-term strategic planning and detailed short- to medium-term operational planning. Without proper planning, a business cannot know that the decisions taken on a day-to-day basis will fit its longer-term objectives. As part of the planning process, more sensitivity analysis is needed to ensure that business plans are robust and can cope with issues like rises in interest rates and reductions in sales and margins.

In undertaking sensitivity analysis, it is easy to obtain the results you want by sensitising down to your bottom line, whatever that may be – minimum return on capital employed, say, or repayment of a loan. The temptation is to stop there; but what happens if you go further? As part of the sensitivity process, there is a need for more contingency planning. Key risks need to be identified and plans drawn up to cope with risk when it becomes reality.

Healthy cash flow

Expect your bankers to look very critically at cash flow in your business –

139

where cash is generated and where it is being used. The banker's prime objective in most financings is to ensure that enough cash is generated to pay interest and repay debt. Banks want to see the source of their exit. The quality of operating cash flow is the key to good lending, not profitability, and not asset values, which can fluctuate with market demand.

This suggests a need for greater mutual understanding and a two-way flow of information between bank and borrower. A borrower approaching a bank for finance should be prepared to answer detailed questions about the business. In future, banks are likely to require more due diligence work before they lend.

The depth of work will depend upon the situation and the perceived risk to the bank. In NatWest, we have business appraisal managers and seconded qualified accountants in each of our 6 corporate regions. Their job is to read behind the business plans on new business proposals presented to the bank. Where a more detailed review is required, we may require due diligence completed by independent sources before lending.

Sharing information

Banks are looking to develop a better understanding of their customers' businesses, so borrowers should really be prepared to share information – both at the time when the borrowing is put in place and on a continuing basis. Banks will normally expect to see a regular supply of management information – we need to hear bad news as well as good. Early advice of an actual or potential problem gives bank and borrower time to work together to solve the problem in a manner satisfactory to both parties. Belated advice can often leave both parties without the precious commodity of time.

If borrowers can meet the bank's requirements for thorough and prudent business planning, demonstrate good cash generation and are willing to share information, they should not have difficulty in presenting a good case for raising bank debt.

So what financing options are available? How will the supply of loans match up to demand, and what can be expected by way of new requests?

Requests are likely to fall into two broad categories:

- *Working capital* to support increased trading levels (likely to be a reality for most manufacturing businesses)
- *Capital expenditure*, either to bring existing equipment back up to standard because investment has suffered during the recession, or to invest in new plant and equipment to support higher levels of turnover.

In addition, there will be other requests to fund investment in new products and markets, and acquisitions.

This is against a background of limited demand for company products, with recovery taking time to work its way through to increased sales and profits. Balance sheets have been weakened by exceptional redundancy and closure costs, revaluation write-downs and high gearing through trading losses. However, there is competition among the banks for good business. Banks have suffered from falling income streams as a result of writing off bad debts, non-performing loans, perceived reluctance from corporates to borrow, and some corporates taking advantage of a buoyant equity market to raise fresh capital from existing shareholders. As a result, there is healthy competition from banks to lend for good quality proposals.

So what options are available to companies when approaching their banks for finance? Historically, banks have provided significant funding on overdraft. This can have drawbacks from the banks' and the borrowers' perspectives. Overdrafts by their nature are repayable on demand and subject to frequent review. They do not provide certainty to borrowers. From the bank's standpoint, overdrafts are difficult to control, have no defined repayment programme, and tend to be fully utilised. So banks will be seeking to lend increasingly on a structured loan basis, probably committed over a term against covenants linked to the borrower's business plan.

They will also be looking to link the life of the loan to the life of the asset financed and will expect to achieve repayment from cash flows generated by the assets funded. Overdrafts are increasingly likely to be restricted to short-term timing differences linked to the working capital cycle of the business; lenders will expect utilisation to fluctuate accordingly. In some circumstances, banks will encourage their customers to raise finance through specialist lending vehicles. Leasing or invoice discounting are obvious ways of matching liabilities with assets.

Despite the impact of the recession, banks are open to write quality business and will compete to win it. In defining quality, we are looking to lend to corporates who exemplify the principles discussed earlier. But what other factors does a bank look at when making a credit decision? It will focus on three key areas: management; non-financial analysis; and financial analysis.

When assessing management we look at (for instance) background, track record, how people work together, whether there are any dominant members of the team, succession, management reporting systems, ambitions and strategy.

Non-financial analysis focuses on the industry and sector in which the customer operates, competition and the customer's market position. NatWest UK has a defined strategy influencing our approach to lending in 30 major sectors, which is fine-tuned for each of our regions. Such an approach does not rule out lending to more difficult sectors – we recognise that there will always be successful niche operators.

A bank will undertake financial analysis based on the historic financial information, and will also look for detailed projections supported by a thorough business plan, incorporating a clearly defined corporate strategy. Our focus will be on robust cash flows, capable of repaying debt after undertaking realistic sensitivity analysis and implementing contingency plans in the event of key risks materialising.

Competitive pricing

Remember what was noted earlier banks will compete for quality business. This is already evident in both the syndications and bilateral loan markets, where pricing for good quality business is lower than it was 12 months ago. Banks are prepared to consider balanced propositions and will not price to recover previous losses. They want to back viable businesses and they want to work with borrowers as a partnership. Moreover, the potential supply of finance will exceed demand. Because of all this, pricing will be competitive.

Simon Bettany is a manager in NatWest' UK's central Corporate Credit Department.

The above article is an edited version of a presentation made at a 'Financing for Growth' Conference held in London in February 1994.

THE ROLE OF THE FACTOR

Paul Hancock

The UK factoring industry offers a professional service to commercial organisations, solving the problems of bad debt risk, the cash flow gap and the credit management task.

The latest figures released by the Association of British Factors and Discounters show that this industry is growing by 20 per cent a year, suggesting that there is a real need within the market served by factors. What is the industry's role in the 1990s? What benefits are conferred upon users? To answer these questions it is necessary to understand the nature of trade credit: simply, when one business sells goods or services to another it is normal to grant trade credit; that is, to allow the customer time to settle the invoice.

Terms vary according to the trade. In fresh food, for example, payment may be expected in seven to fourteen days. In the printing industry 90 day terms were once prevalent, although these have been reduced in recent years. The most common terms of trade are net monthly, meaning that all invoices raised in a month should be paid on the last day of the following month. Thus, if all invoices are raised equally throughout the month and paid strictly on time, the supplier will receive payment on an average of 45 days from invoice date.

Most industry surveys reveal that companies receive payment on an average of 75 to 80 days. Thus customers are, on average, abusing credit

143

terms by taking an extra month to pay. This is free credit to the customer, but expensive for the supplier. As interest rates rise, so illiquid customers seek to extend the payment period. Virtually every company granting trade credit will face the following problems:

- *The cash flow gap* – there will be a need to finance the time customers take to pay. This may mean increased bank borrowings or extending the credit taken from suppliers. In extreme cases it may even be impossible to pay preferential creditors.
- *The bad debt risk* – most companies are dealing with commercial organisations rather than government bodies. In times of economic downturn corporate failure is rife, and many companies have lost money when a customer's business has failed.
- *The credit management task* – sales ledger records must be kept; there are statements, reminders, special letters, telephone calls, finals and even legal action. It all takes time, skilled people, and hard work. It is unproductive.

There are three areas in which a factor claims special expertise, and these are the foundations for a professional service. The first is *credit underwriting*. A non-recourse factor provides bad debt protection through credit limits. If the client trades within those limits, payment will be made by the factor if the debtor fails to pay. A recourse factor does not accept the credit risk but will provide advisory credit limits based on knowledge of debtors. But if the debtor fails to pay, the factor will not pay.

At the heart of any factor's operation is a major computer installation, dedicated to *sales ledger administration and credit management*. Statements must be accurate, regular and up to date. Payments received must be promptly reconciled against invoices outstanding in order to keep the ledger clean and make it easy for credit managers to see which invoices are outstanding and overdue. The credit management function must be sensitively geared to the client's needs and credit policy. That will usually mean similar collection routines for overdue amounts of similar value, with an emphasis on speedier action on larger overdues. There may be individual routines for special customers; in extremes it is even possible to have a different collection routine for every customer, although it is unlikely to be needed.

Pursuing overdue payments is a matter of skilled diplomacy, tact, and persistence. The credit manager will establish the name of the person responsible for payment at the debtor's office and learn of any special payment routines which apply. It is important to discover whether there is a valid reason for non-payment and thereafter to obtain a clear undertaking as to payment date. Members of the factoring industry collect debts in averages of between 55 and 65 days. International Factors collected UK debts in an average of 55 days in 1993. This compares with national average collection cycles of between 75 and 80 days and demonstrates the effectiveness of skilled credit management.

In *international trading*, the Single European Market has provided additional stimulus for UK exporters, and access to an additional market of 370 million consumers. However, buyers will probably wish to buy on Open Account terms – in other words, to receive the goods and an invoice and to pay it when their cash flow allows, just as in the UK. Just as in the UK, this can be a hazardous way of trading. Communications are not aided by language difficulties, nor are collections helped by different trading customs and legal practices. The larger factoring companies have overseas partners with which they work to provide added benefits for UK exporters choosing to use a factoring service.

The services provided by the principal factoring and invoice discounting companies are led by *full service factoring for UK sales*. Total cash flow management is the complete answer to the problems of slow-paying customers. Clients gain full sales ledger administration and credit management, and open-ended finance geared to sales growth. In addition, if the service is what is described as non-recourse, the client will gain protection against bad debt loss on all credit approved sales. With a recourse service that protection will not be included.

Bad debt protection

Companies are helped to grow safely and strongly, first, through bad debt protection. Before making an offer the factor checks the customers in the sales ledger, so that credit limits for existing business are in place when factoring starts. As new customers are gained application is made for the credit limits required. Factors, with their extensive credit libraries on thousands of companies, provide fast and accurate decisions.

Once the factor accepts the credit risk the client can trade safely, knowing that payment will be made automatically if the customer fails to pay. Payment is normally made on insolvency of the customer or 120 days after due date. When sending an invoice to a customer, the client simply sends a copy to the factor, who ledgers the item, and sends statements and reminders in accordance with trading terms. Collection routines are agreed with the client when factoring starts. It is the client's policy which applies, to ensure that customers' goodwill is maintained. If legal action seems necessary the client's consent will be sought. If litigation on a credit-approved invoice is mutually agreed, the factor bears all the costs.

Prepayments up to the agreed percentage of credit-approved invoices – usually 80 per cent or 85 per cent – are available on the next working day after the factor receives copy invoices. The balance, less charges, is paid when the factor receives the customer's payment. These charges for finance will usually cost 3 per cent a year more than Bank Base Rate and are calculated on a day-to-day basis. The factoring charge for bad debt protection and sales ledger service will usually be between 0.75 per cent and 2.5 per cent of factored sales, and is the subject of a formal quotation after an investigation of the business and the workload and risk in the ledger.

The key full-service components for safer *exporting* also include bad debt protection. The factor will check the credit standing of existing customers, and new customers when the client gains them. Decisions are often made by the factor's local associate in the customer's market using local commercial information. Provided that the client delivers goods in accordance with that approval the factor will pay even if the customer fails to. No claims procedure is necessary – payment is automatic, usually on insolvency or 120 days after due date. If the client holds a credit insurance policy, factors are generally willing to accept that as an alternative to including bad debt protection in the service. A formal assignment of the policy may be required. Once the factor has received copy invoices, details will normally be sent to an associated company in the buyer's market. The associates will ledger the item and send statements and reminders in accordance with trading terms. The effect of local credit management, dealing in the customer's language, is often to secure earlier payment of invoices.

Finance for growth is available on similar terms to UK factoring. The client can call on the factor to pay up to the agreed percentage of credit-approved invoices – usually 80 or 85 per cent – on the next working day after receiving copies. The balance is paid, less charges, when the customer pays. Finance can be made available in either sterling or the currency of the invoice. If a client chooses the latter, the cost of finance may be lower, and the currency may be used to reduce the exchange risk. Finance will, again, usually cost 3 per cent per annum more than Bank Base Rate and is calculated on a day-to-day basis. Currency finance will be quoted at a margin above cost of funds. The factoring charge for bad debt protection and sales ledger administration is normally the same as in the UK.

Confidential invoice discounting applies where the business has substantial sums tied up in debtor balances and a fully computerised sales ledger but no need for the collections expertise of full service factoring. The service can provide high levels of finance at competitive rates. The discounter provides immediate payment of up to 80 per cent against good trade debts outstanding in the ledger when discounting starts, and a similar sum against new invoices as copies are submitted to the discounter.

If the company is already doing a first-class credit management job, there is no reason for any change. While the contract continues, the client maintains all contact with customers, and they remain unaware of the role of the discounter. Customer payments are normally banked to the credit of an account in the discounter's name; he will then release the balance of 20 per cent, debiting the discount charge at each month-end.

Bad debt protection may be available as an optional extra. If it is included then, subject to carrying a small first loss on any claim, the client will be shielded against bad debts on any credit-approved customer. This option means that the finance is without recourse and the client will not be asked to repay the funds if an approved customer defaults through insolvency.

Discount charge

There is a discount charge based upon the finance used, and this will be comparable with normal bank overdraft charges. There will also be an administration charge. This will depend upon annual turnover and whether or not bad debt protection is to be included in the service. It will be calculated as a small percentage of discounted turnover – usually between 0.2 per cent and 0.5 per cent. The finance that invoice discounting provides is particularly suited to growing businesses as the funding is linked directly with the level of sales.

Paul Hancock is sales and marketing director of International Factors Limited.

HOW BPR HELPS IN FINANCE

Richard Hawksworth

BPR radically improves performance by evaluating and redesigning each nut and bolt of a core business process to determine its true value to the customer.

The current vogue puts business process re-engineering (BPR) top of the management agenda. Featured in the portfolios of all of the Big Six management consultancies, BPR is certainly making a big splash. But are the claims made for it based on fact or fantasy?

The first step toward evaluating the value of BPR is to define the term. Interpretations vary, but in general BPR is a way of radically improving performance by evaluating and redesigning core business processes – either on a company-wide basis, or by applying BPR to individual divisions or functions within an organisation. BPR assesses how products and services are delivered, but (and this is the crucial point) all processes must be surveyed from the customer's point of view. It looks at the value chain of the business, evaluating each nut and bolt of a process to determine its individual value to the customer.

That is the theory, but in order to prove or disprove it, a practical example of BPR in action is needed. Consider the case of two major international companies which have employed a BPR programme: Caradon plc and Grand Metropolitan plc. In each case, the programme impacted directly on the finance department, and is view ed here from that angle.

First, what is the environment in which the finance department of a thriving business operates? And what are the challenges it faces?

Traditionally, finance and accounting has had a rather staid reputation. However, far from being the final resting place for retired accountants, today's finance department plays an integral part within its parent organisation, impacting on all business activities. The finance manager is often responsible for collecting, consolidating and analysing data on everything from invoices and ledgers through to brand evaluation and human resources. The information that he or she provides forms the basis for planning and ultimately for the strategic direction taken by those at the top of the corporation.

Support systems

These decision-makers have a global frame of reference; they cannot afford to lose sight of the competition and must have access to precise, accurate and timely information with underlying details and explanatory analyses, regardless of where the information is located. In many cases, and in the examples we shall consider, they are reliant on a patchwork of systems to support the operations of the department. Often, each individual system, whether for accounts payable, fixed asset management or data consolidation, will have been selected by different people responding to different demands, and will be optimised for the particular need which it addresses.

While acknowledging that each system is critically important, BPR theory stresses that each is only a component of a larger structure which must be capable of anticipating and responding swiftly to changing business conditions. The real goal is to integrate the systems into a responsive machine – a management tool which can be used easily and quickly to satisfy the demand for information. Here, the customer, the focus of any BPR programme, is the decision-maker whose strategy will be based on the information he receives. When an organisation expands through acquisition, the situation becomes more complicated – and this is where the need for re-engineering often lies.

At first glance, Caradon, a building products group, and Grand Metropolitan, a food and drinks giant, seem like very different organisations, operating as they do in completely different market sectors. What they have in common, however, is that both have established and maintained world-leading brands for many years – and both have made major acquisitions of other companies at some point in their recent history. Another similarity is that, in both companies, the finance department is surprisingly small – far larger resources are employed at the sector and operating company levels. But both departments had to adjust quickly to a rapidly evolving corporate environment while continuing to meet the requirements of users around the globe.

Caradon, a £2 billion group which includes 70 companies and lists Twyfords, Doulton and Everest among its premium brands, had an exciting year in 1993, which marked something of a strategic watershed in its development. Disposing of its investment in CarnaudMetalbox in April, the cash-rich Caradon made a £808 million acquisition of RTZ-Pillar the following October. This move extended Caradon's investment in building products and services throughout Europe and North America. Inevitably, it was also the cause of some disruption, an effect felt particularly by its financial team.

Acquiring RTZ-Pillar increased the number of Caradon's financial reporting sites from 20 to 70, and doubled the size of the financial reporting operation. The finance team found that the number of businesses reporting every month into Caradon headquarters had increased from 16 to 70, but without a corresponding increase in the number of staff or a relaxation of reporting deadlines.

The process for financial reporting required drastic overhauling. The team really wanted a solution that would give greater control to their customers – the analysts, planners and executives – and a better feel for what was going on in the business. Another target was to cut the time taken to construct monthly financial reports; having access to the reports as quickly as possible can make a fundamental difference in the analysis and planning process.

After a period of deliberation, the team at Caradon decided on a consolidation product called Hyperion, designed to optimise the process of collecting, analysing and presenting business and financial information. In theory, this would give Caradon access to a high-performance server database; provide the Windows user interface for ease of use; and employ a client-server architecture to give simultaneous access of the same information to more than one user at a time. In response to strong pressure from their customers – senior management – to implement as much as possible of the replacement system within a period of only one month, the team decided to install its chosen application across the group to give a full working system from day one. Thereafter, it was decided that the application – adding reporting and budgeting tools and an executive information system – would be built a layer at a time.

In May 1994, Caradon began the process of linking the Hyperion system to the new GEIS communications network across the group. A brief period of pilot testing, which involved running the old and new systems in parallel, proved so successful that, by 31 May, Caradon had decided to go live with the new system. For the first time, everyone across the group operates on the same system, which Caradon hopes will save time – and money – in the long term. Progress since has been very smooth; the Caradon group's half-year results were consolidated on Hyperion without any hitches. In effect, the new system has given Caradon a scalable solution, and enabled it to re-engineer totally its financial consolidation and reporting process.

Grand Metropolitan has also undergone considerable reengineering. In 1986, the company was active in 28 different business sectors including hotels, betting and gaming, child care and nursing, pubs and dairies.

Today, it is active in only two core sectors – food and drink – but its premium brands still include many household names: Smirnoff, Baileys, J&B Rare Whisky, Pillsbury, Burger King and Häagen Dazs. Every aspect of Grand Metropolitan – the businesses in which it operates, its core competencies, business strategy, organisation and structure – has been fundamentally re-engineered over the past eight years, a period during which it has doubled its profits and evolved into a truly international organisation. The transformation has had a far-reaching impact on every part of the business – not least for the finance staff. The continuously changing nature of Grand Metropolitan's business poses something of a challenge for all of them – whether at the headquarters in London, or in the operating companies themselves.

Financial challenge

The re-engineering story begins at the start of 1993, when the finance department decided to embark on a process of reviewing and simplifying its existing consolidation and reporting process. The challenge that had been set was to enable Grand Metropolitan to provide information on its businesses to investors on a more frequent basis and to improve the reconciliation process between management and financial accounts at the year-end. Grand Metropolitan's business is structured in sectors – for example, Food America and Food Europe, with many different operating companies grouped within each sector. The change had to be effected on a company-wide basis, involving not just the needs of the central finance department, but those of the operating companies as well. The project was code-named Single Stream and was implemented in three areas: data consolidations and reporting; training and communications; and hardware and software. Each area was global in scale and was tasked with standardising to the single most efficient system across the group. Hence any platform had to be usable internationally and able to cater for evolving requirements in the future.

Before the Single Stream project, consolidation and reporting were carried out across four applications, which inevitably created duplication in the processing of data for financial and management purposes. To eliminate this duplication, and the corresponding staff time and effort which went with it, Grand Metropolitan decided to build a core system on one application to encompass all the corporate information necessary to provide external reporting. This could then be carried out directly from headquarters, saving time and preserving the accuracy of the data. The core system would then be rolled out to the businesses, which would incorporate their individual requirements, reflecting their business area. Grand Metropolitan chose Micro Control as the base for its core consolidation system. The core system has now been built and proved very successful under test.

The experiences of Caradon and Grand Metropolitan illustrate that BPR can be a valuable management tool. Rather than replacing only the weakest components of an ailing or inefficient system – or automating a fundamentally flawed process – BPR can provide a more permanent and productive solution. At the very least, BPR provides an aid to thought. Like any tool, however, it will only be truly successful when it exactly fits needs and will prove cost-efficient in the long term. After all, it is not always appropriate to build a new bypass – sometimes altering the traffic flow is sufficient to solve the problem and requires a far smaller expenditure of both time and money.

Richard Hawksworth is the UK marketing manager of Hyperion Software, leading supplier of financial management software.

THE MICROPROCESSOR
REVOLUTION

RE-ENGINEERING, IT AND TIME

Peter Goldsborough

IT and time are important elements in any successful re-engineering programme; they can help solve a company's process problems and create customer value.

To many top managers, re-engineering and rethinking information technology (IT) are virtually the same thing. It is easy to understand the reason for this linkage: in almost every successful re-engineering programme, the application of IT plays an important role, largely because of the power that information has to reshape an organisation and to alter the way work gets done.

However, it is dangerous to begin re-engineering with the assumption that IT will provide the solution to a company's process problems; technology is an important tool in re-engineering, but it is not the goal. The ultimate goal is the creation of customer value. When IT contributes to the creation of customer value, when it is linked to strategy, it becomes a critical component of re-engineering.

IT creates value and competitive advantage in two ways. It allows companies to:

- Do the same things they do now, but faster, more accurately, more consistently, and at lower cost, and

The power of IT

A leading European financial institution fell captive to outdated, entrenched business processes that were no longer providing a competitive edge. Through an institution-wide rethinking of these processes, it has learned the value of using IT appropriately in re-engineering.

Major improvements in service, time and cost were possible by taking a process view and modifying or redesigning the existing physical processes Having done this, the company uncovered cost savings of more than $100 million.

By combining such physical modifications with IT elements, even greater improvements became possible. The redesigned processes were enabled by major changes in existing computer systems and the incorporation of new technologies like digital imaging and pen-based graphical user interface applications tied to existing mainframes.

Incorporating IT tripled total cost savings to approximately $300 million. Including IT in re-engi-neering does more than increase the cost savings realised by the new processes. Elements like time and quality are also improved. The accompanying charts show how IT enables improvement in several dimensions for one process.

The company also discovered that IT alone does not improve a process significantly. Before the re-engineering effort got under way, it was incorporating new technology at one point in a process to improve delivery of a financial product to the customer. That technology raised 'first time yield' of that step in the process to 100 per cent. Unfortunately, the overall successful delivery of the product only increased from 15 per cent before the new technology to 20 per cent with it. IT must be part of an effort to improve every step and aspect of a process if real value is to be delivered.

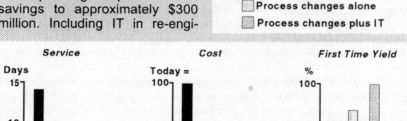

- ■ Today
- Process changes alone
- Process changes plus IT

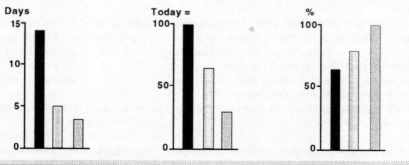

- Do things that neither they nor their competitors are doing now, creating new strategic business opportunities.

In the first role, fast information movement contributes to process speed. Automating repetitive, mundane tasks can improve accuracy and consistency. Continuously reducing the cost of information maintenance and processing contributes to overall cost-effectiveness. Taken alone, however, the application of IT for speed, accuracy or cost rarely generates dramatic bottom-line business results.

Too often the quality of information is compromised by the business processes that create it or by the incentives and behaviours of the customers or employees who provide key inputs. And, too often, the information is not prepared and delivered in a way that is most useful to those who need it. Poor presentation formats make getting the big picture difficult or seeing subtle trends and patterns impossible. Sources of variances are not called out.

Averages are presented instead of distributions. Decision-making support tools are missing or underdeveloped. In many cases, it is only by rethinking the processes which create and use the information that more fundamental impacts from investment in information systems can be achieved.

The application of IT is at its most dramatic when whole functions or activities can be greatly reduced or eliminated; for example, eliminating back offices by pushing order entry, tracking and even invoice printing into the field. By using laptop computers and field-driven software, appraisers can make claims on the spot and print the customer's cheque on site. This eliminates tremendous paper-shuffling and, in addition, provides high customer value. Shrinking logistics functions by live-tracking of goods provides high customer value while requiring lower cost. By bar-coding and then tracking all packages in the shipping stream, the sophisticated shipper can immediately track the whereabouts of a particular package, eliminate the manual effort of attempting to trace it, and identify errors in addressing.

The best assessment of new technology's impact is based on changes to the end-to-end process as seen from the customer's perspective. For example, the most sophisticated new materials scheduling system will be unlikely to improve the order to delivery cycle to any noticeable degree if the time it acts on is only a small fraction of the total time the customer has to wait. Many companies have systematically employed IT in the relentless pursuit of taking time out of processes.

Role of time

Companies that have reduced cycle time over the past decade were pioneers in end-to-end process re-engineering. Since then, companies have thoroughly embraced the objective of time as a diagnostic lens, a powerful new metric, and a driving force for many aspects of performance. Time-based competitors have always worked on processes to create competitive advantage and customer value through speed and greater responsiveness.

Time is a superior diagnostic lens. Almost all activities and processes can be measured in the time dimension. Companies are systems, and time is one of the few dimensions that connects all the parts. Mapping where time is lost or wasted is the fastest way to find service, cost and quality problems. Time is a powerful new metric. Process-managed companies almost always include time as a key measure of performance. It is a unifying concept, a simple measure that everyone understands.

Time drives many other aspects of process performance. First, *meeting customer needs*. The time between the emergence of a customer need and its satisfaction is the most relevant component of service; customers think they know what they want, and when they want it – which is usually as soon as possible. Time-based competitors offer convenience and, in return, can charge a price premium from customers who place a value on their time. That is why convenience stores can charge higher prices than supermarkets.

Second, *achieving quality*. Most problems show up in lost time: parts that cannot be used, information that did not arrive, work that must be done again. Time reduction demands that high quality be built into business cycles from the start. Third, *lowering costs*. Faster cycles lead to lower costs because production materials. and information collect less overheads and do not accumulate as work-in-process inventory. A systematic attack on wasted time will automatically lower costs. It is faster and less costly to do something right the first time.

Companies that focus on time reduction through process redesign achieve parallel improvements in quality. Time reduction and quality improvement compound to produce higher customer satisfaction and market share.

Far-sighted companies have used information and communication technology to improve existing processes so effectively that their performance gains have transformed industries. Wal-Mart's logistics expertise, driven by a network of IT applications, has redefined the competitive landscape in terms of cost, product availability and customer service.

Strategic weapon

IT's second role is as a strategic weapon. Information can create advantages of both position and capability. Using processes to enhance information can lead to position advantages. For example, when information interconnects customers and suppliers in fundamental ways, it often creates barriers to entry. The airline reservation systems represent extremely valuable assets because they translate technology and information into unique business value. Another example is MCI's deployment of IT in consumer long-distance telecommunications. With the ability to price calls specially to an individual's circle of frequently called telephone numbers, MCI not only gained market share but enlisted its customer base as a marketing force on their behalf. By re-engineering information-rich processes to achieve position advantages, companies can gain an edge on their competitors.

At the same time, using information to enhance processes can create

Re-engineering for time

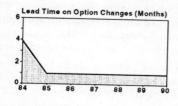

Lead Time on Option Changes (Months)

Total Inventory Turnover

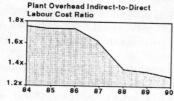

Plant Overhead Indirect-to-Direct Labour Cost Ratio

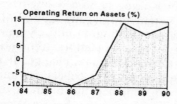

Operating Return on Assets (%)

Sometimes the re-engineering of a complex business process benefits from a strong, early focus on one metric or issue that can get everyone's attention. A US manufacturer of special-purpose construction equipment took this approach when it set out to improve its responsiveness to customers and, at the same time, reduce its inventory levels and overhead costs.

Senior management knew it had to centre the effort around one organising concept that linked an external customer view with an internal process view, and it chose time.

Time was both an analytic tool and a trigger for action. First, it proved to be the best language for describing, and best metric for mapping, the processes that crossed many functional and geographic boundaries. For example, the path that a customer order followed from sales through customer engineering and materials management, and finally to production and shipment to customers, was best captured by a graph of elapsed time that showed how most of it was wasted. Even the stove-pipe die-hards got the message.

Time also triggered a long flow of benefits from the re-engineering effort. The first success was cutting the order-to-delivery time through the company. This allowed customers to order later and dealers to carry less stock. This time compression then triggered asset reduction in the company itself, first in inventories and then in warehouse space. As the order path was simplified and inventory disappeared, overheads began to drain out of the system. When excess assets and non-value-added work are removed, the overheads go with them. Finally, return on assets rose as costs and inventory went down, and price realisation firmed up as less inventory had to be discounted.

superior capabilities. Historically, the indirect link between most mass media advertising and actual sales has allowed marketing to hide behind a smoke-and-mirrors facade of awareness and image. Now, direct response marketing, retail scanners, hand-held sales force computers, and customer databases have made it possible to track the effectiveness of most marketing expenditures, often down to the individual customer. The competitive advantage is shifting to those who can more quickly and systematically learn from customer responses.

Competitive weapon

Time magazine's ability to identify the profitability of customer by promotion led it to drop the number of promotions, shrinking its circulation base, but increasing profitability significantly. And, if you look behind the world's most respected customer service operations, you find superior information systems and innovative use of IT, from optical scanning to artificial intelligence, and from computer-based training to wireless communications.

These top service companies have demonstrated payback from technology investment in their customer-facing business processes. Federal Express has continually raised the competitive stakes in the package delivery business, to the point where, today, the company is now as much in the business of information tracking and management as in package delivery – it now even manages other companies' departments on an outsourcing basis.

Using IT as a competitive weapon means understanding how and when to deploy it. Large investments in IT do not necessarily improve productivity or create new competitive advantage. Nor is using IT in a re-engineering effort as simple as scrapping the existing system and starting again. In fact, few companies have been successful at implementing an entirely new IT architecture. Doing so requires four to five years of effort, tremendous managerial resolve and a commitment to organisational change. It also requires a deep and practical understanding of how collecting, understanding and using information better can enhance the business. Line managers must manage IT architecture as a core asset, funding and continuously improving it as they would their plant operations, distribution channels or sales force.

Far-reaching collaborations

Perhaps the greatest challenge from the management perspective has been bringing line managers and IT experts together to define the opportunities and requirements for bottom-line business performance improvement. As many companies have found, re-engineering's team-based approach to process redesign and integration has resulted in the most successful and far-reaching collaborations in their experience.

Peter Goldsborough is vice-president of the Boston Consulting Group.

DYNAMISING THE DESKTOP

Michael Skok

IT is now a core ingredient in the operations of many organisations, but managers are still frustrated by the gap that persists between their needs and technology solutions.

For the 30 years since the arrival of the first commercial computer, the role of IT has largely been to process data in support of specific business functions. Computers were seen essentially as a technical issue, a separate function that served business processes without actually altering them. This world is changing for a variety of reasons. For many types of business, IT has now reached a level of critical impact. Banks, airlines and the larger retail businesses, for instance, simply could not function without IT. The mission-critical nature of this role demands that companies think at a more fundamental level about IT's relationship to the core processes of the business.

Competitive pressures, particularly for companies operating in global markets, are also forcing change. In particular, businesses need better communications, and they need to use information more effectively to maintain competitive advantage – rather than simply creating data to support other business functions. These competitive forces also demand that companies understand more about their markets, become able to respond faster to changes in the market and draw closer to their customers. Technology is seen as a key tool in dealing with these issues.

161

Recessionary pressures over the past five years have had a further impact, by creating leaner organisations as companies delayer, removing entire strata of management. Having fewer people to manage, each of them with more to do, demands better information and better communications. Managers are starting to realise that they must use information technology to support the structures that remain, with IT taking on more of the administrative burden and helping individuals and teams to save time, communicate more effectively and make better decisions.

Technical advances

The potential exists to meet these challenges. Dramatic technical advances, coupled with equally impressive price reductions, have fostered the widespread adoption of networks and distributed computing solutions, in which central computers or servers are linked to very powerful desktop computers. The result is a many-fold improvement in the facilities that IT can deliver at a fraction of the cost of earlier mainframe-based systems.

Other changes are taking place. Recent research suggests that fear of technology is no longer an issue in the workplace. As technology spreads through the entire organisation and is seen to be important to key processes, users are becoming more interested in how IT can help them. As a result, the manager of management information (MIS) is also evolving, from the sole arbiter of IT policy to being a facilitator as well as a setter and guardian of standards: in a devolved organisational culture, the end-user wants to make the decision about the machine that sits on his or her desk.

All this is driving a continuing and substantial investment in IT. Allowing for internal IT spend by companies, UK investment in 1993 alone is likely to have exceeded £20 billion, while investment in the USA over the past decade is reckoned at more than £1 trillion. But, while the potential to help may exist, the evidence suggests that IT is not actually making the impact expected. Balancing the massive 10-year investment by US companies are studies indicating that office productivity in the country's businesses rose by only 1 per cent, while other studies suggest that IT has yet to change dramatically the way we work. Another study, by Forrester Research in the USA, suggests that, for many companies, more than 40 per cent of IT systems staff are dedicated to maintaining existing applications.

Against this background, changing the focus so that investment is dedicated to ensuring that IT actually supports changes in business processes is a major challenge: simply throwing out the old is not an option for many, perhaps most, companies. But why is there still a gap between the aspirations of IT and the reality? Insights into some of the answers were obtained when European Software Publishing undertook some in-depth research into how companies, and individual managers, actually use IT. A survey of financial directors in 100 of Britain's largest companies identified a number of issues relating to the way these people use IT and the likely constraints on its greater adoption.

The research threw light on a number of issues. First, it is overwhelmingly clear that the directors interviewed are fully committed to the use of computer technology on the desktop. Moreover, they foresee continuing advances in hardware and software performance as their principal source of hope in tackling increasing workloads. Second, research confirmed that fear of technology is no longer seen as the great constraint on its wider use. Lack of time is clearly always an issue, but more significant was the lack of awareness among managers of how the different technologies could be integrated to support wider business processes.

Third, despite the widespread acceptance of technology, more than half the respondents are still dissatisfied with the quality of their current information management. In other words, computers are helping them handle increasing volumes of information – but are the systems adding as much value to the total business process? Fourth, even though the technology is sitting on their desks, still relatively few managers are using the communications and information-sharing capabilities of IT. Large amounts of their days are spent in communicating – meeting, telephoning, and so on – with their work-group colleagues, but few are using technology to support and enhance these activities. Linked to this, there is clear disillusionment with much of the time currently spent with colleagues. When a sizeable proportion of the sample admit that they spend more than a month of their working year wasting time at meetings, something is clearly wrong.

Next, there is clear evidence of the evolution from central to devolved, from the MIS specialists to the end-users, when it comes to developing, implementing and supporting IT strategies. Managers increasingly expect to look after themselves and are expected to: this is the success of the PC revolution – that users now appreciate the key role that IT has to play at the individual level. It is clearly seen to be a beneficial move for the long term. In the short term, however, it is reducing control of the IT investment. Departmental managers do not have the skills for this new role, and they certainly do not have the strategies. In fact, only 16 per cent lay claim to a departmental IT strategy. It is clear that something must fill the vacuum; and that, unless a more effective solution is found first, chaos will result.

ESP's research showed that companies need a strategy to deal with these challenges, which is what prompted the development of the WISH (Work-group Information Sharing) strategy and the BusinessWare range of products and services. WISH is an enabling strategy for companies, allowing them, in a logical and painless way, to link IT development to business strategy. BusinessWare provides the means and the tools to integrate computer applications with business processes in order to meet specific business objectives. Underlying WISH and BusinessWare are three key components of effective information management which apply to all businesses using IT today:

- *Work-groups.* The spread of local area networks to support small teams and work-groups has created the need for software that enhances inter-activity and task-sharing within these groups. But, first, the relation-ships within the specific work-group(s) involved must be understood.

- *Information access.* Data processing is no longer the productivity bottle-neck. The real issue is information access, with a multiplicity of data-bases and hardware, software and networking environments providing the real barriers. The need is for understanding at the detailed level what types of data are required, what the sources are, and how the data is to be consolidated or presented – all these must be addressed before practical solutions that make a lasting contribution to the business can be installed.
- *Intelligent sharing.* Technology has, for many, already created informa-tion overload. Yet people must share information. The trick is to use technology intelligently, using smart communications media that will help decide who needs to see what and what result is needed – that means sorting, prioritising, routing and delivering enactionable infor-mation.

Much of the technology to manage the above tasks is now available. The task of WISH and BusinessWare is to provide the framework within which these existing technologies can deliver the benefits of integrated work-group computing, without jettisoning existing legacy systems where the latter still have a role to play. The starting point is a methodology – a BusinessWare AudIT – to establish the gap between the business need and the technology solution, and to identify ways to bridge the gap. Once the structure is effective, the applications that will deliver most in relation to the real business needs of the organisation can be put in place.

We have also found that it is important to develop our own additional software bridges, or BusinessWare Solution Packs, between specific appli-cations, again to ensure that the technology really does contribute to better business processes and communications. One recent example of this is a solution that enables the integrated and efficient handling and distribution of the vast amounts of information that now comes into companies by fax. The enthusiastic response to BusinessWare provides evidence that it touches a soft spot, that companies are indeed waking up to the fact that intelligent investment in technology, linked to clearly defined business strategies, can at last provide the productivity and other gains that have been the Holy Grail of IT for too many years.

Michael Skok is chairman and chief executive of European Software Publishing (ESP). He has worked in the computer industry for 14 years, co-founding Skok Systems and later founding ESP. He established Symantec UK, which he sold to Symantec Incorporated in 1992 for $27 million.

MANAGING THE IT RISKS

David Clarke

There are risks associated with the introduction of any new IT system. It is essential to understand what these are, how serious they can be, and what management action is required.

Information technology (IT) has become so central to the success or failure of a business that installing any type of computer system involves risks. Some believe that, moving from a fully integrated solution provided by one computer manufacturer to buying best-of-breed components to assemble an optimum solution, is inherently a higher risk. This is a fallacy. It is just a different risk, and approached carefully it can be a much lower one.

The first element of the fallacy is the idea that migrating systems to smaller, more cost-effective platforms is something new. In fact, there has been a steady progression, from the mainframe computers of the 1960s, to minicomputers in the 1970s, to standalone PCs in the 1980s, and now to networks of PCs. Nobody would seriously suggest that migrating from a mainframe to a minicomputer is inherently risky. So why should migration to a PC be any more so?

The second error is to worry that PCs and Unix systems are not powerful or resilient enough to support mission-critical applications. Today's top-of-the-range PCs are many times more powerful than their forebears of 10 years ago – more powerful even than the minicomputers or mainframes of previous generations. Indeed, it is not unreasonable to speak today of the personal mainframe on the user's desk. Small wonder that PC sales now account for more than half the total IT hardware spend.

PC software has similarly advanced. Operating systems such as Novell

NetWare and Microsoft Windows NT have developed to a point where, together with systems such as Compaq's Insight Manager, they can rival minicomputers in areas such as system management, multiprocessor support, multi-tasking and security. And on the desktop, there are more than 60 000 different application programs available for the PC alone.

Proprietary systems

The third, and perhaps most serious, fallacy is to believe that old-style proprietary systems do not themselves involve a large element of risk. If the old, hierarchical computer model of the early 1980s had been entirely satisfactory, then the huge change which is now taking place would not have happened. In fact, there are several risks associated with proprietary technology.

First, if you buy a fully integrated solution from one company, you are locked into taking that vendor's technology in all parts of the system, regardless of whether or not it is the best available. The investment required to be the finest in every element of a solution is so high that it is extremely unlikely to find any one company best at more than a few of those elements.

Second, the cost of a proprietary solution is generally higher than an amalgam of best-of-breeds. Competition from this more open approach has forced proprietary vendors to reduce their prices in recent years, but their solutions are still nowhere near as cheap as best-of-breed.

However, the principal risk of proprietary systems is their constricting effect on the business itself. There is no doubt that in the 1970s and early 1980s the way in which businesses were run and organised was constrained by their IT structure. If you have a mainframe computer system, you are forced into a mainframe, hierarchical way of running your business. Under the new, best-of-breed model, you can choose at each layer how you implement, what you buy and how the system runs, so you can match your IT system to the way you want the business to run. That could be hierarchical or decentralised; empowering people at the customer interface; making more controlled decisions centrally; or, commonly, a combination of all of these.

So the real advantages of the new style of computing lie not so much in better technology, or reduced costs, though these undoubtedly exist, as in being able to match your IT systems to your business, so that they become allies in moving the business forward, rather than constraints on how it is organised. However, as stated earlier, there are risks associated with the introduction of any new IT system, and PC-based systems pose their own set of problems. As with all risks, it is essential to understand what these are, how serious they can be, and what management action is required.

The first risk lies in the quality of your hardware. If it fails, it is not just a question of paying to fix it. There are also issues of lost working time, lost staff confidence, lost customer confidence and, most serious of all, loss of potentially irreplaceable data. Despite the tag 'IBM PC-compatible', some

PCs are more compatible than others. If your PC system turns out to be incompatible with future releases of software, or current ones, the hidden costs could be huge.

Even if their hardware is compatible, not all PC manufacturers are committed to being first with the latest technology (indeed some well-known names are committed to *not* being first), or to making sure that it works properly. If your supplier does not keep up, or your PCs are incompatible with new processors or other hardware developments, you will be faced with the expense of changing suppliers or needing one-off fixes. And several big names in PC manufacturing have gone out of business since 1990, with more failures on the cards. If your supplier should be among the failed, you may have problems obtaining spares and support.

You can protect your business against all these risks, but not by buying the cheapest PCs on the market. Quality, compatibility, innovation and stability all carry a certain premium, but they will repay the investment in the long term. So ask your PC supplier about its quality assurance procedures, not only in manufacturing, but also in:

- Component supply (does it have relationships with a small number of quality suppliers, or does it bid on the open market?)
- Product testing (it is impossible to build and ship a PC in 24 hours and still test it thoroughly)
- Compatibility (does it have compatibility and connectivity labs, and partnerships with major industry trend-setters like Microsoft, Novell and Intel?).

Then check the vendor's record on technological leadership (is it regularly first to market with new processor technologies, for example, and how much testing does it do?). Consider whether it can provide a desktop, server or portable PC to suit every facet of your business (does its PC range consist of six models, or 60?). Does it have dealers and support personnel in every country where your business operates? And how well are those dealers selected and trained (is there, for example, a meaningful accreditation scheme, or a special type of dealer experienced in supplying mission-critical systems)?

Invisible costs

Hardware, however, is only one element in the total cost of a system. Several studies have been made on the life-cycle costs of PC-based systems, and they have all concluded that the visible costs of the hardware and software are far outweighed by invisible costs. According to Gartner Group, hardware accounts for 18 per cent of the system cost, and software 10 per cent. The rest is swallowed by training (7 per cent), data access (2 per cent) and support (a massive 63 per cent). Supporting users of PC systems is inherently more expensive than supporting traditional mainframe and minicomputer users. Part of the reason is that the PCs may be dispersed throughout the organisation, in departments and locations where hands-on support was not required before.

But many PC users make more demands on support resources simply because they are doing more. As PCs, with all their variety of available applications, have replaced terminals on people's desks, the scale and scope of what staff can do on their computers has been multiplied hundreds, even thousands of times. This places a greater emphasis on providing adequate training and support for users, but if they are furthering the needs of the business that is no reason for not introducing PCs. It is simply necessary to strike a balance between management control and individual liberty. Ideally, all staff should be using the same set of software packages – word processor, spreadsheet, database, and so on. But if one individual or department needs a different package in order to do its job better, this should be seen as one of the benefits of PCs, not as a problem.

A further potential risk of the 'mix'n'match' approach to IT is the possibility that nobody else has mixed'n'matched exactly the same elements as you. This may require considerable systems integration skills, not just to pull together the disparate components, but to ensure that this process supports the objectives of the business. This level of skill is quite different from the kind of skills required in developing conventional systems. It may be found in-house, but to ensure a successful implementation it may well be necessary to buy in skills or consultancy from outside.

Finally, the most insidious risk of systems based on PCs is to fall into the trap of treating them like any other PC. Desktop PCs have traditionally been seen as quick and dirty. Everyone knows the data they hold is sometimes inaccurate and not properly backed up, but nobody cares because the business does not stand to lose much if things go wrong. Critical PC systems are different. They must be managed by professionals, and treated with the same respect as any other core system, which means effective security, regular back-ups, professional software development, preventive maintenance and contingency plans.

From the above, it can be seen that open, PC-based systems can potentially bring much greater benefits to the business than their centralised, proprietary counterparts, and that the risks involved can be minimised, as long as you keep your eyes open. Above all, it must be remembered that minimising these risks is a management issue, not a technical one, which means that you, the business manager, can stay firmly in control.

David Clarke has been UK marketing director for Compaq Computer since 1990.

THE MAIN TRENDS FOR MAINFRAMES

Peter Robinson

With the data explosion of the 1990s, mainframes are vital. They can provide the necessary memory, power and data storage, as well as support thousands of users.

Business strategies are continually under review and subject to change. The role of the mainframe has, for the past 30 years, adapted to those strategies and will continue to adapt. Before 1980, accounts and financial reports were often the basis for company decisions and direction, and the mainframe provided fixed format reports and processed predefined requests. Management support functions were added to these basic functions in the form of database-searching facilities and 'what if' criteria. As business moved into the 1980s and away from the accounting or operations era, the mainframe became a strategic tool.

Now, the 1990s are seeing a massive information explosion. Information is at the fingertips of all levels of the workforce, and management teams are hungry for information for better management of their businesses. Competition has become sharp, fast and intense. Computers are called upon for immediate design calculations, optimum quantity calculations and rapid solutions, because speed and accuracy are of the essence. Technology now has an immense capability to manipulate, analyse, store and display information. Information has become available to the ordinary man and woman, to the point where it is difficult to imagine a working day without access to high levels of technology. Cashpoint banking, direct parts ordering, stock control and airline reservations present just a few of the technology areas without which society cannot manage.

All these areas exist using the computing power of the mainframe. Reflecting this, demand for mainframe processing power is growing at 20—25 per cent annually, belying its unfashionable image. Access to information in the 1990s has become key. Managing the vast amount of information now accessed at the workstation and controlling data changes, updates and duplications have become very important. Knowledge is invaluable – gaining the right knowledge from your business information systems is essential. This information can only be co-ordinated and managed from one place, however: centrally.

Question of control

The question of control makes the continuous debate on centralisation or decentralisation irrelevant. Changing business and social trends throughout the 1990s mean that new technology options will become available. Demand for emerging technology and improved implementation is growing with the increasing sophistication and influence of the user. This centralised position of power will control and direct the destiny of the enterprise while exploiting all other technologies. The true cost of decentralisation, which includes support and organisation as well as hardware and software, though still unquantified, is becoming more apparent.

Within a few years, there could be a move back toward the mainframe for this reason. The client-server solution, in which networks of PCs are served by a more powerful microprocessor-based machine, must be justified through the benefit to the business of the restructured application, not on the arguments of hardware and software costs.

The changes are not only technological, but organisational. In the 1980s, management structures were hierarchical. The IT centre mirrored this structure, with the mainframe sitting at the top. Management structures of the late 1980s and early 1990s became divisional. The mainframe also claimed a role in divisional IT structures, with different groups pulling appropriate information down from the system.

Management structures of the mid-1990s and into the immediate future are becoming increasingly networked. Units now feed from each other and are linked. The power of decision-making and control, however, still rests in one place. The mainframe has evolved to address this latest change in management structure and can provide the necessary power, access, control and security, while deploying greater ability to share data across organisations by way of open and networked units.

The mainframe is, as it always has been, the solid foundation upon which good business systems are built. It offers high performance based on continuous improvements to current technologies – for example, increased chip densities, faster cycle times and design enhancements. The power, heat and size of mainframe systems are becoming so efficient that, physically, the mainframe is starting to look more and more like a mini-computer. But the more powerful machine carries with it the high levels of reliability and data integrity demanded today.

In terms of technology directions, it is clear that, long-term, the industry is likely to migrate to highly parallel CMOS architectures. New technologies will further lower the cost of computing. Organisations could be looking to make both this technological move and also a move into an environment featuring more open systems. In the shorter term, a hybrid system will emerge which will combine the current fast, but heat-intensive bi-polar technology with the cooler, denser but slower CMOS technology. Such a system would provide a natural growth path for today's mainframe users and would allow time for the newer parallel architectures to mature and for associated software to become stable. Application changes, software changes and staff training, which are necessary to use the future highly parallel architectures, could then be made gradually, which would allow companies to migrate at their optimum rate.

The information highway is the future. British Telecom has announced that it is considering major expenditure (in the region of $15 billion) in information highway technology, as are other major cable providers worldwide. Massive communication networks, not just within companies, but around the world are influencing business and social trends. Computer power will become a utility like plugged-in electricity. The mainframe, or even a network of mainframes, will be at the centre of enterprises, occupying the role of server to the servers that cover a wide range of users.

As companies move to open system IT environments, the mainframe will provide open system server capabilities – that is, a server for data management and distribution, applications management and distribution, and network management and distribution. In an open system environment the mainframe plays a crucial role. Downsizing, or transferring smaller system applications closer to the user, also places new but substantial responsibilities on the mainframe, again in the areas of data and network management. And the mainframe will continue to be the best place for intensive and repetitive commercial operations. It is very good at transaction processing against a large database and can handle thousands of transactions in seconds.

In addition, the mainframe will continue to be used for back-up and archiving, while also providing organisation-wide data management and data security functions.

For many large enterprises, mainframes are essential. Only the mainframe can provide the memory, the power, the data storage and the ability to support several thousand users and a multiplicity of tasks. The data explosion caused by the move to the paperless office will continue. Huge amounts of data are stored, managed, accessed and then transmitted across networks to other offices and departments. The growth in this data area is typically 60 per cent a year. Newer applications such as voice and image mean that growth is more likely to be 200—500 per cent a year. All this explains why Hitachi Data Systems has made the R&D commitment and broad development plans needed to provide a wide array of products to meet customer needs across multiple platforms. Most large corporations across the world are committed to the mainframe into the next century, and we are likewise committed to satisfying their requirements.

Peter Robinson is vice president of marketing for Hitachi Data Systems, Europe.

THE NETWORK'S THE COMPUTER

Ben Smith

A computer network used to be a simple way of swapping files and sharing peripherals such as printers. But today, it is not an exaggeration to say that the network is the computer.

That 'the network is the computer', is more than just the latest catch-phrase. For many companies, maximising the potential of their huge investment in computer networking is one of the critical paths for business success. Why has the network become of such strategic importance? If you look at all the traditional functions of even the most basic computer, there is clear evidence that the network has become the system, which the individual workstations, printers, servers and other elements within the network serve to drive.

Feeding the network

In any computer system, there are four major elements to its function: input, output, processing and storage. Today's network systems – most of them based on Novell NetWare – fulfil the criteria needed to handle all those tasks. The workstations provide a high volume of input to the network system from a vast and increasing variety of sources. These include keyboards, screens, scanners, fax modems and other input devices. The devices can be as simple as a diskless workstation that exists simply to store data on a server, or as complex as an engineering workstation that handles the display and modification of sophisticated computer-aided design models. But at the end of the process, it is the network, and not just any single PC or workstation, into which the data is fed.

Data is a company resource which must be captured quickly and accurately, maintained efficiently, and worked on by many users simultaneously. Information must then be communicated to the right parts of the organisation, enabling timely decisions by the appropriate employees. It is the network that manages this flow of business-critical information. As work-group applications become more commonplace, moreover, this change is accelerating. The role of the network as computer becomes more vital still. Work-group applications become the engine which helps collect data that can be used by the network in services of the enterprise (which, rather than the individual, is now the user of this computer). Electronic mail alone provides the network system with a high volume of complex input that it can then manage and process.

Outputting data produced on the network has been a key feature of network systems since their inception. In fact, the objective of sharing printers drove the growth of early network systems in a big way. These days, however, data generated by any one of the myriad of input devices and workstations on the network is just as likely to be heading for a network printer as it is to a plotter, a fax modem, an electronically published document or an electronic mail system, or to be routed to an external on-line system. In the interests of managing enterprise-wide resources, it is the network which often handles this output. It often makes much more sense to have a single, high-speed, high-volume, multi-line fax modem, or a high-performance laser printer serving a group of PCs than it would make to equip each PC with a mediocre modem and printer.

Sitting between and around the input/output functions of the network as computer is its vital role in processing data. This is a modern role for the network, which started life as a fairly dumb system that could only do what it was told. These days, however, networks often include servers with multiple processors (the upcoming version of Novell's NetWare 4 will include symmetric multi-processing support to make the most of this technology). The systems can thus effectively act as application servers. This role has for many years been filled by Unix in the mini-computer and high-end PC environments. In application server-based systems, processing work is farmed out to the servers on the network that are best-suited to handle given tasks (usually those high-performance servers that have spare processing capacity).

Vital to processing

In such a system, the network is vital to the processing of data, for it is the network that parcels out where and how the data for a given task or process is handled. Without the network, the application would simply not exist. That is perhaps the most important change that has started taking place in recent years. Many new applications require the existence of a network to operate properly, and these applications treat the network as the computer. You install and configure the application to the network, with various types of workstations listed as users of the application. Now the application actually runs on the network; instead of multiple instances of the application running on workstations on the network and merely using the latter to transfer data files between them.

Thinking of the network as the computer also changes your view of applications and the data they create. Modern applications, such as Lotus Notes and the new PerfectOffice from Novell WordPerfect, install themselves in a network and run on top of a network-operating system in the same way that the desktop applications of the 1980s installed themselves on a desktop PC and ran on top of a disk-operating system. Those 1980s applications could not have run without DOS – and today's network application cannot run without the services provided by the underlying network operating system. Meanwhile, the view that applications take of the data available to them does not end at the edge of a desk. Given the right LAN (local area network) and WAN (wide area network) connections, users of the network as computer are just as comfortable accessing data that is physically stored halfway around the world as they are retrieving whatever resides on their local hard disk.

In many cases, particularly when documents with links to other documents on the network are opened, users will probably not even be aware where the data actually resides. They just know that it is somewhere in the system. As always, the system in the modern context is actually the network, and one part of a compound document may be in one physical location while the rest is thousands of miles away.

What you could call reliability with flexibility is yet another major reason why this view of the network as computer is a particularly positive development. In other times, the phrase 'the system is down' would send terror and anxiety into the hearts of users, with visions of late nights and missed deadlines. The modern network has enough reliability, fault tolerance and local processing power in its components to ensure that no single component is indispensable. It is a very rare set of circumstances indeed that would make network computer users of the 1990s unable to work with their applications and data. Old mainframe and mini-computer systems cannot boast such reliability, while desktop PCs are islands unto themselves and often cannot help one another out when one goes down.

Fault-tolerance

Today, though, even when a bomb goes off in the City of London, fault-tolerant networking means that the Stock Exchange continues to function. Organisations take the security and reliability of their networks for granted. A good example is the Automobile Association (AA), the motoring organisation that markets itself under the slogan 'The UK's Fourth Emergency Service'. The AA has 11.3 million members and customers and has invested in Novell's System Fault Tolerance (SFT III) as part of a £500 000 network to guarantee the effective deployment of its Relay Fleet Rescue Services. The computer network enables it to respond to and manage more than 13 000 breakdowns a day. The Novell software is responsible for securing all information on the AA's Relay Service, so that it is managed effectively and efficiently. So, next time your car breaks down, it might be worth offering a prayer of thanks to the reliability of today's networking software.

In summary, today's networked systems are designed from the outset to be flexible, expandable and responsive to the needs of the enterprise. They do not require mass migration to upgrade only some elements of the system. If you have a system using DOS and Windows workstations running NetWare, adding an Apple Macintosh-based desktop publishing workstation is no more difficult than adding a printer or fax modem. The enterprise network is the computer and the added hardware is merely another device to support, not a cause for major network restructuring.

In the era of open systems, network operating systems are designed to operate with a number of hardware and operating system platforms, so that phrases such as 'appropriate solutions', 'co-existence' and 'co-operation' become the bywords of the enterprise's network management team. The role of the network as computer can only increase. Enterprise-wide computer systems cannot function effectively without a strong and flexible network as their backbone – and the fast pace of development in the network-based applications sector will ensure that it is very much in firms' interest to think of the network as the computer. If organisations still think of the computer stopping at the edge of the desk, they will be doomed never to move beyond that desk. And that would not give anyone much of a future.

Ben Smith is area director for Novell UK, which he joined in 1987, working as sales director for four years, and then as UK country director. He is responsible for Novell's sales and marketing programmes in the UK, Scandinavia, English Africa and the Middle East. Before this, he worked in ICL's Retail Division and, before that, he headed up public sector sales of networking solutions for Digital Microsystems.

THE FUTURE OF SOFTWARE

Paul Gardner

While software has become feature-rich, it often doesn't meet the needs of the user. In the future, it will be simpler and more powerful, with unimagined flexibility and intelligence.

Thanks to PCs, millions of people now have unprecedented access to information and information-gathering tools. Sophisticated software applications allow them to organise data, crunch numbers, publish documents with pictures, graphics, sound and even full motion video, and then communicate that information locally or around the globe. But even with today's clever generic software it is all too easy to focus on the tools rather than the tasks to be accomplished. In a competitive market-place, software developers have continued to add more and more features to their applications, which in turn has created increased complexity and considerably higher memory requirements.

As a result, although software has become more powerful and feature-rich, it has also become more difficult to use and update. In many instances, it includes a wealth of features and functions that most users neither want nor use. Despite the plethora of features and functionality, moreover, no one piece of generic software can do everything everyone wants. This has left many users longing for a new kind of software which allows you to take your favourite features from several different applications and combine them into one single personalised working environment that works precisely how you want it to, when and where.

Companies such as Apple, WordPerfect, Lotus Development, Novell, Xerox and IBM all now share the common goal of making the computing experience as easy and productive as possible. But in recent years, making this goal a reality often seemed to have become increasingly elusive.

We all know that people are using PCs for more and more complex tasks involving multiple programs and an ever-increasing variety of media. The isolated image of the desktop computer has been replaced by an increasing number of users working together on computer-based projects demanding new and improved capabilities and collaborative resources. There is also evidence of a growing dissatisfaction with the prescriptive nature of most shrink-wrapped software. Apparently no matter how powerful and feature-rich an individual application may be, there is still increasing demand for customising capabilities to meet the emerging needs of today's specialised users.

Traditionally, PC users would choose a word processor for text documents, a database application to keep track of contacts and addresses, and a spreadsheet for numerical modelling. But as users expectations grew, with the emergence of more powerful and specialised applications such as desktop publishing and graphics applications, so the demarcation between word processing, page layout, database, spreadsheet and graphics capabilities and so on began to blur and merge.

Many users began to ask, 'Why can't I simply use one application to do everything I want? Or at least, 'why can't I work with a number of types of applications in one place?' Today, more and more computer users engage in creating what might be called compound documents. These consist of parts containing various media such as text, sound, graphics, full motion video and tables, all in a variety of software file formats.

Currently, each requires users to work in different ways and often in separate applications. Despite the increasing ability to cut-and-paste or even drag-and-drop information, moving data from each creator application to the final document can involve a demanding, labour-intensive and cumbersome process, which can be long-winded, error-prone and downright frustrating.

As recently as 10 years ago, most of what people did with PCs essentially centred around text and numbers. When the Macintosh was launched in 1984, its unique graphical user interface (GUI) introduced a fresh new emphasis to working with graphics on the computer, allowing easier manipulation, editing and integration of both words and images. But today personal computing is pushing the limits of current hardware and software technologys.

OpenDoc

Major developments are appearing, such as Apple's System 7.5, which will replace passive GUI with an intelligent interface that actually offers active assistance at the end of 1994. What will follow is an evolution in desktop computing that provides an object-based framework for developing applications that are fully integrated and inter-operable across platforms and distributed networks. This framework will be capable of reducing the complexity of computing today while supporting the development of tomorrow's more advanced and flexible software applications. As a first move in this direction, Apple, in co-operation with major computer industry players such as IBM, has developed a compound document architecture called OpenDoc. It addresses all these software issues by reducing the complexity and increasing the flexibility of software for end-users and developers alike. OpenDoc offers an evolutionary approach to restructuring software away from today's monolithic applications into smaller independent modules or parts which can be flexibly combined in a variety of ways.

Users will then be able to combine conveniently their favourite component parts from different vendors, just as they might combine the components in a stereo system, to create a personal, unified, customised workspace that can accommodate multiple media and functions. With OpenDoc, it will be possible to edit any data type directly in any document without having to switch applications. This means that users will be able to create a single document containing word processing, spreadsheet, graphics and other functional types of areas. When you select any of these areas within your single document, you will automatically be presented with the appropriate tools from the original program to edit that particular data type. For example, clicking on a spreadsheet area would bring up all of the spreadsheet program's specific menus and tools. And best of all, since everything is live or real-time in a single document, there is no cutting and pasting required to consolidate information types from several applications.

OpenDoc fundamentally changes the meaning of the term document from a single block of content bound to a single software application to a totally integrated entity composed of smaller blocks of content or parts. One of the fundamental principles is that OpenDoc is designed to enable the construction of compound collaborative and customisable documents which are inter-operable across hardware platforms and with other compound document architectures such as Microsoft's OLE 2.0.

Like OpenDoc, OLE looks toward integrating different applications. However, in contrast to other major efforts along these lines, Microsoft's OLE 2.0 is concerned with inter-operation between monolithic applications and not with fundamentally altering the dynamics of the software business. Users would still be faced with huge applications from a small number of large developers, clogging up their PC. OpenDoc gives small developers the chance to market innovative software on a level playing-field; today only the large players can compete in this market. This stifles innovation and leads to long gestation periods for applications. The development time for creating an OpenDoc part is considerably less than creating a fully compliant OLE 2.0 application that ends up taking lots of hard disk space.

179

While Apple is not alone in recognising the problems with software development today, its stated intent is to make OpenDoc technology not only cross-platform, but also truly open. This means that both systems vendors and independent software vendors will be able to obtain the source code easily and without restrictive licensing.

Inter-operable

Since OpenDoc will also be inter-operable with OLE 2.0, developers can take advantage of OpenDoc's broader feature set and additional supported platforms without sacrificing OLE support. As a matter of fact, part of the work currently undertaken by the WordPerfect and Novell OpenDoc teams is to implement OpenDoc on Microsoft Windows in such a way that it will inter-operate with OLE 2.0. Software applications that support the additional capabilities found in OpenDoc will have the ability to inter-operate at a higher level of functionality on Windows or the Macintosh and to inter-operate across multiple platforms or distributed systems as well.

The software market is already seeing a major shift away from monolithic applications to more component-based software, and third-party developers have already begun work on component applications that support OpenDoc. Because compliance with the OpenDoc specification will be verified by an independent company – Component Integration Laboratories (CI Labs) – software developers will be able to write OpenDoc parts that run on Macintosh, Windows Unix and OS/2 platforms and networks. From the user's point of view, the OpenDoc approach will simply streamline the whole computing experience.

The benefits of widespread adoption of the OpenDoc philosophy could be revolutionary for both users and developers of computer software. But to be truly successful, this will have to be a quiet revolution without dramatic upheavals.

Fortunately, the OpenDoc approach is designed to work with all existing applications and document types: and OpenDoc parts will behave much like current software applications, enabling users to upgrade without having to go through a totally new learning process. The idea is that, as users become more familiar with the full potential of this new software approach, they will begin to build new, convenient, efficient and personal work environments while still maintaining their current software investment.

In the very near future, Apple will build OpenDoc into the Macintosh operating system, allowing users to take advantage of new system features such as 3-D graphics with existing applications. OpenDoc components will also become smarter about what kind of document they are actually in, and what sort of task the user is trying to accomplish.

Today's profound changes in both hardware and software technology will take users well past current barriers and permit personal computing to make even more beneficial contributions to their work, education and entertainment. We feel that the best software of the future will conform to Apple's own strategy of 'fitting in while standing out', combining innovation with backward compatibility. OpenDoc software capabilities, by 1995, will act as the foundation for future Macintosh operating system releases. And, as always, the primary concern for each of the companies involved in this venture remains the experience of the user, not merely technology for technology's sake. Without a doubt, software, in future, will be simultaneously simpler and more powerful with unimagined flexibility and intelligence.

Paul Gardner is a former director of enterprise solutions and software at Apple Computer UK Limited.

THE NEW WAY FOR NETWORKS

Alan Roach

As companies struggle for competitive advantage, close links between organisations and their customers are more important. This is achieved with ATM communications technology.

A new technology in computer communications is set to revolutionise the way the world does business. Asynchronous Transfer Mode (ATM) links businesses together and enables fast, secure and sophisticated communication of voice, video and data. Current networking is weighed down by the enormous complexity of the many different kinds of computers and networks being used. Telephone companies, personal computer companies, and major computer system vendors such as IBM and Digital Equipment use many different kinds of communications technology.

Modern business computing relies on two very different networking systems. Local area networks (LANs) link people together within their buildings. They can be built very quickly and provide extremely high-speed communications between many different kinds of computer system. However, when companies want to link these LANs together, they need to work with the telephone companies, which have built national and international voice and data networks, and which provide the long-distance links needed to build wide area networks.

Across the world, the major telephone companies and corporations are committing to ATM, believing it to be the technology for the future. In turn, this view has been enthusiastically endorsed by the companies providing local and wide area networks. For the first time in the history of communications, the opportunity exists to build global networks based on the same core technology. From the local office to the far reaches of the world, ATM is set to become the universal language of high-speed data communications. Major communications companies such as Sprint, MCI, AT&T, BT and Alcatel have committed to providing networks using the technology, and the majority of LAN vendors are moving to exploit the power of this communications revolution.

When change is the only constant, technology has to be powerful and flexible enough to cope with the dynamics of that change. ATM brings three vital elements to modern communications. It can handle high volumes of information at far greater speeds than ever before. It is also the first network designed to handle many kinds of traffic, including voice, video and data. Finally, ATM provides a flexible switching platform, which means that the network can change and evolve to reflect changing relationships with customers, suppliers, partners and competitors around the world.

The need for ATM is being driven by the rapid pace of change in the modern business world. As companies struggle for competitive advantage, close links between organisations and their customers become ever more important. The pressure of time now hits every part of the business process. New product concepts need to be quickly converted into prototypes and transformed into real manufacturing processes. Sales and marketing teams need to increase demand swiftly in the face of stiff competition. Everything must happen at once. The key element to all these aspects is communication, both inside the business and across the vital web of relationships with customers, suppliers and business partners.

ATM is the core technology that ensures that information gets to the right people quickly and accurately. It is also flexible, so that, as your business evolves, your ATM network can be dynamically redesigned to reflect the business realities that your organisation has to face every day.

Businesses are beginning to see that their communications networks are not a necessary evil, but an opportunity to give added value to their customers by improving quality, service and time to market. At the same time, there are real dangers in investing in technology that will create communications roadblocks by its inability to support tomorrow's business applications.

Multimedia

Unlike today's existing networking technologies, ATM can handle many kinds of information, from maintaining a live video conference to updating a detailed engineering drawing instantly. As businesses move to exploit new computer applications that rely on sound, colour and video images, ATM provides a network robust enough to carry this complex information, as well as traditional data communications traffic.

THE MICROPROCESSOR REVOLUTION

This kind of application, known as multimedia, will play an increasingly important part in the future of business. Although there are no truly accurate predictions of the rate at which applications will become available, it is generally accepted that organisations which embrace them will gain a significant competitive advantage.

ATM technology solves today's communications challenges, yet is powerful enough to absorb even the most demanding multimedia applications of the future. It will give real business benefits by allowing existing networks to be consolidated into a single service, dramatically reducing the cost of network ownership and increasing application availability. These two factors will combine to make staff much more productive. Trials using ATM show its versatility:

- Enabling medical specialists to study X-rays on a computer screen and provide rapid diagnoses on-line
- Allowing engineers to develop products jointly using a shared computer model, even though they are working in different countries
- Distributing and giving access to graphical data, such as location drawings and survey maps: utilities companies will be able to pinpoint underground cables, relay or extend them and update the data
- Providing interactive tele-teaching, giving students access to the best tuition, even in remote area
- Giving High Street shops the means to produce compact discs locally in minutes, as they are selected by a customer: the entire range will always be available, with no transport costs or unused stock.

The greatest problem faced by existing networks is running out of capacity. Today's networking technology was designed for computers that were far less powerful than those now available. Both applications and computer systems have dramatically increased in their power and scope since the personal computer was first invented in the early 1980s. Basic silicon chip processors, the engines of the computer age, have at least doubled in power and halved in price every year since their invention, and the trend is continuing. This means that yesterday's supercomputers have become today's Apple or IBM personal computers. Network technology has struggled to keep up, with the result that many modern networks are choked with excess traffic. This can cause transmission error and affects performance, but it has also slowed the deployment of new applications.

The first wave of computing rapidly increased the speed and accuracy of business processes, replacing calculators with spreadsheets, typewriters with word processors, and filing systems with databases. Networks have been created to link together these applications, and are partly responsible for the massive increase in the speed of modern business transactions. However, a new wave of applications is becoming available that does more than automate existing processes. This means that you can create links between people as and when they are needed, and change them to meet new business circumstances.

Linking people

If you have an engineer in Tokyo and a designer in Washington, they can be linked via the network to your marketing team, providing a dedicated work group with access to the same information. When the project is over, the work group can be dissolved, because an ATM network enables virtual links, liberating you from the cables and computers which make up the physical network. This saves the time and money involved in the messy business of physically moving computer resources around. It also enables a more flexible approach to solving business problems. ATM will deliver a future-proof network solution for businesses of every size and kind, one that is scalable to meet changing business needs and not the needs of technology fashion.

Many of today's computer networks are like crowded highways, on which different kinds of information have to struggle to complete their journeys. Many existing networking systems were built on the idea of contention – the notion that different types of data should compete to get access to the network. Technologies such as Ethernet are now showing signs of strain as they struggle to cope with the increasing demands of the modern information world. ATM networks can provide a private road for everyone on the network, bringing an end to congestion and liberating the power of existing computer systems.

Many organisations have invested vast amounts of money in high-powered computers, only to use low-speed computer networks to link them together. ATM networks are so fast that they remove the wide area network bottleneck and free up the processing power already present within the organisation. They can also cope with all kinds of traffic, over short and long distances, providing a completely scalable solution. The technology will be available for linking together scientific workstations in an engineering department, for providing live news feeds for financial organisations, or for providing a global information link for the entire organisation.

The new technology is also more efficient. With current wide area networking technology, you are frequently paying for bandwidth on the wide area network that you are not actually using. ATM provides bandwidth on demand, which means that you only pay for what you use. The network can respond to the changing needs of business by providing the network resource that you need, when you need it. A switched ATM communications infrastructure is like having a digital network on tap.

Smooth migration

The challenge to the modern business is clear: how to exploit the emerging power of the new network technology while protecting its existing investment in computer technology, networking and applications. ATM products and services are designed to provide organisations with a smooth migration path from existing local and wide area networks to the emerging networks of the future. A current wide area networking technology, Frame Relay, provides a major migration path between today's networking technology and ATM. Many existing computer and networking products and services may already support Frame Relay networking, and many public network providers have increased their investment in it because of its central role as the stable, cost-effective stepping-stone to ATM.

Frame Relay and ATM systems, when added to existing networks, will help consolidate voice and data networks into one cost-efficient, seamless enterprise. As the needs of business communications change, the architecture will perform the vital function of supporting smooth evolution and growth.

Alan Roach is UK managing director of Alcatel Data Networks. He was formerly sales and marketing director of Hutchison Mobile Data Limited and sales director of General Datacomm Limited.

USING BUSINESS INTELLIGENCE

Rod Whyte

With the wealth of data and technology now available through business intelligence systems, management is coming close to the Holy Grail of information access and delivery.

For many years, executives have sought to reap the benefits of their investments in data and information technology – often seen as a black hole of never-ending requests for funding. The ultimate goal, however, has always been the broad implementation of easy-to-use technology enabling non-technical managers to obtain real decision-making value from their corporate data reserves. Significant advances in computer technology and communications have now seen electronic mail and word-processing systems move into the mainstream.

This has spawned an environment which is right for the growth of 'business intelligence' –managerial applications which provide real marketplace insight and facilitate swift decision-making and communication between management and support staff on a large scale.

One of the key reasons for the growth of enterprise-wide systems is the blurring of boundaries between three previously separate technologies. They comprise decision-support systems (such as Express and System W); personal productivity tools (such as Lotus or Excel spreadsheets); and executive information systems (EIS). All these constitute successful 'point' solutions in their own right. However, each of these three separate groups has sought the benefits enjoyed by their counterparts.

For example, users of pc spreadsheets have demanded enhancements in their connections to corporate databases. Conversely, users of highly functional decision-support systems have sought to broaden the use of their capabilities for robust data manipulation and analysis. Practically every vendor of such systems has improved the ease of use of the pc front-end.

Lastly, executive information systems (which were frequently 'islands of isolated automation') lacked real analytical flexibility if users wanted to move beyond the realms of canned, preplanned reports. EIS are now being significantly upgraded to cope with the demand for sophisticated ad hoc analysis through improved data integration with back-end decision-support systems that are functionally rich.

Easy-to-use applications

The success of PC local area network and Windows technologies have provided a further catalyst for this new breed of enterprise-wide information delivery. Indeed business intelligence solutions are set to bring a whole host of easy-to-use, intuitive, highly functional and robust sets of applications to the desk-tops of an organisation's key decision-makers.

It is now being recognised that the flat, record-oriented model of data on which relational systems are based was not designed to either address the needs of sophisticated business analysis effectively or efficiently. These systems were optimised for data access and retrieval. The missing ingredient has been a focus on interpreting the data, rather than simply reporting it.

This has led to a new buzz-word for the computing industry. OLAP stands for on-line analytical processing. It unites the power of decision-support systems with the ease of use inherent in enterprise-wide intelligence systems (EIS). Slotting in seamlessly over existing relational databases, it acts as a data broker to any number of applications, across any number of operating platforms and for any number of users, regardless of computer literacy. The primary feature of the OLAP architecture is a multi-dimensional approach to data analysis, which has significant benefits over the relational model. This approach:

- Presents data more intuitively
- Delivers greater analytical power
- Performs analyses faster
- Requires less support from IS departments.

OLAP and multi-dimensionality are the cornerstones for successful business intelligence solutions. The multi-dimensional view enables sales, for example, to be viewed by product, time period, region, and so on. A true multi-dimensional database offers users an unlimited number of dimensions, such as time (which may be broken down by week, month and year), product (product group, sub-group or category) and area (TV region, county or postcode). Because data is stored only once, the multi-dimensional array in which it sits can be rapidly and efficiently viewed from many directions – and sliced, diced, rotated and pivoted from any perspective. This multi-dimensional user view facilitates model design and analysis, allowing users to manipulate models more easily and intuitively.

Multi-dimensional databases and graphical user interfaces (or front-ends) provide users with the ability to explore their data easily and quickly in order to discover critical business information. The resulting ad hoc interaction with data not only produces dramatically faster responses to key business challenges – by highlighting the news in the data – but can also reveal new levels of specific cause-and-effect relationships. Cutting response times to real business problems, business intelligence provides managers who have direct responsibility for distinct units and processes (such as lines of business, geographical entities, special markets and brands) with the ability to function as first-hand analyst of that business.

Kraft Jacobs Suchard provides just one of the examples of successful business intelligence applications with its enterprise-wide information strategy. In the UK, it is not unusual for retail buyers to be armed with better information, in areas like product performance and profitability, service levels and market share, than manufacturers selling to the chains.

Redress the balance

Part of the world's largest consumer goods company, Philip Morris, Kraft Jacobs Suchard uses IRI Software's Express technology to redress the balance between retailer and manufacturer. It sees the exploitation of IT in support of sales and marketing functions as a primary route to achieving its principal aim – that of achieving preferred supplier status in all categories in which it trades. Based on client-server technology, a single corporate DB2 data warehouse is being created that can be accessed by a series of Express applications across a whole range of sales, marketing, finance, planning and executive support functions.

The first application to go live was the customer account management system, focusing on basic sales information viewed by major customer or trade sector for all products. The information systems manager, Alan Rawlinson, explains that 'It's very easy to use and provides a wealth of reporting options for analysing customer and product sales information. Consequently, it helps us to improve the accuracy of our forecasts, as well as assess the impact of differing pricing and promotional strategies, through a better understanding of customer and market dynamics'.

Following the acquisition of Terry's confectionery business from United Biscuits, the system significantly speeded delivery of key sales information to Terry's management. Kraft has also developed applications for customer account profitability analysis and is using prepackaged Express applications for financial planning and budgeting, and multi-source sales and marketing analysis.

At NatWest Markets, the corporate and investment banking arm of the National Westminster Bank Group, the aim was to network a sophisticated reporting and analysis system to more than 150 executives in London and New York. This would help them to test the effects of business decisions on assets portfolio, risk and profitability. The bank has developed a graphically driven system using the Express multi-dimensional model, which enables executives to handle portfolio analysis, short- and long-term planning, performance reporting and monitoring, trend analysis and modelling, as well as the control and monitoring of risk exposure levels.

The system is fed by general ledger applications and provides access to monthly financial data allowing examination of loan books by customer, team and region, as well as at summary level. The system also enables marketing teams to generate 'what if' scenarios on the current portfolio and expected yields. Overall, the system is providing NatWest with a significant advance in delivering timely, accurate key performance information across the division.

Planning for profit at Quaker Oats is now enhanced by its ability to analyse data on all of its food products worldwide using multi-dimensional technology. According to the manager of finance and planning systems, David Brieg, 'We now have an overall worldwide competitive picture that we never had before. We now know where we stand relative to our competitors, and we understand our total profitability picture. We used to know how much we sold in total in Germany or France, but we really couldn't break that down for each product in individual countries – we simply didn't have the tools to do it'.

Quaker can now decide almost instantly which products it should market and in what part of the world – and at what price – to beat its competitors. The company has now rolled out Express to about 60 users in its marketing, sales and financial divisions. Where the previous system showed general trends in Quaker's overall business, Express lets users drill down to product details by brand and even by product bar-code.

Glaxo Pharmaceuticals, Britain's most successful drug company, has also recognised the potential of OLAP technology, using multi-source marketing data analysis to help monitor patterns and trends within the UK pharmaceutical market-place. Described as one of the central pillars of Glaxo's commercial information architecture, Express is used to combine more than 28 data sources (both internal and external) for a large range of reporting, tracking, modelling and forecasting activities. The system is truly enterprise-wide (the user community numbers more than 1000); its applications are being developed across sales, marketing, finance and production.

Marketing Reports System

The Marketing Reports System is probably one of the most frequently used analytical systems within the marketing department and is used to look at market share and competitor activity over 10 years of history. The system contains data on more than 2500 products and 8000 pack sizes across 1700 geographic areas, and produces invaluable analyses based on shared, accurate and consistent information in all markets in which Glaxo operates.

As these examples show, the rewards for users of business intelligence applications can be substantial. Full data access, sophisticated analytical and modelling capabilities and ease-of-use all combine to deliver real competitive advantage to an organisation's key decision-makers. With the wealth of data and technology now available, management is coming close to the Holy Grail of information access and delivery – and is finally beginning to see the return on IT investments that has been promised for so long.

Rod Whyte is executive vice-president SPG Europe for IRI Software.

PCS: FACING THE SECURITY ISSUE

John Bruce

A desktop computer in any organisation is a potential entry point into valuable corporate data. Can users be trusted to ensure complete data security and protection day after day?

In both management and computing theory, it is pretty well accepted across the world that empowerment of the individual is the way forward for corporate growth and success. In management theory, this decentralised approach has been developed by a whole range of programmes, from mentoring and upward appraisals, to quality circles and national qualification structures. In computing, it has been most clearly demonstrated by the growing importance of the personal computer.

Only a few years ago, most employees of a given organisation only had access to company data through a mainframe system, if at all. Today, hundreds of thousands of people have vast amounts of corporate-sensitive data, plus vital forecasts and plans, which are nestled inside their PCs.

Trusting the individual

That is giving a major responsibility to a lot of people for crucial data that is vulnerable to workstation or disk malfunction, viral attack, sabotage, or outright theft, every single day: data which if lost, corrupted or stolen could be desperately damaging to an organisation's well-being. It is fortunate, therefore, that each PC-user has access to back-up utilities, antivirus programs and security locks to ensure the safety of his or her own machine and its contents. Or is it fortunate? Can an organisation be really confident that each and every individual will take daily responsibility for ensuring the complete security of vital data? Can it be certain that mistakes will not be made, concentrations will not lapse, and consciences will always stay clear?

A recent study showed there to be an average of 1.4 back-up facilities on every PC, a fairly healthy figure. However, it also showed that each user actually used the facilities on average only once every 13 months. Such a high level of negligence and carelessness on the part of end-users effectively renders these back-up programs useless. Most antivirus programs are excellent at dealing with known viruses. Yet figures show that, on average, three new viruses are created every day. Antivirus packages age rapidly. They need to be updated regularly to cope with these ever-new threats – but so few are. It only needs one employee to take a disk home for personal use, and the entire system could be affected.

In a study last year of corporate financial problems in the USA, more than 25 per cent of companies surveyed reported fiscal loss through data sabotage or workstation fallibility. Organisations are vulnerable to costly security violations, not only from disgruntled employees and industrial espionage from within, but also from external hackers who break into corporate computing networks via use of a modem.

According to Datapro's *Computer Security Issues Survey* of 1993, unauthorised access is the chief concern of corporate data security staff. A further survey of computer security specialists held by COMSEC revealed that as many as two-thirds of the respondents had experienced a data break-in in 1993 alone. Such security breaches are not just damaging to corporate confidentiality, they hurt the company financially, too. The average cost of a break-in runs to tens of thousands of pounds. These losses not only come from damaged materials, repair costs and time wasted, but can come from newly transmitted viruses, credit card fraud and theft of computer-registered goods such as airline tickets.

A 1993 US survey showed that 22 per cent of organisations with more than 5000 employees had registered losses of $100 000 or more from malicious acts, system failure or simple carelessness. Even worse, 78 per cent of organisations with more than 1000 staff reported that data risks had increased at a rate equal to or greater than the rate of growth in their computing resources in the past five years. That is a horrendous statistic. Because networking across Europe is rapidly approaching levels in the USA, figures such as these will inevitably become a European problem as well, if the real lessons are not learnt.

Onus on the company

The problem is clear. Most end-users quite simply do not feel as protective about their data as the company does. Although companies are right to give more and more computing power to the individual, the responsibility for the complete security of the data involved must lie with the company itself.

The answer is to find a method of ensuring complete network security which can be controlled from one centralised point without compromising the independence of the end-users, at a cost which can be thoroughly justified by the savings incurred. Put like that, it sounds like a particularly difficult solution to find.

Put like this, it doesn't. To begin with, most end-users are not interested in the slightest in PC security. Many will spend their working days suffering, if at all, only a handful of data problems, certainly not enough to worry about. And when something does go wrong, there is always the MIS manager to sort it out. Losing responsibility for data security will not lose many users much sleep. In addition, the costs incurred simply in installing, upgrading and maintaining security programmes on behalf of end-users on each individual workstation are vast – an estimated £40 per application per workstation – and that is before data loss and corruption costs are taken into account.

So the need is for software that provides centrally controlled security without destroying the freedom of the end-user. But for such a product to work, it will need to justify several criteria. First, most organisations have a mix of platforms, often including DOS, Windows and Macintosh systems. For a central security product to work, it must be able to operate across all platforms on the network, thereby simplifying training and support, and ensuring consistency. There is no point in buying software that offers, for example, antivirus protection for DOS, only to find that support for Windows is minimal, and that full Windows protection costs extra. Not only are extra costs incurred, but so is extra installation and management time.

Enterprise software

Because organisations are increasingly laying the foundations for integrated enterprise network management systems, the tools they need to use must be designed with the enterprise network in mind. This essentially means three things. The enterprise software must initially be able to permit distribution management from a central console to every unit across the network. But that is not all. It needs to encompass logging and reporting to and from that point, so that administrators can monitor the network and quickly identify attempts to breach security. Finally, the software must be able to integrate with other management tools, both in terms of sharing data, and sharing the space available on the management console.

Once this has been established, the actual security itself within the tool needs to have several available levels. In many environments, users share work stations, yet still need to conceal confidential or private files from other users. Within the same environment, however, there may be other users who work with extremely confidential data, and who need the type

194

of top-level security offered by encryption. A flexibility of password protection and security level is therefore paramount. In addition, the product should provide a way for trusted personnel, such as the MIS staff, to access workstations in emergency –as when a password has been forgotten.

The product should also be simple to use for the end-user. There is no point in setting up complicated procedures if, for example, they take up so much time that individuals might not bother to log out properly, leaving their machine open to unauthorised access. Once the security software has been implemented, users should be able to access their workstation quickly by supplying the appropriate security information.

All this seems like a lot to demand from a piece of software, but there is good news. Such products are already available, and are improving and increasing in number all the time. At Symantec, for example, we are providing local area network-based tools that meet the needs of organisations, to help them prevent the security breaches not only of today, but also of tomorrow. Based on the concepts outlined above, and using the core product base, network versions have been developed of each of the main utility tools successfully used by individual users for years. As a result, key products such as The Norton AntiVirus and The Norton Utilities can now be run across an entire organisation, operating from one centrally managed console.

As international network management develops, so the strategy will grow. The company is developing an underlying architecture that will allow theme tools and others to interconnect into an overall enterprise system that operates over wide alta networks.

This complete systems management and administration solution will work through a series of LAN-based tools each designed to bring costs under control. Within this family of network tools, there are several products that concentrate on data security and protection, such as antivirus software for NetWare. Another product provides data protection and security features, automatically performing a series of quick tests on each workstation's hard disk upon network log-in. In addition, a central database on the server containing specific information on each workstation is automatically stored and updated, which ensures automatic protection and repair of disks and files across the entire corporate network.

Norton Administrator

Norton Administrator for Networks is a single automated solution to costly, time-intensive and repetitive manual LAN administration tasks. It includes three key network administration features – a network inventory for gathering both hardware and software information to the server from user machines, software distribution to users on the network, and permissive or restrictive software licence metering together with other features. A further product enables LAN managers to install and monitor the full range of DiskLock security options across the network from one console.

The trend toward more and more workstations within organisations is healthy. It gives people more responsibility for their work, a stronger sense of achievement, and a higher degree of productivity. The data security risks are greater, however, which makes the trend toward centralised, enterprise-wide security control a healthy approach, too. The time and costs saved, and the extra security provided, are vital. It also means that employees can concentrate on their work without having to worry about system controls. Enterprise-wide security is here to stay.

John Bruce, marketing director, Europe for Symantec Corporation, has worked within sales and marketing in the IT industry for 20 years and has been a director of IT companies for half that time. He joined Symantec in 1992.

TELLING THE TALE

THE DYNAMICS OF STRATEGIC IDENTITY

Peter Zentner

To make strategic identity work, there must be support and loyalty from customers, employees and suppliers alike. If you want satisfied customers you need satisfied staff.

'Strategic identity' is a dynamic management tool. It harnesses an organisation's energies through the behaviour and interlocking attitudes of all who help generate the company's income – employees, customers and suppliers. It is, by definition, strategic. It grows the business. To understand strategic identity, it is helpful first to define corporate identity (CI).

The latter always leads to a visual solution: a logo, a visual clarification of structural relationships, ideally a reflection of the company's personality. Traditionally, when management is reconsidering its corporate identity, it turns to a design consultancy. You go to a surgeon and the advice is 'cut'. You go to a designer and the advice is 'design'.

In the 1980s, CI attracted millions of pounds of companies' investment and enormous opprobrium from the media. CI is either money wisely spent, or the story of the Emperor's clothes. The chief executive of Prudential Insurance has said that 'We have no way of measuring the value of the millions we spent. We think it has been worthwhile'. Evaluating the success of a new corporate identity has never been easy. Wally Olins, chairman of Wolff Olins, major CI consultants, has always maintained that evaluation is not possible.

Strategic identity is a harder concept. It is the motor which drives the company, and its purpose – to increase the profitable business done – can be measured. Identity and strategy should be the mirror images of one philosophy. However, there is often a mismatch between boardroom strategy and reality on the ground. For instance:

- One well-known High Street retailer claims that his company's 'pile 'em high, sell 'em cheap' policy has been superseded by total customer service. Shoppers in his stores, however, continue to complain about poor service.
- One European member company of a multinational chemical group shows a similar dichotomy between strategy and reality. The chief executive's view was: 'We're dynamically pursuing an acquisition programme'. His managers' perception was: 'We're going nowhere. We back off. We cut costs'.

So why the gap? Boardroom delusion? Boardroom public relations? Or a tendency to become cut off from the real world – like Hitler who slept as the Allies landed in Normandy on D-Day? Whatever the reason, top management strategy can become divorced from internal and external reality. Many companies unwittingly restrict their employees' potential contribution by practising top-down communication and an authoritarian, if polite, management style. They may also, without realising it, ward off wise external counsel, through NIH, the Not Invented Here syndrome. The more successful a company, the more its success can be a barrier to new ideas.

Strategies come to grief unless they have the support of customers, employees and suppliers. Moreover, these different groups, which influence the generation of the firm's income, are interlocking. They form one structure. Store employees reflect the views of customers; suppliers reinforce customers' perceptions; and customers, in the end, are the ones who pay the bills. Giving due attention to the architecture of business relationships makes for a successful strategic identity. That means listening, and responding, to all perceptions expressed about the business.

Yet most companies would claim to do this already – recognising the importance of their customers, employees and others in the chain. The rhetoric is right: 'the customer is king (or, presumably, queen)'. But if that is so, when did you last feel like royalty in any shop? Every retailer claims to do customer research, and does, but the methodology does not lead to red-carpet treatment.

The company sets the research agenda. It drafts the questions and gets the answers within its own predetermined framework. This is true for quantitative research based on scripted questionnaires. It is also true for qualitative research. This, though based on free discussion, is likewise preprogrammed, running on preordained tracks of chosen themes. The customers are only partially heard. The company duly gets its partial answers.

Satisfying customers is basic. It is twice as important to avoid dissatisfying them. Satisfied customers tell six people of their good experiences. Dissatisfied shoppers tell no less than eleven. But possibly it is not the customer horror stories which are the most significant. The difference between the very satisfied and the satisfied customer provides the really important clue to success.

In the USA, Xerox (which uses a 1—5 scale for its Customer Satisfaction Index), sets out to convert all its customers to satisfied fours and very satisfied fives. Within two years, this was achieved. Then research revealed the startling data that fives were *six times more likely to repurchase than fours.* Clearly, aiming at fours *and* fives is not good enough. Yet there is no shortage of companies which do just that, proudly proclaiming the combined figures in annual reports. Yet, to be truly customer-driven, strategic identity must specifically strive for very satisfied customers only. A 5 per cent increase in customer retention, according to recent research, equals anything between 25—85 per cent additional profit. The pursuit of fives is no luxury, rather a commercial necessity.

Just as companies profess to be customer-focused, so most claim a policy of partnership with their suppliers. The theory of long-term, close co-operation with suppliers to bring mutual benefits is not controversial. The practice often is. The supplier is, of course, the junior partner. 'We are both equal, but some are more equal than others', or 'We are part of the family, but we know our place' – these are just some of the perceptions expressed by suppliers. Yet, if the company is to draw maximum advantage from its supplier partnerships, it needs to listen to those voices, often only faint for fear of losing orders – or even of jeopardising the total relationship. As one supplier to a leading chain has said: 'If we were not kept at arm's length, we could do so much more for them'.

If customer' and suppliers' views need to be allowed maximum expression, employees' views are key. They lie at the centre of all company experience, and deserve even more active consideration. Employees' perceptions, their attitude to their customers and their job satisfaction feed directly into the customers' satisfaction. They are the mirror image.

Yet the retail sector, for one example, is hierarchical and structured. Store employees tend to be told, not consulted or debriefed about their customer experiences. They have literally an untold wealth of relevant observations. Research shows that two-thirds of managers never talk to staff about their jobs, a recurring feature among even the most prestigious High Street names.

Hence the gap between head office view and front-line employee perception. 'Are we a friendly store? Not when we're short-staffed, harassed and can't achieve what we want to.' And (an especially perceptive comment): 'Our strength is we're customer-focused. Our weakness is our customer service'. That in turn leads to the mirror image of one customer's observation: 'The staff are not unfriendly. But they're not actually friendly either. They won't waste time on the customer'.

Low morale among front-line employees, clearly, can have a strongly adverse impact on a store's customers. Research by PepsiCo's fast-food subsidiary, Taco Bell, shows that staff turnover directly affects profits: in the 20 per cent of retail chain stores with the lowest staff turnover (which must surely mean the highest morale) sales are double and profits 55 per cent higher, compared with the 20 per cent of stores with highest staff turnover. Front-line workers, as the interface with the customer, should be, according to a Harvard Business School report, 'the centre of management concerns'.

Design and visual impression

The strategic identity means the interface between all the company's main revenue-creating stakeholders – suppliers as well as employees and customers. Its effective management encourages their loyalty in an increasingly competitive market-place. Design has an important role in reflecting that interlocking identity. Design cannot act as a substitute or a cosmetic veneer. If design loses touch with the reality, it merely exposes the strategic identity's flaws.

British Rail is an example: the best of design and creativity exposing the less-than-best reality. The simple BR logo provokes the unkind witticism: 'BR don't know whether they're coming or going'. And the superbly dreamy, unwise commercial 'We're getting there' which BR wisely withdrew when the gap between dream and BR reality had simply become too great.

What is the visual component of strategic identity? On the one hand, it is the logotype and the visual system which clarifies the web of internal relationships of subsidiaries, divisions and products. Ideally, it should be pleasing, should differentiate from competitors, should be in keeping with the ethos of the organisation, be implemented throughout, and be painstakingly maintained.

The visual element is the servant of identity, not identity itself. It acts as signal and packaging for the company for the benefit of employees, customers, suppliers and others. However, the most important aspect of strategic identity's visual manifestation is the one directly experienced, the design and visual impression of corporate headquarters, offices, factories, shops.

For example, one clearing bank is developing a futuristic branch, which divides its prototype space into three: the walk-in customer area – ample, highly attractive, nothing but the best; the look-in 'kitchen' behind glass – high-tech, mouth-watering; and the working area – out of sight from the customer, relatively cramped, referred to by the workers as the dungeon.

Then there is a hotel built around a colossal atrium, with dwarfed rooms for the workers. Or the company HQ where directors travel by separate lift to reach the carpeted sanctuary of their offices. Or the canteen showing less concern for the employees than the adjoining store does for the customers. All give their messages to the workers, and through the employee/customer chain, to the customer and others in the business relationship. Management may simply not be aware of the full implications and impact.

Organisational management depends on who is truly following and with what degree of loyalty. Strategic identity is management's tool to ensure that any gap between management's thinking and that of its crucial followers – employees, customers and suppliers – is eliminated. At the end of the day, their combined loyalties are the route to maximum customer retention and to increased profits.

Peter Zentner is a consultant specialising in corporate identity and business strategy. He is managing partner of Strategic Retail Identity

ASSESSING THE VALUE OF PR

Mike Beard

Not enough attention is given to PR as an element in management development. Some managers are unable to define PR adequately or assess the role it can play in their plans.

Currently there is a lively debate among PR practitioners about evaluation of results. This has been stimulated largely in the marketing communications area. Marketing managers are accustomed to evaluation of their advertising. When moving budgets from the ad agency to the PR activity they seek measurement methods to justify the switch. However, the needs of this specific area of communication should not be allowed to cloud the wider issue of evaluation of the total contribution of PR to the organisation.

To place the issue in context, you need to examine the changing role of the PR practitioner. The Institute of Public Relations has recently reconsidered its traditional definition of PR, which has tended to overemphasise the process, rather than the substance of what we do. The new and alternative version defines PR as being about reputation – the result of what you do, what you say and what others say about you. It is the discipline which looks after reputation, with the aim of earning understanding and support, and influencing opinion and behaviour. That is a vital final qualification. There is little point in being loved for the sake of it: little point in being loved unless the investment actually changes behaviour.

204

Today, almost every organisation is aware of the vital need to take care of its reputation. In major companies, in local and national government, in public bodies, charities and many other organisations, PR has become a key management discipline. Research continually demonstrates the crucial importance of reputation in influencing business decisions and personal preferences. Inevitably, therefore, the demands and expectations placed upon our capabilities have grown significantly. In return, we are increasingly involved in strategic decision-making at the highest level.

It has always been clear that monitoring is a key stage in the classic approach to managing the PR function. It starts by researching and assessing the situation before establishing the strategy for the specified area of business activity. Once the function has designed and obtained approval for a programme and budget in line with the strategy, the implementation phase begins.

It has always been understood that the next and vital stage is a process of monitoring and evaluation which feeds back into the refinement of strategy, to begin the cycle again. What has not been so clearly understood or agreed has been a formal process for completing the evaluation phase of the programme. In the early days, subjective assessment dominated this process. If everyone felt good about the outcome, this was the key factor. The next step was the growth of more formal management reporting. As the PR function became more strategic (and expensive), line managers expected the same kind of reporting disciplines that were demanded of other management functions.

In the 1960s and early 1970s, PR teams began to justify their efforts by quoting an advertising-equivalent value for the press coverage they generated. This was driven by a desire to show how useful and relatively cost-effective the function could be. Of course, media relations was a more dominant element in PR at that time. Unfortunately, the advertising-equivalent analysis was often used in a rather crude way, ignoring the quality of message delivery and whether the coverage had reached the target audience. In 1969, however, Bob Worcester set up MORI and then launched a series of attitude-tracking studies which are still highly relevant to public relations. Over the years since then, both in-house practitioners and consultants have filled the air with exhortations to include evaluation in programmes. At the same time, they have searched for the Holy Grail of an affordable and reliable system.

Evaluation systems

In recent years, the chorus advocating evaluation has been strengthened by a whole new raft of specialist companies. A recent feature in *PR Week* listed 10 evaluation systems on offer, all of them apparently concerned only with media coverage. This leads to the key point that media relations is only one important element in most PR programmes. If that is all you measure, then you are only measuring the implementation of one part of the programme – and not measuring its effects or effectiveness at all.

What else might be measured? Before answering that question, a word of caution: do not become over-obsessed with evaluation. The present emphasis could be a symptom of the insecurity of a relatively new management discipline, feeling a need to justify its hard-won position. Other functions such as finance and human resources have come through this process. Having said that, there are a number of areas of measurement which together make up a comprehensive package. Perhaps the most important is the normal personal appraisal carried out by the individual's employer, whether in-house or in consultancy. Clients will also appraise consultancies just as they appraise other specialist external suppliers.

The next brick in the wall is the evaluation of the execution of the agreed programme – whether we did what we said we would do. From here, you can move on and research whether the programme increased the knowledge of its target audiences and, even more important, whether it influenced their attitude to the organisation, product or issue in any measurable way. After this, some clients and suppliers might be prepared to make an act of faith and assume that it probably all did some good. It is much better however to establish some measures of behaviour which will confirm that real results have been delivered.

Management awareness

A more detailed look at the various levels should begin with the premise that PR practitioners are professionals, who should be properly paid and made subject to the same management appraisal as other executives. They should have personal action plans which can be monitored to facilitate this process. Also, PR strategy should be reviewed by the executive board from time to time. For such reviews to be successful, general managers need to have a sufficient knowledge of PR to be able to sit in judgment. This is one of the many reasons why the IPR will be giving increasing attention to improving line management awareness and understanding of the discipline. And the guidelines within an organisation for administering PR should be formalised into procedure manuals, just as they normally are for finance and personnel.

Media evaluation ranks high on my own list of programme execution measures. Media relations is one of the most important things we do, but it can never stand alone as a sound basis for evaluation, even if the particular programme is mainly media-based. There are wide fields of PR, such as government relations and internal communication, where media is unlikely to be a major element in the programme. Indeed, it can be equally important to measure the number of times an expensive video was viewed by target audiences – and how they reacted.

And then there are all those expensive publications and information packs. Were they actually used as intended, and what readership was achieved? Did they have the desired effect on the readers, and how many are remaindered in the basement? How well are direct mail programmes measured? Is the material even arriving – and if so, how quickly and in what condition? If the programme involved events or visits, how many actually took place, and how did the attendees respond? None of this is intended to denigrate media evaluation, just to put it in context. Many of the media evaluation services are well-structured. They measure quantity, content, delivery of message and actual reach of target audience. There are also products on offer which are simplistic and potentially misleading.

The next level of measurement tracks the attitudes of specific audiences. The MORI tracking studies, which measure familiarity and favourability, how well you are known, and how well you are regarded, are particularly useful. The advantages of these studies include the consistent approach over many years, allowing comparative tracking, and the collaborative structure which helps to obtain top-level responses and significantly reduces cost.

However, there are audiences for which this approach is not appropriate. It is very difficult to structure meaningful low-cost research of employee attitudes, for example. Even if you succeed, there is some chance that it might never be repeated when the results are disseminated. This could be because the information generated looks depressing in isolation, but in fact would look relatively good if you had access to comparative data. Often the only affordable option is to structure a simple study on a specific issue and cover a small sample of the audience. Such ad hoc studies, if done well, are much better than no evaluation at all.

Research suppliers need to understand that programmes are becoming far more refined in the way they target audiences. In other situations, there are secondary audiences which may be of more relevance. For example, the views of city editors on a medium-sized company are valuable and interesting. Equally relevant are the views of the specific financial journalists on the same publications who follow that company and actually write the pieces which appear.

The research industry needs to respond to these changes by providing more sophisticated and affordable tools, even if this only involves clearer packaging of services which they can already offer. A package of attitude studies covering all corporate audiences, with a few extra questions thrown in, might cost £30 000 or more – extremely good value for money, but not always affordable when budgets are tight. For some, it could be a choice between doing the programme or doing the research.

Behavioural change

Finally, the real beef in the measurement sandwich is the ultimate test, which identifies behavioural change. That, after all, is what we say we are aiming to achieve. In the financial communications area, such measures include price-earnings ratios, relative measurements of share price performance, or changes in the structure of the share register. In marketing communications, it might be sales volume, or recruitment of new stockists. In employee relations, you might look at employee retention rates or unit labour costs. In government relations, the tests can be legislation obtained, amended or avoided. In community relations, it could be the numbers of complaints received from neighbours about a particular site.

The mix of evaluation techniques is complex and the right balance needs to be used without becoming obsessive on the matter. Evaluation is only one element in managing the PR function – and managers may need to develop broader skills in this whole area.

Mike Beard is president of the Institute of Public Relations and director of corporate communications at the Taylor Woodrow Group.

WINNING WITH WORDS

Jean Hilder

Word-based communications are the nerves and sinews of any organisation. Information mapping digitises document creation and management, making it possible to win with words.

The world is in the Information Age: information has succeeded manufacturing as the motor of the economy. The information industry is highly skilled and highly paid, and has the potential – which was once the preserve of manufacturing – to exploit resources and create wealth. Its raw materials are knowledge, information and training. As in the early days of manufacturing, the way to get ahead is to be the most efficient at exploiting raw materials.

From E-mail to memos to procedures, proposals and on-line help text, a significant amount of corporate information is carried and stored in words. Unfortunately, words have been their own worst enemies. It has been estimated that the average manager reads or skims about a million words a week. Anyone who works in an office and routinely receives forgettable memos, turgid reports, junk mail and E-mail, or who has wrestled with unusable user manuals, is likely to resent the poor quality of the word supply.

For many companies, creating, maintaining and publishing the words used to communicate and store information is almost a second business – they spend between 6—15 per cent of their budgets on creating and maintaining documentation. In an information-led economy, words are not *less* but *more* important than ever before. That would be fine if this 6—15 per cent of budget were being used efficiently, but often this is not the case. Words have had a bad press for a couple of reasons.

First, words are not static things – they do not sit still, but are part of a process or flow. They have to be created, maintained, distributed, archived, retrieved and even reused. They must be managed. Second, people go to art school to learn how to paint pictures, to music college to learn how to compose and play music, but nowhere, it seems, are they taught how to write documents. It is assumed that everyone can do it as a birthright.

Manage the flow

More or less everyone can write; some people can even write well, but few can write efficiently without being shown how. It is just as depressing to create bad documents as to receive them. A method and document management strategy which addresses these concerns is required. The important thing is to manage the flow.

In the past, the flow has often been uncontrolled. Words have not been thought to require management or special attention. They are simply a means to an end. They have flowed from all areas of organisations without particular regard for their audience or purpose. Managing this undisciplined flow is impossible because there is no standard way of understanding what the words are supposed to be doing in the first place. Document management needs to define all aspects of a document, from its content, structure and purpose to its audience.

There is an analogy with analogue and digital methods of recording. Information which is recorded and transmitted by analogue processes is vulnerable to noise, distortion and decay. Digital processes cut information into definable chunks which can be precisely checked and easily reproduced without distortion or decay. A viable document management method must *digitise* the flow of words and information to make it controllable. Using such a process makes it easier for document management to take care of the creation, amendment, approval, distribution, archiving, retrieval and reuse of documents.

Although the paperless office has proved to be a myth, paper is in retreat, and electronic systems of document storage and retrieval are on the increase; 45 per cent of respondents to a recent survey had on-line systems, and 32 per cent were planning or designing on-line systems. Companies such as AT&T are finding that their customers are driving the need for on-line documentation. But this gain may not be much of a boon if garbled electronic communications merely take the place of garbled paper ones.

While it is an exaggeration to say that the medium is the message, it is certainly very important in communicating the message successfully. Documentation experts agree that it is not a good idea to transfer existing

paper-based documents on-line without considering the special characteristics of on-line documents. Information for use on-line, such as help text
or groupware, must be divided into modules that can fit comfortably on to
a single screen or series of screens, and which are easily retrieved and suitable for reuse in a variety of contexts.

Information presented in this way – for example, as help text – has
to be sharply focused on the needs of the user and the task which is being
carried out. There is even less room for vagueness of content or purpose
than in paper-based documentation. Extra words merely clutter the screen
and confuse the user.

The information to be communicated electronically must first be carefully analysed and structured. Increasingly, the way information is structured is just as important as the way it is written. Perhaps this was always
true, but we did not notice. Certainly paper-based documentation has
nothing to lose in learning from the stricter disciplines required in
creating electronic documents.

In 1967 (almost before on-line documentation was dreamed of), an
American named Robert E Horn developed a methodology for structuring
and writing documentation. By one of those coincidences that often seem
to occur in the history of ideas, his non-linear approach to information
development –information mapping – turned out to be ideal not only
for paper-based, but also for electronic documentation.

Information mapping

The information mapping method is simply the application of scientific
principles from the psychology of learning and perception to the handling
of information. It holds that writing business and technical documents is
less an art than a science, whose aim is to maximise the efficiency of the
delivery of information. Writing is not a gift, but a skill which can be
acquired by anyone given the right training. In a word, information
mapping *digitises* the document creation and management process.

Horn's discovery was that information is more easily communicated if
you can see what it is doing. If the art of novel writing consists of melding
the elements of a text into a seamless narrative, the science of information
mapping consists of separating out the elements so that their function is
obvious. Text creation consists of three stages –analysis, organisation and
presentation:

- *At the analysis stage,* the information is broken down into chunks and
  analysed according to its type (there are seven basic information types)
  and subject. At this stage, too, the intended readership or audience is
  assessed and analysed in order to identify the information it needs and
  wants to know
- *At the organisation stage,* the chunks are put into clearly labelled blocks
  and grouped in maps according to principles of relevance and consistency

211

- *At the presentation stage,* the text is clearly laid out using such aids as formatting tools; each type of information – such as concept, process, procedure or structure – has its own most effective way of being presented to make it instantly recognisable.

The difference between an unmapped text and a mapped text is like the difference between a slightly blurry photograph of a landscape and an Ordnance Survey map of the same location. The creators and consumers of information mapped texts often feel that they know where they are for the first time.

The process of mapping information is a salutary one. Existing documents treated in this way prove to be full of inconsistencies, duplications, holes and grey areas which can now be identified and put right. Even new information is often sharpened up by the process. The training and discipline of mapping are welcomed by information providers,who find it helps them to clarify their thoughts.

At the end of the process, words and tables and diagrams exist in maps which contain only a graspable number of blocks (seven plus-or-minus two blocks for paper-based information, and five plus-or-minus two blocks for screen-based information are the numbers endorsed by the findings of perceptual psychology). In this form, the information is readily portable. Because each map is only about what it says it is about, it can be taken out and reused for other purposes. For example, a procedure for using a particular piece of software can easily be extracted and incorporated in on-screen help text. Or, once sets of company procedures have been created, subsets can be extracted and given to particular groups of users.

Mapping a company's knowledge assets can be a liberating experience for the people and the company. Often there is more knowledge there than might have been thought. The whole is greater than the sum of the parts. The whole of a company's information expertise and experience, amalgamated into a textual knowledge database, can form the core of an overall information management strategy. Placed on a network, an on-line textual knowledge database becomes an even more powerful way of sharing, distributing and creating information. Networked or not, mapped information is readily identifiable, properly organised and can be treated as a fund to which people contribute, and from which they can borrow and benefit instead of a morass into which they fear to sink. People are empowered.

Semantic network

Mapping all of a company's information is in effect building a semantic network – a set of working definitions – for that company. In other words, it is not just tidying up documents, it is helping the company to identify itself to itself in all its aspects, from the way it communicates internally through memos and reports, to the way it operates in procedures, and to the very nature of the tasks it sets itself in user manuals. A company which has scrutinised its information so closely and methodically has achieved a new level of self-awareness which eliminates confusion and doubt and encourages purpose and progress.

In the realm of the self, self-knowledge produces the ability to communicate successfully with others. Likewise, confidence in information means that a company can communicate its role and position effectively to the outside world with which it has to transact business. The company and the people in it can say what they know. In other words, the efficiency of knowledge and information – the words we love to hate – is maximised. The 6—15 per cent of budget spent on document management is not simply another part of the company budget, but part of a keep-fit programme which ensures continued health. With information mapping, it is possible to win with words and not to drown in them.

Jean Hilder is director of TMS Computer Authors Limited.

THE NEW DRIVERS OF ADVERTISING

Jonathon Hoare

As consumers become more sophisticated and the battle for shelf-space grows, brands and their marketing tools must anticipate or react very quickly to emerging trends.

A recent *Economist* article mourned the death of the brand manager. Recession, it would seem, has transformed companies into cost-cutting ogres and the consumer into a cynical discount junkie. Even superbrands like Marlboro and Coca-Cola have been unable to shrug off the advent of value marketing and the growing market-share of supermarket own-label brands. So, is this the end of brand advertising as we know it? Should companies slam the doors on image marketing and invest in database modelling and price wars?

The answer seems to be yes and no. Yes, the brand, the brand manager and his various advisers must adapt to survive in this brave new world. No, because it is the advertising industry's challenge to reassure senior management that brand investment *will* secure a commercial return, a basic business principle that did get partially lost in the roaring 1980s. So what are the driving forces of change in our approach to marketing?

First, the consumer. 'Grey panthers', 'thirty-somethings', 'Generation X', 'Nineties Butterflies', 'Tyrannokids'. Each week the marketing press tells us about newly discovered stratas of society differentiated by their age, lifestyle or habitat, all of which have highly individual spending habits. God help the agency media planners...Whoever he or she is, today's consumer is more sceptical and more thoughtful, willing to consider new alternatives and concerned with quality and benefits, rather than badge status.

This scepticism extends to advertising – corporate puffery and expensively produced extravaganzas are recognised for what they are and rejected. The Henley Centre has just completed a consumer attitude survey across Europe that charts a marked decline in people's favourable attitudes toward luxury brands. David Baker, head of planning for JWT in Europe, comments that: 'Consumers have become more sophisticated, they know more about marketing and don't purchase brands just on name: they are nowhere as naive as 10 years ago'.

Bloody promotional wars

Second, the market-place. Supermarkets/warehouse clubs rule with a market share of grocery sales nearing an average of 25 per cent in the European Union. International research by BBDO reveals that European consumers now perceive own-label goods to be almost as good as the brand leaders. The battle for shelf-space and the bloody promotional wars are increasingly common on the High Street as well, as any retailer will tell you. In the UK, for example, the new mobile telephone giants all talk value, give discounts and continuously woo new avenues of distribution.

Third, technology. Interactive media, supermarket trolley-loads costed and brand-assessed in seconds, ATM-style ticket and product sales kiosks – punch-button selling – have transformed how we buy and what we buy. Dell Computers believes that by 1997 it will be selling more than 30 per cent of its equipment via high-tech sales booths in airports, shopping malls and even hotels. Coca-Cola and Pepsi have invested heavily in vending machines anywhere and everywhere as convenience marketing takes hold.

Fourth, media. I recently hosted a course on marketing at Management Centre Europe in Brussels and invited our media director to give a one-hour presentation on media trends in Europe. The result? A mind-boggling torrent of facts and figures, new media launches and opportunities. Cable TV, Satellite TV, Home Shopping TV, the PC as tomorrow's info-screen, electronic newspapers, in-store promotions, laser sky posters, in-car entertainment, in-flight entertainment. People are bombarded with more and more messages each day, which means that brand marketing *must* be different, relevant, motivating and memorable just to get to first base.

Fifth, internationalisation of brands and services. Quite naturally, companies believe that a similar product distributed across a number of countries could be supported by the same advertising. This makes sound economic sense, and more than 60 of the top 100 advertisers in Europe have merged and purged their national marketing teams accordingly. Global advertising campaigns abound, and advertising agencies are racking their brains for headlines that will translate into German, Hungarian and Chinese.

Sixth, media comments. The media have been busy with their own headlines, marvelling at the success of Sainsbury's copycat Cola – increasing a 26.2 per cent market share to 74.7 per cent in just four weeks. They gleefully wait for other superbrands to suffer similar indignities, pouncing on any evidence of discounting or sales decline. People read such articles and wonder even more about what to buy – and so the vicious circle continues.

So, why is it that some established brands are prospering, and why is a whole clutch of new products and services gaining profitable market share across Europe and other continents? Quite simply because, as the world turns faster and faster, for every door that shuts another one opens.

Go out and give it to them

In short, brands must anticipate or react very quickly to emerging consumer trends – and so must their marketing techniques. Confectionery has moved into the chiller cabinet, carbonated drinks vie with bottled water and new isotonic brands for the growing refreshment market, prescription medicines have gone over the counter, skin creams now feature a whole ranges of skincare products. Marketing has always prospered when based on a relevant sales cycle. This is where the beleaguered army of advertising and marketing professionals should start. To coin an old sales phrase 'Find out what they want, then go out and give it to them'. (You could now add '...in the right place at the right price'.)

Image and sales marketing must now work in close co-operation, with telemarketing and database prospecting used as essential tools of the trade. Specialist marketing companies multiply accordingly, while advertising agencies agonise over whether to integrate or not to integrate. Of course, companies which have built up brand equity can afford to milk short-term profits via promotional activities – after all, what is the point of investing in a brand over a number of years if you can't make hay while the sun shines? The art is knowing how much hay can be made.

British Airways seems to have achieved a fair balance between premium branding and specific offers that represent genuine value. Some so-called experts have criticised the Air Miles initiative, but nearly every other airline has followed suit. At the other end of the spectrum, General Motors was revelling in the success of its small car brand launch in 1992. Saturn cars were sexy, well priced and energetically marketed. A decision was taken in 1993 to reduce marketing expenditure, as the cars seemed to be selling themselves. Sales dropped like a stone – why? The Saturn brand was still embryonic; it desperately needed the profile and excitement of a heavy advertising spend to stand a chance of doing battle with the big boys on the forecourts. The marketing dollars have been speedily returned.

Young & Rubicam has recently launched its Brand Asset Valuator – a study that measured the attitudes of 30 000 consumers in 19 countries relating to 450 global and 6000 local brands. The findings were that familiarity must be backed by relevance and esteem, with brand building working outwards from specifics (differentiation) to a more general proposition (familiarity). Clever stuff, but I still like that old sales phrase I coined: to repeat 'Find out what they want, then go out and give it to them…in the right place at the right price'.

Here are two examples of where canny marketing has optimised a product or service market share. In the mid-1980s, an entrepreneur called Peter Woods spotted an opportunity to undercut the major financial institutions' prices on motor and home insurance. Cost and convenience were the twin pillars of a formidable new direct service. However, after a year or so it became evident that only a limited number of people would risk insuring with an unknown company, even when backed by the Royal Bank of Scotland. Direct Line needed to invest in branding, to become better known and trusted.

Chris Wilkins (now the creative vice-chairman of TBWA) came up with 'the little red telephone on wheels' branding device that personified the service offer. The first television advertisements attracted an astonishing response level that was swiftly and courteously handled. Since then, the branding device has been at the forefront of Direct Line's meteoric growth, and has so far proved to be adaptable to new markets and new product offers as the company has continued to expand. The little phone now enjoys more than 90 per cent recognition among Direct Line key target audiences, and the distinctive jingle helped to sell more than 1.8 million motor policies off the screen in 1994. The brand marketing is still working hand-in-glove with the company's sales strategy.

Hello Boys! Hello Girls!

Wonderbra faced a different problem. In 1993, Sara Lee reclaimed the brand from Gossard, which promptly launched its own version of the old classic and called it Ultrabra. Wonderbra seemed doomed to lose market share to its sexy young rival, suffering from a 'bra my mum would wear' image. The marketing budget was limited, but two trends in the marketplace offered some opportunity. The curvy look was back in vogue, and our research showed that girls of all ages wanted to look good – for their own self-esteem and well-being.

The resulting campaign was purposefully controversial, because we hoped that the media might help promote the brand. Posters were used specifically to provoke comment. TV, radio and press coverage was unprecedented, giving free coverage calculated as worth more than £15 million. Sales more than doubled as women identified with the model and her obvious confidence in life. Kaliber, the non-alcoholic lager, has even paid for 300 'Hello Boys!' posters to run in tandem with its 'Hello Girls!' campaign.

It is clear that some of the rules of advertising have changed for good. Certainly the marketing armoury has expanded. Everybody must accept that companies are demanding new levels of marketing support that range from pure marketing consultancy to specialist niche targeting. Accordingly, brand departments and advertising agency structures must alter to meet these new demands. But companies ignore classic brand investment at their peril.

By concentrating on the sales cycle dynamic, management and their advisers can assess the competitiveness of any given product, and then the role for brand marketing. Shorten the ad-to-sale chain and you will have a sales director, a larger marketing budget and a stronger brand.

Jonathon Hoare is managing director of TBWA.

NEW PRIORITIES IN PROMOTION

Iain Arthur

Sales promotion is more serious than it was 10 years ago. The distinction between strategic and tactical aims is recognised, and clients expect strategic input from their agencies.

Before considering the trends that are now coming through in sales promotion, it is important to understand what happened in the 1980s – the age of Thatcherism, consumerism at its most extreme, a boom economy, lots of cash to spend, and marketing increasingly building on the glitz and glamour of the product. Brand names particularly associated with style were able to command a substantial price premium over an unbranded product.

Against this background, there was growth in direct marketing and in design, in the relevance of public relations and in the sales promotion industry itself. One of the sectors to become heavily committed to sales promotion was petrol retailing, which saw a continual flow of promotional activities based on either games or free gifts. There was more sales promotion all round: and from more sales promotion, more and more experienced agencies emerged, along with more and more experienced clients.

The sales promotion product got better. Agencies had never had it so good. Lots and lots of independent agencies, freed from advertising big brothers, developed. From those agencies came other agencies in the form of breakaways. Some went onto the Stock Exchange, and brought financial investment to the sales promotion industry. In this dynamic time, the entrepreneur led the manager, and sales promotion agencies developed skills across a broad range of marketing disciplines. Their clients began to be more aware of the power and effect of sales promotion, which had always been handled at junior level in the marketing department (perhaps to compensate for lack of involvement in the more serious strategic issues of advertising and public relations – to give them a little bit of fun in their job).

In the early 1980s, all sales promotion activity was reactive, responding to market dynamics. But slowly toward the end of the decade, the proactive sales promotion campaigns developed. The techniques began to proliferate. First there were the games; millions and million of games – every newspaper started running games to build circulation. Then there were the scratch cards; billions and billions of scratch cards in packets of tea, with bottles of beer – everywhere people were scratching and winning. Then there was the multi-bag, the opportunity to create a point-of-sale promotion without any physical change to the display or the pack label, a multi-purchase incentive where the consumer was invited to, in this instance, buy six and save 15p. The handle of the bag was punched out and became the coupon for use as a control at the check-out. And then the win-a-car, win-a-bike, win-anything-a-day competitions. Heinz was particularly fond of this mechanism; so you would buy your beans, enter the competition, and every day a car would be available as a prize for 100 days.

Then there were the off-the-shelf incentives, the free tickets to come into a leisure park, or a zoo, the free weekends in hotels around the country. There were free films, free accommodation, free travel, free tickets – in fact this was the beginning of a new five-letter word: Free Asterisk. The asterisk means, yes, it is free but you have to do something else; you can get into a leisure park without charge, but you have to bring a paying customer with you; you can have a free weekend in a hotel, but you have to eat the meals and pay for them; you can have a free film, but must pay for the developing and printing. With the beginning of Free Asterisk (free, but not quite free) came the development of sales promotion agencies which were really *selling* promotion agencies. Their product was a weekend-away voucher which they then tried to sell. They were trying to sell the technique, and not really offering sales promotion consultancy.

During the 1980s, the less popular techniques were coupons, along with pack offers, tailor-made activity in the large multiple grocer market, self-liquidating premiums and charity promotions. At the same time, retailer power was growing, with retailers building their own brands and taking command of marketing the supplier's products. The decade also saw brand marketing at its strongest. The importance of the brand was finally appreciated; the value of the brand was frequently brought on to the company balance sheet. Trade marketing evolved, with manufacturers committing themselves to understanding the marketing needs of their customers and devising their own marketing strategies to match those needs.

And what are the trends for the 1990s? There are fewer promotions, but they are bigger. Research and evaluation are now playing a crucial part. People want to know what they are spending money on and what benefits they are achieving. They are looking for brand value benefits, not just sales or just short-term stocking objectives. They are concerned with cost-effectiveness now (not just with cost), with marketing and not just technique. Promotions are not technique-driven, but marketing-driven, with techniques chosen to suit the strategic positioning of the product.

Creative synergy has evolved through marketing campaigns where sales promotion now follows the lead of the advertising, extending and developing the theme created by the advertising campaign. Far more discerning consumers are not easily fooled by Free Asterisk. They are looking for tangible added value; they want to see, understand and compare the benefit they are going to have when they buy the product. Following on from the growth of retail power in the 1980s, very powerful chains are dictating and managing sales promotion within their estates. The communication explosion has meant new media appearing everywhere; more magazines, more newspapers, more television channels, satellite television. Everybody is looking for less wastage, too, and more precision. The clients will not accept communicating to 10 000 of whom only 1000 are genuine. You fish with a line, not a net.

What techniques have come through in the 1990s? Coupons are up and coming once again, because they are now more sophisticated, more controlled, more direct. The free draw is back and popular, along with the on-pack lottery, as agencies and clients appreciate the mechanics for presenting the technique within the law. Immediacy has become enormously important. So while price reduction is still the number one technique, extra-fill, extra-product free is now the second most important sales promotion technique next to price.

Charities are back in fashion, and so are strategically relevant joint promotions, where two products with a similar target market and similar brand status come together to cross-promote and support each other. The consumers are responding to, first of all, reduced price; second, banded pack – equal with extra quantity of product free; fourth, a re-useable container; fifth a free gift with purchase; and the sixth most powerful mechanism, the coupon. The next ranking mechanisms do not fall into the immediate category, making it very obvious that immediacy is important – indeed, it has never been more important in sales promotion. However, power to excite response still exists, while at a lower level, for the free mail-in (seventh), the self-liquidator (eighth) and contests and games (ninth).

Table 1 shows a range of promotion techniques and objectives, and is far more accurate in that it identifies the real strength related to the real objective. For instance, if repeat purchase is the objective, then cash-back and free mail-in share the position of most effective technique, with free draw being totally inappropriate. If purchase frequency is the promotion objective, then cash-back becomes stronger than free mail-in. If consumer

Technique selection	Trial	Repeat purchase	Consumer loyalty	Purchase frequency	Trade up to larger	Consumer awareness
Couponing (off-pack)	8	7	6	1	8	8
On-pack coupon	6	8	7	1	8	4
Cash-back	5	10	8	9	5	5
Special price	8	5	3	5	7	5
Extra-fill pack	8	5	6	6	7	6
Multi-pack/bag of	2	1	8	7	3	2
On/in-pack premium	8	9	8	8	8	6
Self-liquidating prem	5	7	6	5	6	6
Free draw	1	0	2	0	1	8
Competition	4	0	4	2	4	8
Instant win	8	5	4	0	1	8
Personality	7	4	6	3	1	9
Phone-in	6	2	4	2	5	9
Free mail-in	7	10	8	8	6	6
Charity link	5	6	7	4	4	8

Table 1. Promotion techniques and objectives.

awareness is the objective, personality promotions and phone-ins become the most powerful technique.

Sales promotion's marriage to, absorption and use of direct marketing is a major trend. The 1990s have seen a continued merger of the two skills; in fact, there is some argument about whether direct marketing is just a different expression for more precise sales promotion. The demand from clients for less wastage and more precise targeting has generated continued growth of the promotions led by direct marketing. Fast-moving consumer goods are now managing databases which for the first time allow direct marketing techniques to be economic and available .

Clients understand direct marketing now, and a sales promotion campaign that does not contain at least a small percentage of direct marketing is extremely rare. Sales promotion agencies have now developed their own direct marketing expertise, which is frequently far more strategic than the traditional science of direct mail, bringing a greater depth of creativity and increasing the effectiveness of direct marketing campaigns. Agencies continually encourage clients to build databases, increasingly building database enhancement into sales promotions, planning for the future, and gradually making communication with the consumer more economic and more precise. Clients are now willing to run a number of different approaches to a particular sales promotion technique, so establishing and testing effectiveness by measurement of response. Direct marketing and sales promotion working together have moved from a simple expression of tactics to a strategic necessity in marketing planning.

The power of the retailer, though, has continued to grow. More and more superstores, megastores and hyperstores are opening with sophisticated marketing and traffic-building support. Not only do they offer value, but also convenience, freshness and quality, removing one by one the advantages of the individual retailer. This increased retailer power is accompanied by increased competitiveness between the retailers and continual enhancements of the shopping experience. Shoppers, being aware of the extra benefits that come from retailers, are becoming more selective. They are demanding that their shopping experience be interesting, informative and fun; and the retailers are continuing to develop their own brands. Own-branded product is no longer a cheap alternative; the retailer's own brands now have premium brand images in their own right. And, of course, the retailers are now taking over marketing activity from suppliers' brands.

Two major retailers in the UK have appointed sales promotion agencies which suppliers must use if they wish any sales promotion activity to take place in the retailer's outlets. This in turn has provided extra revenue for the retailer, as he takes a percentage of the supplier's fee for the use of the sales promotion agency. The retailers are getting to know their customers better, building up lists of their customers, and selling the lists. In the stores, the increased sophistication of electronic point of sale has now made mechanisms like the multi-bag redundant. The 'buy six,get one free' offer can be controlled by the check-out, switched on and off at the retailers' discretion. Their traffic-building frequent shopper programmes are being funded by the suppliers, who in turn are ready to understand and co-operate, for they have been developing their own trade marketing approach to retailer customers.

The development of sales promotion may be leading into a legal minefield. Brussels could legislate in the future to restrict promotion and direct marketing activity. But there is no room in the sales promotion industry, anyway, for the con, the misleading of the customer. There is no room for the cowboys, for amateurs, for the unsophisticated. All sales promotion must be straightforward, clear and honest in its presentation to the consumer. And with the client's understanding of the impact of poor sales promotion on consumer attitude to the brand, even greater effort must be made to ensure that fulfilment of the sales promotion proposition is efficiently and effectively handled – that consumers receive what they expect to receive, if not more.

In the agency world, itself, there has been a polarisation. A lot of the small agencies have gone out of business. The rule is back to the basics of the industry, with more attention given to client servicing and less to expansion and acquisitions. More European and Japanese companies have come into the UK. Clients are demanding and getting a greater degree of client service, and the brand value, not the technique, is being recognised as the most important consideration when planning a campaign.

The clients have become the agencies' partners. The sales promotion agencies are no longer working at junior brand manager level; they are now involved in the strategic planning of their clients. They can then understand the brand objectives, be proactive and develop the brand portfolio. Sales promotion is no longer reactive, but planned, and there is a far greater depth of input by the client when briefing the sales promotion agency. The latter is the partner of the marketing department, not a function of sales.

In conclusion, sales promotion in the 1990s is a much more serious business than it was in the 1980s. The differentiation between strategic and tactical objectives is recognised, and clients expect a strategic input from their agencies, thus providing a far greater contribution to overall marketing. The rise in contact point from junior brand manager to marketing manager, and even marketing director, has meant a far greater level of strategic communication between client and sales promotion agency. But it is still fun!

Iain Arthur is director of Fleming Arthur Limited.

THE FUTURE OF DIRECT MARKETING

Michael York Palmer

New technology will continue to excite and inspire today's direct marketing pioneers. A glossary, from A–Z, is needed to understand the future impact of this technology.

Any look into the future inevitably needs to be put into perspective by a brief glance at the past, particularly so where direct marketing is concerned.

After 30 years calling itself *The Reporter of Direct Mail Advertising* the pre-eminent US publication changed its name to *Direct Marketing* in 1968 to recognise the total activity of direct mail users in employing all media to acquire and identify customers and prospects, then to communicate with them regardless of medium.

Direct Marketing is now defined as an interactive system of marketing using a variety of media to effect a measurable response and/or transaction at any location, with this activity stored on a database. Thus the main medium of direct mail has been supplemented by inbound and outbound telephone marketing, interactive direct response television and radio, print media, and a variety of miscellaneous media stretching from outdoor posters, business pages, PC discs, CD Rom, even sugar bags and book-matches.

Despite this expansion across the media spectrum direct marketing is still measured by the growth in direct mail year on year in the UK. Royal

Mail direct mail growth statistics show a steady growth pattern during the 80s from 961 million items in 1980/81 to 2082 million in 1989/90. Then, reflecting the recession, the growth is almost static until 1993/94 when it surges again up to almost 2400 million.

As a percentage of overall advertising expenditure direct marketing will soon break through the 20 per cent barrier and many predict will hit 50 per cent before the millennium. Bearing in mind the number of press advertisements where a coupon has been added as an afterthought, advertising which incorporates a direct marketing element may well be over 40 per cent of the overall expenditure already.

One of the essential strengths is the element of secrecy and confidentiality, and when allied to personalisation of messaging, direct marketing will continue to be a difficult medium to quantify. So what will be the predominant influence on direct marketing of the future?

To plagiarise the well-known quote from Sir Charles Forte on location of catering premises being vital, the main elements will be technology, technology and technology.

The computer in its various guises and sizes has been in use for database direct marketing in the UK for more than 30 years. Only those coming into the industry from outside, with no knowledge of direct marketing, have regularly astounded the cognoscenti by bravely (and consistently) re-inventing database marketing, with an entirely new approach dedicated to the applications available from their own bespoke software. From now until the end of the decade, a mere five years there will, however, be a great deal more technology to excite and inspire today's direct marketing pioneers.

Even a SWOT analysis would be difficult to construct given the immense parameters that will influence the future developments in direct marketing. No amount of superb relational database management and state-of-the-art technology can ever beat the warm friendly voice of a skilled order clerk or salesperson — what may not be obvious will be the on-screen script or prompt they may be reading which has stored up all the personal customer data.

Inevitably there will be few media that escape the march of direct marketing techniques and technology. Media integration at all stages will involve the use of direct marketing in some form or another, and many believe that it will become the catalyst that generates the synergy between all the diverse media.

In order to understand the increasing impact of this technology on the future of direct marketing an A-Z is required.

A. Artificial intelligence is the branch of computer science that deals with using computers to simulate human thinking, and is concerned with building computer programmes that offer creative solutions to problems. Once human reactions and responses to aural and visual experiences can be harnessed, the tedious and risky testing of different direct marketing approaches can be minimised.

B. Bar codes are already in extensive use on product packaging and now under test by Royal Mail with selected DMA members for address and delivery application. Future plans may include bar code readers in smart letterboxes and the use of more sophisticated Glyph technology, which has both outbound and inbound systems activation potential.

C. Customer care needs technology of increased capability as the demands of direct marketers escalate. RFM, Chaid and Multiple regression analysis will lead to ever more personal and specific offers being made to customers such as timely bulk buying offers to combat competition.

D. Digitisation will enable marketers to send more words, pictures and data ever faster into television sets, through fibre optic cable or even on old copper wires — thus making interactivity easier and faster for home shopping, banking, remote learning, video games and telephone response services.

E. Electronic mail is here already in business, but consumer electronic mail boxes will become a medium in their own right. In return for the free provision of this service the company that maintains the mailboxes will have the right to give the name to a selected number of advertisers who then place messages in the box, first having obtained the recipient's permission.

F. Fax has come a long way very slowly in the last 25 years, but is now set to flourish. Plain paper machines giving high definition full colour capability when interfaced with an auto-dial in-house database will make old fashioned newsletters obsolete. Fax on demand response facilities will expand rapidly world-wide, especially for business marketers once touch-tone technology is in place.

G. Geodemographics applications for direct marketers continue to expand. Acorn type systems will be the basis for many different types of data overlay, each one making the individual consumer's preferences ever more clear and targetable. Businesses will know exactly where to site a new sales office, retailers when to open and executives moving house exactly which roads in their new town to target for a new house.

H. Holographic tills and barcode readers will feed the developing supermarket customer clubs and give the vital data flow to the relational database regarding the family preferences, product purchases, and can map the lifestyle progression that an historic flat file database can never achieve.

I. Interactive PC discs, videos, CD-ROM and other physical electronic media will enable direct marketers, both consumer and business to business, to relate with the needs of customers and prospects by giving them a method of buying or enquiring via the personal electronic medium of their choice.

J. Junk mail as we know it should disappear in the cloud of technological advances available for direct marketing.

K. The Knight Ridder Syndrome based upon the Viewtron system tested in Florida in 1980. A sophisticated, expensive videotext machine for the home, positioned to provide a substitute for newspapers on the theory that electronic media would replace the printed word. Right in principle, wrong timing. Pioneering is rarely successful.

L. Loyalty programmes will increase in efficiency and profitability and the power of relational databases will facilitate timely and appropriate offers and rewards.

M. Multi-vendor integration will end the competing vendor situation whereby computers cannot exchange data or programmes because they use a unique operating system. Open systems will give easier access for electronic direct marketing by offering computer gateways and world-wide networking.

N. Neural networks are information processors that mimic human learning, finding patterns in incomplete or unstructured data. Vital cluster analysis on relational database is an obvious discovery, and with the growth of neural networks that develop and create themselves like bacteria in a Petri dish, there are great opportunities as well as some underlying threats.

O. Optical scanning helps the inept direct marketer who currently uses Apple Mac technology in a non creative way, to add the depth, dimension and movement to direct response advertising that it requires.

P. Parallel processing or, as it is now being called, massively parallel processing technology can offer cheap and fast processing because it acts like several hundred PCs operating simultaneously. Applications for direct marketers are diverse: on one hand a 5 million database can be scanned in a few seconds and on the other language/translation computers can scan the possible 100,000 variations on the meaning of a sentence in Japanese in less time than it takes to input.

Q. QVC, the shopping channel, is now fully operational via satellite TV across the UK and Europe and can be recommended for the direct sale of products 'not available in any store' or simply to cure insomnia. More such channels will develop with the growth in direct response TV.

R. Relational database management technology will be the most popular database management system within five years. It presents data in tables that lets users define, view and query the database. Being very flexible they can navigate through the available data in the way that is most important and meaningful to the direct marketer at that specific time. They make hierarchical or flat file databases look antiquated and past their sell by date.

S. Selective binding, pioneered by R. R. Donnelley in the USA, enables the reader of a publication to select only those interests, sports or hobbies to be covered in their personal copy that they require, and it enables the magazine to personalise any article, advertisement or offer to their reader and his family.

T. Telephone systems providers will offer fully integrated media opportunities to the direct marketer via digitised technology transmissions, videos, TV programmes and cabled networks, viz. the recent purchase of aging film companies by major world wide telecoms conglomerates. This will enable video to be called up on telephone lines with additional advertising opportunities becoming available.

U. User friendly technology will mean the demise of the PC and keyboard. Apple Newton and its competitors will take the technology out of electronic communication. Already it is possible in USA to hold your telephone next to the TV while the touch tone bleeps are broadcast to ensure immediate response dialling.

V. *Voice-activated response* is already in use and has been successful in sales promotion tele response campaigns for Marlborough cigarettes. At present it is crude and impersonal but once developed and empowered it will be capable of handling huge amounts of peak time telephone response and data gathering. Misuse of overlong questions on high tariff calls is the downside risk of ultimate credibility.

W. *Workstation technology* means that workstations and high-end personal computers take over the database functions once performed by main frames or mini computers. Thus more companies are empowering individuals and departments to manage their own stand-alone database, especially marketing databases. Relational databases will restructure the repositories of information power in business. Problems will result due to the lack of personnel capable of operating these systems.

X. *Xpert systems* encode the knowledge of human experts into logic that non-experts can use, and are used in pattern matching in predictive modelling techniques by a database direct marketing analysts. They can aid the design of new formats, credit screening and scoring, fraud detection by financial direct marketers and for instant onscreen data for inbound telemarketing calls.

Y. *Yuppie syndrome* is a classic example of hierarchical database mentality that is overcome by relational database management. They still exist, but their lifestyles and consequent lifestyle needs will have changed and should have been tracked. Yuppies used to become Dinkys (double income no kids yet) but are now more likely to be Acorn Group B4.10 Affluent Working Families with Mortgages, or if less successful Acorn Group E.12 36 White Collar workers, home owning in multi-ethnic areas with young families.

Z. *Zap*-proofing your TV direct response advertising to prevent an immediate and almost involuntary button pressing syndrome when the ads commence involves techniques developed over the last 10 years by both stations and their advertisers. The key lies in timing the station announcements, programmes and advertising so they are both seamless and unpredictable. Otherwise the technique of 'roadblocking' is used with simultaneous airings on multiple channels, plus the use of half hour 'infomercials'. Roadblocking is already in use on the satellite channels whereby commercial breaks are synchronised between several channels.

Michael York Palmer is managing director of Response Marketing Limited.

MAKING LOYAL CUSTOMERS

David Perkins

Loyalty marketing is the key to customer retention: a long-term approach which focuses on profits and centres on better customer targeting through the collection of vital choice data.

You may not realise it, but your best customers are those you already have. Keeping them will cut costs and boost profits dramatically. Indeed, if you can retain an extra 5 per cent of customers, you will nearly double your profits in around five years. Winning new clients is an expensive business; losing old ones is more costly than most companies ever know. Yet, ironically, in most areas of commerce little attention has been paid to the long-term benefits of the concept of loyalty marketing.

It is not just more profitable to retain a customer than to win a new one. The longer you keep a customer, the more profitable he or she becomes. In the credit-card industry, for instance, it takes almost two years to generate enough business from new customers to pay for the costs of acquiring their custom. So, if a rival woos the customer away within that time, the original company loses money.

The loyalty, or otherwise, of customers has a direct – and measurable – impact on your bottom line. One programme, run by Carlson Loyalty Marketing for a bank wanting to enhance its credit-card business, achieved a 12 per cent increase in transactions, a 20 per cent increase in renewals and an 18 per cent increase in outstanding balances, with a commensurate increase in interest earned. In another case, a life insurance company raised its customer retention rate by 5 per cent, lowering its marketing costs by 18 per cent.

Improvement of customer retention rates rests on a number of things: knowledge of the individual customer; tailoring of products, promotions and rewards to that customer; and continuity of communication. This is where the advantages of a loyalty programme, as opposed to short-term, mass-marketing techniques, become clear. Knowledge of the customer requires the development of a continually expanding and enhanced database of information. The initial, and most important, source is applications for membership. Most loyalty programmes invite people to join a club. To join, they have to complete an application form, which asks for demographic information.

Loyalty programmes

Names, addresses, demographic characteristics and purchasing habits are analysed to identify the customers most likely to buy further products, and the products or services which they are most likely to acquire. The products, promotions and incentives are tailored accordingly, to support a regular flow of information to individual customers. Successive responses generate more information about their preferences, which is, in turn, fed back into the database so that the customers can be targeted evermore accurately.

Such extensive individual customer profiles help to reduce costs in two ways. First, a company is more likely to retain customers, rather than being forced to spend money recovering them from its competitors. Second, once the initial database has been set up, the company can serve its customers more efficiently and hence more cheaply. But loyalty programmes are not just about boosting profits through greater customer retention. They also provide an invaluable vehicle for cross-selling and new sources of profit generation.

Take the proliferation of frequent-flyer programmes after their introduction in the USA 12 years ago. The device of awarding points per flight, which could then be redeemed against further flights, encouraged customers to remain loyal to the airline. So successful have these schemes proved that many airlines now work in partnership with other operators, such as hotel groups and car rental companies. These partnerships are needed to increase revenue and to gather more information about customers' preferences.

The information provided when customers enroll in frequent flier schemes provides additional selling opportunities. The Northwest Airlines Worldperks programme, to take one example, now has more than 10 million members worldwide. The Worldperks database stores information about their geographic origins, gender and age. It also records the number of flights they take, the routes on which they fly, and when they do so. With this information, Northwest Airlines is able to stimulate business on a sluggish route or revitalise a particular market sector.

When winter route revenues are weak, for example, it can match known lifestyle data with details of past flights to preferred ski resorts and send out mailshots precisely targeted to the tastes of those members. Similar programmes cater to the interests of golfing enthusiasts. With such accurately pitched offers, the take-up is very high.

The airline industry operates some of the longest running and most sophisticated loyalty programmes. In the USA, indeed, 32 million frequent flyers have joined loyalty schemes, notching up 620 billion free air miles between them – enough to fill 590 000 Boeing 747s. But airlines have also learned the importance of investing selectively, because not all customers are equal. The well-known Pareto principle applies here, with 80 per cent of the profit usually generated by 20 per cent of customers.

For various reasons, some customers do not stay, no matter what added value or service benefits they receive. Referred customers, for instance, are often more loyal than those who buy on price promotions. Similarly, some customers generate greater value – a fact acknowledged by the various grades of membership which the airlines provide. BA, whose Air Miles programme is familiar to most people, even has a category of Platinum Card holders. They receive their membership by invitation only and are reputed to qualify by spending over £50 000 a year. Clearly, such customers are more valuable than those who fly from Heathrow to Manchester twice a year.

Loyalty programmes can be applied equally successfully in other, less obvious areas of business. For example, the Harvest Partners customer loyalty programme, which is operated by Carlson Loyalty Marketing on behalf of American Cyanamid, a US agrochemicals manufacturer, has attracted 370 000 members since its launch in January 1993. This scheme works with magnetic-strip membership cards which are wiped through a terminal to record details of the transaction, including what products are bought and by whom. But the technological complexity of loyalty schemes can vary enormously. A number of schemes use very basic smart-card technology. One such instance is the system operated by J Sainsbury in its Homebase stores. There, cards are used to record points corresponding to the amount customers have spent. They can then put those points toward further purchases. Mobil Oil operates a similar scheme in conjunction with Argos, and other oil companies are set to introduce their own electronic forecourt loyalty programmes.

These schemes encourage customer retention, but they fall far short of the true potential for building business, because they fail to collect data about participants which can then be used in the design and targeting of future products and promotions. More sophisticated programmes are operated by a number of hotel companies, including Marriott, with its 'Honored Guest Program', Westin Hotels and Resorts, with its Westin Premier, and Holiday Inns, with its Priority Club. On joining such programmes, customers receive a PIN number which enables operators to record and analyse subsequent purchases by type. They also complete personal preference profiles, which are automatically taken into account when customers make reservations.

Preference data collection

So if, say, a businessman wants a no-smoking room and a copy of *The Telegraph* each morning, he will receive them without having to ask. He gets the added benefit of a reduced check-in time, since the reception desk already has those personal details which would normally have to be recorded on a registration form. Similar schemes are operated by some of the car rental companies, with the same advantages of speed and convenience. Avis operates the Avis Express card, which allows operators to record a customer's home and business addresses, driving licence details and preferred class of car. Clients are thus able to check in and depart very rapidly.

Customers do not object to the collection of data on their preferences. On the contrary, it makes them feel that the services and offers which they receive are personalised. In fact, with the use of sophisticated software and database analysis, promotions are tailored to their individual wants. All this is a far cry from the so-called customer care programmes of the 1980s, whether they took the form of mints on pillows or fixed smiles at the reception desk. Such practices were certainly an improvement on the impersonal service of previous years, but they were also indiscriminate. When every company started using them, and every customer became a target, they lost their value as a differentiating feature.

By contrast, the feel-good factor generated through a loyalty programme is as personalised as its promotions and incentives. In addition, the benefits to the operator are quantifiable; one hotel which recently implemented a loyalty programme achieved a 2 per cent increase in occupancy, a 15 per cent increase in spend and a 24 per cent increase in length of stay. Try measuring how many customers a smile brings back!

A number of US car manufacturers have now taken the refinement of loyalty programmes a step further, with the application of tools from the finance industry. They have launched dedicated credit-card schemes which work like normal credit cards in every respect save one; the benefits accruing to the customer are tied exclusively to the car maker's products.

The General Motors scheme, launched in the USA in September 1992, and now followed by a British version, for Vauxhall, lets users credit 5 per cent of any purchase, up to $500 annually for seven years, toward the cost of a new GM vehicle. In this way, they could secure a long-term discount of up to $3500 on the purchase price. However, GM is not just securing future business from existing customers. Its database showed that half the first six million credit-card holders recruited did not drive GM cars. The company believes this is a harbinger of better sales prospects, since customers will naturally want to redeem the credit they have earned.

Even the most successful advertising campaign could not have delivered such long-term loyalty. GM has effectively attracted millions of potential new customers and locked them, together with existing customers, into a relationship that may last as long as seven years.

As the cost of media space soars and the threat from competitors demands repeated efforts to woo the public, a company may find its marketing budget spiralling, with very little to show for the extra money. The benefits of loyalty marketing are more tangible. They include a long-term approach and focus on profits. The various elements can also be measured, with demonstrable improvements in customer retention rates. Loyalty schemes are ultimately a valuable weapon in the struggle to grow profits.

David Perkins is managing director of Carlson Loyalty Marketing Services.

OPTIMISING PEOPLE
PERFORMANCE

WINNING THROUGH LEADERSHIP

Will Carling

Leadership is the main factor in enhancing human performance and is the all-important key to unlocking the latent potential of individuals, both in business and in sport.

Every individual has considerable potential which is seldom tapped and never fully utilised. Whether in sport or in business, everyone is capable of achieving more than they are at present, regardless of their capabilities, their education or current success and achievement. At Insights, we asked ourselves why and how coaches can elicit greater levels of achievement from sports people, and if these same principles can be applied to business people in business situations. Our conclusion was – yes.

Our research suggests that what people do, or fail to do, mentally, has a much greater impact on their success than what they do or fail to do physically. Everything that people are, or ever will be, depends on how well they use their minds. Psychologists believe that men and women use only 5 per cent of their potential brain power and, in searching for a key to unlock this vast untapped source of improvement, we have developed a simple formula.

The formula is widely applied in sport and has since been proven in the business world. It is based on the 'inner game' principles expounded by a number of writers, most notably Tim Gallway. There are three functions in the formula:

- Peak performance (PER) – this is the ultimate performance level which people are capable of achieving, but one that few ever achieve
- Personal potential (POT) – this is the latent mental and physical capability within everybody. It is variable and changes according to their experiences, achievements and environment
- Opposition (OPN) – this is the barrier which inhibits utilisation of potential to achieve peak performance and manifests itself in many ways. The most common is self-doubt, the effects of which can be devastating in both sport and business.

So our formula reads, quite simply: peak performance (PER) = personal potential (POT) — opposition (OPN)

By minimising the opposition, you can use more of your potential and maximise your performance. Your own worst enemy is yourself. It is you and how you think of yourself that directly affects your performance. You control your potential and you control your opposition. To minimise the opposition, people need to think of the self as two separate entities.

Two entities

Those who control the primary self, the entity that is the source of our self-doubt, and combine this with the secondary self, the entity that evokes confidence and belief, will find that nothing can stop them achieving their potential. But in management, as in team sports, that potential cannot be realised without involving others. And the collective potential demands something else – leadership.

In the cut and thrust of today's economic environment, leadership skills are more necessary than ever before. Leadership is the main factor in enhancing human performance and is the all-important key to unlocking the latent potential of individuals, both in business and in sport. Companies are now addressing the important issue of personal development, primarily because they want to recruit the most talented individuals they can find.

Those individuals are now more demanding, analytical and ambitious than ever before and consequently require more involvement in the results and direction of the team. Team members want to know the game plan, to understand their role and status in the team. They want to be part of the decision-making process, and to know what success will mean for them. They are willing and ready to work for it, but they need to be inspired, if the vast source of untapped potential within them is to be tapped. To understand leadership, however, you first need to recognise that there are two types of leaders:

- Transactional leaders – who get things done
- Transformational leaders – visionaries who can turn visions into reality through inspiring and empowering people to achieve more than they ever dreamt possible, and to enjoy doing it.

A truly successful leader is a mixture of both, one who inspires people into action, who converts followers into future leaders, and develops transactional leaders into transformational ones. Leaders, however, are subject to the same self-doubts as anybody else. Of all the judgments passed on a daily basis, in fact, none is as important as the one that people pass on themselves. Their potential is a direct derivative of self-esteem _ they perform in accordance with the image they have of themselves.

Lack of belief shows in the way people walk, talk and act. Since others see in you what you see in yourself, you can grow smaller in the estimation of the people around you. Leaders want to be the best they are capable of being. Start extending yourself, and you start to become all you could be. The task is to recognise your strengths and weaknesses – capitalising on the strengths and compensating for the weaknesses.

A leader will recognise the difficulties that some members will have in working as a team. By setting and achieving challenges, and in turn exposing the benefits of the team as a whole, a successful leader will generate good team morale and so build his team. By involving the team at each step of the goal-setting process and by both asking and listening to its members along the way, a leader creates a team in which individuals can channel their energy in pursuit of the combined goal. Teams thrive on challenge, where individuals may avoid risk. The outward signs of an effective team are:

- Trust between team members
- Pride that raises morale and generates a desire for quality in all activities
- Urgency that creates performance
- Enjoyment that generates persistence.

A successful leader has the ability to develop the bridge that takes his team from the present to their shared vision of the future. A vision is a picture of a realistic, credible attractive future – better than exists at the present. The leader must articulate the vision, inspiring and empowering the team to commit to that vision. Past visions determined the choices you made and the actions you took, resulting in where you are right now. Vision expands the horizons: the greater the vision, the greater the goals that will be achieved.

The purpose of goals is to focus the attention. Good leaders will have determined the defined goals and objectives with the team and identified the actions necessary to reach them. The task is to generate an environment of intense activity by inspiration and motivation, while clearly focusing on the final result. Leaders and their teams should together formulate a very precise and realistic set of goals to be achieved in a specific, agreed time-frame. The five key steps in goal-setting and achieving are:

- Determine the desired result (it must stretch and inspire)
- Agree the supporting goals (they must be measurable and achievable)

- Create the urgency, support and direction
- Monitor and measure the outcomes
- Fine-tune or change direction as and when necessary.

In sport, too many teams focus on the negative and consequently do not take risks and do not improve. Fear of failure is a major barrier, but players have to learn that failure is part of progressing. All the great teams and players have failed at some time. The best, though, never make the same mistake twice. It is important to calculate the risk involved. After that, a leader must concentrate on the positive outcomes, rather than the negative implications.

Optimists and realists

Once players have a positive mental image they can understand the reason for stretching themselves and take the risk. Sport is about competing and winning a game, not about competing to draw. In business, too, good leaders see opportunities in every challenge and are prepared to risk whatever it takes to make the vision a reality. They are not afraid of failure – failing is learning. The courage of a good leader inspires and motivates his team to take more responsibility for their own actions and so improve their self-esteem. The best leaders are optimists and realists. They focus on succeeding instead of trying not to fail.

Trust is the vital element that will sustain performance in the team. Integrity is the factor that will result from maintaining trust and credibility in whatever a leader may do. Without integrity there is no trust and so there can be no credibility. In sport, players are very perceptive. If a leader is not honest with them at any stage, they will sense it, and his credibility falls generally. In business, credibility is the foundation on which all leadership skills are based.

A leader must be visible to his team in order to inspire and interact and to become a role model for all the players. He must also accept that he is continually being watched by his team and that its members will pick up confidence or anxiety from his behaviour and manner. What stops leaders being more visibly effective? Insincerity, favouritism, lack of motivation, lack of recognition, poor response, or no response, lack of time – all these are enemies of progress. But there is plenty that you can do to improve:

- Think how the team will benefit from your actions
- Plan your actions
- Set aside specific time in your day to talk with team members
- Show them that you want rather than have to spend time with them
- Be a good example – behave as you expect them to behave
- Involve the team as a whole whenever possible
- Help the team to celebrate its successes
- Have faith – you are probably a better leader than you think you are
- Don't pass your personal doubts and fears on to the team.

Leaders recognise the talents and capabilities of individuals through inter-action with them on a day-to-day basis. This interaction will also produce immediate response in the pursuit of the goals.

Good leaders set the goals, commit themselves to these goals and pursue these goals with the assistance of the team and with all the ability they can muster. They know that the goals are achievable and the team is capable. Commitment is contagious. It gives a good leader the power to tackle and overcome the problems encountered, and its impact will remain long after the desired goal has been surpassed. Commitment and persistence are a prerequisite for good leadership and good teams – and both prerequisite and means of reaching any goal.

England rugby captain Will Carling is managing director of Insights Limited.

THE ACTION OF LEARNING

John Stanley

While management has become action-orientated, business school education remains unchanged. Action-learning programmes, with live consultancy work, are an alternative.

How should managers be trained, educated and developed? At first sight, the answer seems clear. They should go to business school. In the USA, the latter have continued to boom in numbers, soaring by 23 per cent to 670 in the latest decade, with their graduates rising by a third to 80 000. Yet the worth of MBAs and their training is being questioned – by employers and academics – more deeply than ever before.

From both business academics and, even more, from top managers, the argument heard today is that management has changed, but business school education has not: that the age of the highly numerate analyst, which the schools specialised in producing, is over, and that the day has arrived of the visionary, multi-faceted, team-working leader who makes things happen; in other words, who is action-oriented. That strongly suggests the need for 'action learning', a phrase coined long ago by Professor Reg Revans.

He argued strongly against traditional business school education, and rammed home the case for a quite different approach, in which students study real-life problems in other organisations and, most important, produce real-life solutions. There has been plenty of empirical evidence to support Revans' belief that action learning is highly effective. When tried, it seems to have satisfied all the parties – the students, their employers, and the sponsors who receive the action learners into their companies. This general satisfaction all round is certainly validated by our experience at the International Management Development Consortium.

The IMD Consortium now has several years' experience of using the action learning approach across many client companies in several countries. The first such consortium in Europe, and probably in the world, to be formed by a select group of the leading organisations who are its members, the Consortium is not tied to any business school. Its first programme, the Strategic Awareness Seminar, is now in its seventeenth year. It aims at directors and senior executives of recognised, significant potential who need to add the strategic dimension to their operational and functional experience: 642 delegates have attended during this period, and 30 per cent are now at main board or equivalent levels.

The Senior Executive Seminar started in 1984 as a parallel programme to the Strategic Awareness Seminar. It is targeted at senior executives who have experience of predominantly one to two functions (for example, sales/marketing, manufacturing/operations, research and development, finance, and administration), and who would benefit from broadening their commercial awareness; this course is where action learning came on the scene. The seminar revolves around the very issues which American business schools are now striving to include in their curricula – above all, the action-oriented management of change.

The live consultancy work, originally suggested by three of the committee members, has three prime objectives. First, it enables course members to apply in practice the techniques and approaches to general management issues taught in the first week of the two-week seminar. Second, the consultancy assignments enable delegates to determine which, if any, of these techniques and approaches are robust enough to use in their own companies on their return to work. Third, it provides an opportunity for teamworking and development to a challenging timetable.

In 1989, it was decided to extend the scope of the consultancy work and develop the programme to include a more international focus. Accordingly, this seminar was moved to Switzerland. The student/consultants have since worked on everything from professional hi-fi equipment to woodcarving and a cable railway. The client firms benefited in the usual way: for instance, in September 1993 one of the Consortium companies, Parker Hannifin, let the students into its Stuttgart factory – improvements and savings worth £250 000 a year followed in factory operations and marketing.

Action learning projects

For the client company, the live consultancy projects provide an excellent opportunity to obtain practical advice from a group of highly experienced senior executives, whose knowledge and know-how extend across a complete range of management functions. The team, moreover, is wholly objective in its findings: there is no possibility of individual influence or bias. As for the delegates, 20 per cent are now at main board or equivalent levels. The action learning projects have clearly developed their consultancy skills and achieved greater appreciation of how to improve business efficiency.

As a result, to give two examples, Ann Widner of the BBC was promoted to head three departments and became Head of Features for BBC Radio, having used several techniques learnt on the course, including SWOT analysis. Chris Earnshaw has become a main board director of British Telecom and chief executive of COMCERT, a joint BT/MCI company which is developing global communications from a base in the USA. The fact that these, and several other careers involved, have flown higher after attending a seminar prompted IMD to focus on younger potential high-flyers, too – managers, specialists and administrators.

The initial concept has been modified over the eight years since the programme was first run (in June 1987 in Cambridge) to reflect the changing development needs of delegates and the increasing demands of working for larger companies. Redesigned in January 1994, the programme now consists of three days of faculty input and eight days' working on the live consultancy projects. The days with the faculty are spent mastering the requirements: how to analyse businesses and other organisations in relation to their strategy, marketing, finance, organisation structure, internal systems and operations; plus the development of team-working and consultancy skills.

Consultancy handbook

The faculty of Bill Ball (business and financial strategy), Terry Mills (people strategy), John Stanley (organisation and human resources strategy) and Mike West (marketing strategy), has developed a consultancy handbook which includes models, approaches and techniques for use both in the company analysis and also on delegates' return to work. West, Stanley, and Sue Venables, the Consortium's training and resources manager, work alongside each project team for one or two days each. They assist with the initial definition of the project concerned, helping with the business, market, financial and organisational analysis, and challenging the team's findings.

Twenty-two courses have been held since June 1987, and 312 participants have attended. More than 80 per cent of this total population have received significant promotion – 20 are group or divisional directors and several have attended the Consortium's most senior programme, the Strategic Awareness Seminar. Perhaps somewhat surprisingly, given the consistent high calibre of delegates, less than 5 per cent have left their sponsoring organisations.

Delegates have been unanimous in extolling the benefits of live consultancy work, with comments like these: 'For the first time, I have been able to examine a whole company and understand the interrelationship of different activities – a challenging method of learning'…'I gained considerable value in working in another function (marketing rather than finance) and this has increased my confidence to seek a general management position'…'I satisfied all my personal objectives set before the course and was surprised at the high quality we achieved as a team. I look forward to seeing our client next year and learning what he has done with our recommendations'.

'The concept of the seminar is brilliant and the amount of learning that has taken place is immense. The collective input of the faculty was of a very high standard and I welcomed the practical approaches we applied to our client'…'An excellent project which stretched me intellectually, and I gained new knowledge which I can apply on my return to work'…'To me, working with my peers from a variety of companies on a challenging and live project confirmed the high praise I had heard from other colleagues who had previously attended'.

The success of working on live consultancy projects is indicated by the number of people who have used their new skills on their return to work. This success is also reflected in the overall value rating of the projects, which has ranged from 4.2—5.0 (the maximum possible) on average over the past four years. More than 45 projects (nearly half in Switzerland) have been carried out in a wide range of industries – electronics, publishing, manufacturing, furniture, hi-fi systems, design, transport, air conditioning, hotels and restaurants, leisure and tourism, retail, engineering, cable systems, railways and trade associations.

Project sponsors appear as pleased as the participants. For example: 'We were impressed by the speed with which each team came to understand our business, the depth of their market and business research, and the professional way they handled our staff and customers. We will recommend the consultancy work to other companies'…'We were highly delighted with the tremendous detail of the analysis, knowledge of our business, and originality of the recommendations'…'We were very impressed with the way the team related to our business and understood our key problems – this was clearly reflected in the action plan they recommended'.

Reports of success

'The quality of the analysis and the professionalism of the approach of the team has emphasised to us the value of action learning live consultancy work – the hallmark of this programme'. As this comment bears out, action learning teaches above all the application of management knowledge in practical situations (without which, obviously, the lore is useless). IMD's Business Management Seminar has plainly achieved its purpose of equipping team members with skills and attitudes that they can apply in their own companies.

Their experience goes to the heart of the business school dilemma.

OPTIMISING PEOPLE PERFORMANCE

The participant, quoted above, who said that he had never before been able 'to examine a whole company and understand the interrelationship of different activities' put his finger on the central reason why the IMD Consortium members have backed the action learning approach with such enthusiasm – and why the schools wish to travel the same road.

The IMD Consortium members feel that they and the students they sponsor have established a model which is well ahead in accumulated knowledge and relevance, and which is surely right. In developing better managers, action is where the action has to be.

John Stanley is a partner in the International Management Development Consortium.

THE REALITIES OF EMPOWERMENT

David Laking

Empowerment is accepted as a clear management aim for enlightened companies in the 1990s. But the realities of empowerment are far more difficult to identify.

It is one thing to say that staff are empowered, quite another to follow through and make sure that it is happening. With this in mind, organisations should be asking themselves what empowerment means in practice, how it happens, and what tools and mechanisms are available to support it. An ancillary question should be asked about why empowerment is happening, and whether companies have any choice when it comes empowering the organisation and its people. The answer is, first, that greater competition, globalisation and improved information technology (IT) and communications are putting pressure on companies to look at new ways of winning business.

There are also changes in the way that people work, and the way in which businesses face the customer. The automation of menial tasks means that staff today can spend their time in more meaningful work than in the past. A traditional manufacturing production line would not have benefited greatly from empowerment, for example, because each person carried out specific, precise tasks crucial to the whole process. In a 1960s office, people in the typing pool were not encouraged to think as individuals, but to plough through work at a steady pace as it arrived.

Contrast those two examples with a 1990s financial services company, where every member of staff is encouraged to put the customer first, rather than concentrate on the narrow margins of their particular job specification. Instead of turning the customer away with a 'you've come through to the wrong department' brush-off, anyone in the company can convert an incoming call into a sales opportunity. It may not mean selling an actual product that day. But building a good relationship between your company and any potential customer is a must in today's competitive times.

As well as empowering people, organisations are empowering their businesses. They recognise that regional offices or retail branches need access to information which allows them to make their own decisions, rather than just obeying inflexible orders from head office. The need for accountability is also driving empowerment. Individual parts of the business can hardly improve their performance if they are still being forced to toe the company-line in all aspects of decision-making. Given the evident force of all these factors, organisations which ignore the move toward empowerment do so at their peril.

How many companies in the UK have already discovered the benefits of empowerment? What mechanisms have they used to achieve it? And how successful are they really following this strategy? Following on from these questions, who should manage the process of empowerment? From where in the organisation should it be controlled? What role should the human resource (HR) department play in the empowered organisation? Research from Peterborough Software (*Bridging the Information Gap*, 1993) has already identified a severe communications problem between HR departments and line managers, many of whom feel that they are not given easy enough access to HR information. Without that information, say these managers, they are not fully empowered, nor can they empower their staff.

One of the problems emerging from our further research (*Bridging the Information Gap, Stage Two*) is that newly empowered managers do not always have the experience or knowledge necessary to manage people. They may no longer have access to central HR services, but they still have to perform HR-type services. Nevertheless, the research has found that the majority of UK organisations are already devolving responsibility for people management to individual line managers. The main reasons given for doing so include the need for line managers to feel more ownership of their people (34 per cent), to make local areas more accountable in terms of performance (31 per cent), to reduce the cost of the central personnel function (14 per cent) and the need for swift reaction to new opportunities (10 per cent).

Mixed feelings

'We believe that it is inherent in a line manager's role that he is responsible for his people,' is the word from one manufacturing site. 'The personnel function hijacked the line manager's responsibilities and it is time to get them back.' Another view is that '[empowerment] is a progressive thing within our industry. It has not got into full swing here – we have a long way to go to get shop-floor managers to accept a caring role for their own staff – they still think that support and training is a HR function'.

While most organisations may well be thinking about empowerment, this is very much a transitional phase. Some line managers welcome the new responsibilities which empowerment brings, others are confused by the process. They were never managed in this way themselves, and some may find it difficult to relinquish their power and authority to tell staff what to do. Over half of the line managers interviewed by Peterborough mentioned confusion and uncertainty as reactions to their new responsibility for people management.

All of this only stresses that empowerment is not something which can happen by accident. It is a strategy which must be understood and implemented from the top down, and followed through properly. Just throwing reluctant line managers into the maelstrom of new management techniques could do more harm than good. But Peterborough has found that the majority of line managers are already being asked to take on specific tasks which would traditionally have been handled by the HR department. Our researchers identified a list of 13 specific tasks from preliminary research, and respondents were asked how much line managers were responsible for these. Full responsibility was measured as 2.0 and no responsibility as 0. Most line managers were responsible for appraisal (1.63), absence control (1.42) and short-listing candidates (1.32). They were far less involved in tasks such as wage negotiation (0.54), succession planning (0.84) and dismissal (0.97).

Properly equipped

The first lesson to learn about the mechanisms of empowerment is that line managers being asked to take on these responsibilities must be guided through their new role properly. They need to know why they are being asked to increase their workload and administrative burden, then asked again later whether the new policy is working out. Making sure that line managers have the right competencies to empower their own staff is a crucial element for any organisation which needs to move forward. The research tackled this issue by identifying eight specific competencies and asking respondents to rate their importance, again on a scale of 0 to 2.0.

The most important attribute was seen as having good communication skills (1.92), followed by abilities to generate trust (1.84), develop team spirit (1.83), overcome barriers (1.65), develop a climate of openness. Also important were the abilities to build links between teams (1.52), think creatively and innovate (1.38) and gain credibility through specialist knowledge.

Apart from making sure that line managers are properly equipped, what else should senior management do to make sure that empowerment works? A first step could be to introduce the idea of a training, competency and personal development framework into the organisation. It is impossible, for a start, to understand the individual skills, achievements and potential of each member of staff without detailed records on a human resources management (HRM) system.

This kind of system can track a person's personal development, matching the training necessary to help that person progress to the level needed by the organisation. Competencies can be worked out for each job title, and a matrix designed to show whether skills held by people doing that job are suitable, or good enough. If they are not, then it is up to senior management to make sure that training is given to bring everybody up to the necessary level.

By implementing a networked HRM system such as Peterborough's Open Door, organisations can give line managers on-line access to this information. If a line manager needs to assemble a project team, he or she can work out from the system who has the relevant experience and skills, and whether they will be available at the right time. A second point to make is that organisations which have been successful in empowering individuals get the best results by involving everybody in the process. After all, doing so, rather than imposing one management's view on every member of staff, is a form of empowerment.

Senior management may think they know what every job entails, but it is those working at the coal-face and serving the customer who really know what goes on. By appointing somebody from the department to record competencies and training matrices, organisations can encourage a more effective buy-in to the whole process of empowerment.

When an organisation begins to dig below the surface in this way, and starts actually to communicate with its staff instead of managing them, it may unearth some disagreeable truths. Staff may be demotivated, because they have neither the competencies nor the resources to do their jobs properly. They may be delivering a poor quality service to the customer because they do not believe that they are treated well by their managers. They find it difficult to see why they should work hard for a company which seems to ignore their contributions.

Staff surveys

Brave senior managements faced with these issues are beginning to use the empowerment mechanism of surveying staff about their perceptions of management. As they would with any quality drive, they devise a questionnaire which asks for ratings about the performance of senior management. When these surveys are carried out every month (or even every week) senior managers can hope to start seeing their ratings improve, as new empowerment initiatives are introduced.

This is a crucial time for UK organisations. They appear to be on a continuum from little or no empowerment to something approaching the real thing. But they must be aware that talking about empowerment and making it work are two entirely different things. There are pitfalls to overcome, particularly in helping line managers and HR departments to change without a perceived loss of status and without confrontation. Proper training for all concerned is essential, as is a genuine commitment by senior management. Using the evidence presented by our research, organisations can begin to work out where they actually are on the empowerment continuum, and what benefits empowerment could bring to their businesses and their employees. Without that view, it may be impossible to keep up with those competitors who are already further down the track.

David Laking is managing director of Peterborough Software.

MAKING TEAMWORK REALLY WORK

Denis Bourne

Traditional team-building techniques are frequently ineffective, but modern-day psychometry using graphics workstations has produced some dramatic and surprising results.

Everyone believes in teamwork. Companies and their executives talk about it – some even build company slogans and advertising campaigns centred on the concept. The essential rules that will allow effective, coherent and mutually supportive teams to develop are well-known. Many businesses have invested heavily in new methodologies to encourage the emergence of good teams, and many have succeeded. Others have not.

What is so often (although not universally) observed is that where group members are at odds with each other, communications breakdowns are common and groups fail to sort out their own internal difficulties. Paradoxically, this can occur even where team briefings are applied, vision and values are expressed and emphasised, and objectives are clear. Supervisors work well and closely with their teams and provide the assistance and support that tradition demands – and still the result is one of fractured teams and lack of integration into the wider organisation.

Further observation suggests two common reasons why using all the traditional team building techniques still does not produce the required result. First, the processes that the organisation uses to get out its product are sending contradictory signals about what is and what is not important.

Second, the informal communications within the group are not supporting team-playing: this often arises from lack of skills in this crucial area.

To illustrate the first barrier, consider the case of performance-related pay. If this operates, with individual performance being measured and rewarded, especially if the measurement is less than totally objective or fair, two possible outcomes are likely. The first is indifference to or manipulation of the scheme within a work group whose members are in close physical proximity, do similar work and can operate in a mutually supportive way. A team may form, but it is more likely to be pursuing its own objectives, at the cost of the company's. If, however, at least some of the work-group members take up the PRP scheme with some enthusiasm, probably because the conditions noted in the first case do not exist, the result, more often than not, is going to be competition rather than collaboration.

The second reason for the non-formation of effective teams is closely related to the strength of the informal working links set up between people within organisations, based on their own needs to be successful and seen to be so. These links can exist between members of a work group and equally can and should exist between members of the group and employees elsewhere in the organisation. Moreover, the links are so strong that they can and do survive organisational changes that are designed to create new working structures and deliver specific business objectives. In such conditions, the old working links can actually be counter-productive to the achievement of the desired new objectives.

The problem, in the team-building context, occurs when these linkages start to produce tensions between the needs of the team and the needs of the external links. From one perspective, there is little harmful about these tensions, which many observers regard as productive – providing that the tensions are out in the open and subject to cross-functional negotiation where conflicts in objectives and priorities occur. The open confrontation of these conflicts and their negotiated resolution is actually beneficial to inter-team working and collaboration.

As common is the simple lack of needed communication and working links within the group itself. This appears mainly to arise through inattention to their development by the team leader. It is often assumed that if all the basics are put in place the rest will follow automatically. Sadly, the reverse is more often true. Many pressures on employees mitigate against the development of all the needed links within the team. These include excess pressure on getting results out; feedback systems including formal appraisal methods; failure to emphasise the need for developmental action focused on improving methods instead of just operating the status quo. That is closely associated with short-term, repetitive results, and can often be delivered by solo actions; improvement nearly always needs people to work in collaboration with their peers, in both the design and implementation stages of the change process.

Informal links

The whole difficulty with the informal links which develop within organisations is that they *are* informal and mainly invisible to the team leader. Short of personally supervising everyone in the team every minute of their working day (impossible as well as totally undesirable), there is apparently little the leader can do to measure the informal links between team members and between them and their colleagues outside the team. At least that was the case until recently.

Psychometry is not a new invention: Moreno did all the essential work back in the 1930s. The technique was first used for treating disturbed individuals, in cases where observation showed that they had few social or other contacts with other people. Psychometry maps the linkages between people in both formal and informal groups, and it worked well where the numbers of people involved were small. The technique languished unused for many years, however, because the cheap computing power which is available today only started to appear decades after Moreno did his pioneering work. The early, manual applications were limited to no more than 10 or 20 people and the number of different ways in which links between them could be qualified was minimal. But the use of new software and powerful graphics workstations now enables detailed analyses of all the working links within groups and even whole organisations to be measured and assessed, with often dramatic and surprising results.

Databases

Typically, databases containing 250 000 to a million bits of information are used, with the number of links that can be presented and analysed in different configurations being anywhere from 1 million to 10 million. That is all possible in the space of a few hours work. Quite apart from the obvious fact that handling such volumes of data manually would be a touch difficult, the ability of graphical presentation to render large data sets into meaningful information and displays subject to easy interpretation is perhaps the key to the value of the whole process.

However, completing highly valid analyses of teams in organisations and their informal work patterns is little use if that information cannot be converted to positive development action. The power of the technology is best seen when its use is based on certain fundamental assumptions about the nature of the innate attitudes that employees have toward their work. The occasions when employees can be seen working passionately in order to fail are few and far between. When they do, the root cause is more likely to be something to do with how they are being organised or managed than innate to the individual. A safer set of assumptions would start with the belief that all employees would like to be very successful in their jobs, would like to deliver high-value contributions to the business (which they would want to be a successful business) and would like to have those high-value contributions highly valued by the organisation.

Where this is not the observed behaviour, the root causes are nearly always in the nature of the organisation and its systems and processes, which is where any sensible investigation of cause would focus.

The logical conclusion from the above is that employees are also likely to want to work in highly successful, integrated and mutually self-supportive teams, since this is a prime route to realising the other desires related to their own success. In which case, if the informal, communications and working links that exist within the team and between them and the outside world are a limiting factor in team development, then all that is necessary is to show members the nature of the problem, and they should work out the solutions themselves, which is exactly what happens in practice.

Network analysis is the modern-day application of Moreno's psychometry, and uses graphics workstations to measure and evaluate informal working links. The technique is questionnaire-based and very fast, so that information generated is used to change organisation behaviour well before it reaches its sell-by date. Because the design of the applications is always based on front-end research completed within the user organisation, the outputs generated always relate directly both to the needs of the business and its strategy, and to those of employees and their desire to be more successful.

Because the design of the developmental action that flows from the work is based on interpretations of the information generated by the team members, it is always based on their daily realities, and not on some distant and inaccurate vision of how the organisation is supposed to operate.

The outcomes achieved are often dramatic and always employee-driven. The issues of resistance to change, which so commonly accompany top-down initiatives, are completely by-passed, as ownership of the whole process is assumed from the start by the employees involved in the various stages of the application. Typical outputs include:

- Individual team leaders who discovered that they had a personal, one-way-only, top-down style that was inhibiting team formation and performance: the fault was recognised, accepted and fixed immediately by agreement with team members as new processes were adopted.
- Teams which discovered that certain necessary key working links between two teams that related directly to business priorities did not exist – this was fixed by team members while managers were still discussing the significance of the information.
- The strategy for change designed by an executive group was rejected by employees as representing too little change, not radical enough, and far too slow. The employee-designed plan was adopted by the executives and implemented with total enthusiasm by the working teams in the organisation – which was no surprise at all.
- The removal of redundant layers of management, after the analysis had demonstrated that they were inhibiting the ability of working teams to produce more output.

OPTIMISING PEOPLE PERFORMANCE

In all cases, performance did improve, often dramatically. Employee motivation also improved, although whether that was the chicken or the egg remains a moot and unimportant point. And in all cases the performance gains were free of any management intervention – except, that is, the intervention that gave employees and their teams the opportunity to take intervention-free action in the first place!

Denis Bourne is the managing director of The Management Exchange.

THE CONFLICTS OF CORPORATE CULTURE

Klaus Leciejewski

Globally, it is clearly emerging more and more that corporate culture represents a competitive edge for companies. Interim managers can help to create change.

In a world with increasing technological and economic harmonisation, corporate culture is one of the last remaining differentiators and, perhaps, the most difficult to harness and exploit. Indeed, for many it is impossible even to define. Corporate culture is, in fact, bound up with a variety of factors which are closely interrelated, specifically: the degree to which employees identify themselves with the company; the extent to which the company wields external influence; the type of management in the company; and the extent of the company's political responsibility in society.

According to the old Greek philosophers, *panta rhei* (everything flows) refers to the fact that the status quo is subject to permanent change. As the century draws to a close, men are more and more aware of the perpetual change in the environment. There is an increasing requirement for regular control, adaptation and thorough modification of even the most successful structures and behaviour patterns. Man is now bound to constant change – and this is also true for corporate culture.

The degeneration of corporate culture occurs from two ends: externally, it is threatened by the increasing number (and sophistication) of competitors. Internally, continuous success within a company leads to a change in the attitude of employees; for example, by confronting management with successively higher wage demands or taking advantage of a previously achieved status quo and disregarding the daily input necessary to maintain it. For many members of staff, a corporate culture which is apparently but superficially perfect will encourage insensitivity, increased demands and the tendency to become complacent. In this context, one can only wonder about the existence of a perfect corporate culture.

Moreover, there are some companies which have maintained a successful corporate culture for decades and then all of a sudden, apparently overnight, are confronted with competitive disadvantages. These types of companies fall into two separate categories of corporate culture: those with a clear-cut hierarchy and principal father figure, who then face the consequences of disorientation and managerial chaos; and those whose staff have developed a high degree of self-confidence through successful company performance, but then suffer from arrogance and loss of contact with the market (for example, IBM).

Every company should seriously question its specific corporate culture at regular intervals. This self- analysis is one of the most difficult processes a company can go through, since investigation of one's strengths and weaknesses can easily lead to doubts about overall company performance. The process of continually adapting one's corporate culture to the changing economic environment can be compared to a permanent balancing act – an effort which most companies try to avoid.

A company's culture reflects its inner state of affairs. First of all, it is determined by the company's management style, although corporate culture implies far more than that alone. The different styles ranging from 'law and order' to more co-operative styles are well-known. In most cases, management styles develop as a combination or variation of several different styles, and none of them exists to serve an isolated purpose. In the end, it is the company's long-term successful performance that determines whether one or another management style is suitable. A comparison of companies with respect to their long-term success over recent decades clearly favours the co-operative management style. The style determines the culture of a company, even though it forms only a part of its overall culture. An enquiry carried out by the Institut der Deutschen Wirtschaft in Cologne lists the 12 key elements for a model corporate culture (see Table 1).

Companies complying most closely with these key elements tend to be successful. This is the reason why corporate culture always constitutes a competitive factor; a company running into difficulties within its market, or a company expecting a decrease in profits, cannot avoid seeing such developments impacting on, and changing, its corporate culture. Our experience of change and crisis management at EIM shows that any attempts to modify corporate culture without implementing changes will not be successful. The crucial question is how the required changes can be implemented as quickly as possible in order to improve the company's actual condition.

Promoting staff's own responsibility	96.7 per cent
Teamwork	93.4 per cent
Increased participation of staff in decision making	92.5 per cent
More information on internal structuring of operations	91.7 per cent
Development of one's own potential at the place of work	89.2 per cent
Free scope for the structuring of your own work	86.3 per cent
Humanisation of working life	84.2 per cent
Consideration of the company's socio-political responsibilities	79.3 per cent
Labour organisation	78.4 per cent
Consideration of ecological questions	68.0 per cent
Flexitime models	53.5 per cent
Participation of staff in company earnings	48.1 per cent

Source: IW-Enquiry 1990, Elements of Corporate Culture, (N=241; several answers; shares 'important/very important').

Table 1. Twelve key elements for a model corporate culture.

Two-edged sword

Corporate culture and the demands which it places on senior managers provide a two-edged sword in today's tough economic climate. A strong corporate culture demands outstanding personalities at the top of companies – personalities whose very particular role is to take responsibility for continuity in the company. Equally evident, however, is the trend for companies to use skilled outsiders, such as interim managers, in very senior posts to effect necessary changes. Often their task is to ensure corporate development and survival in ways not possible without external influence. There is a tension between these two trends. The first demands a degree of consistency, personal commitment and leadership from the top. The second often necessitates radical change, complete objectivity, and a compulsory shock to the corporate system.

This tension is illuminating for many business leaders who are having to alter their companies radically to face a different future, but need to do so without losing the positive attributes which their firms already have. Is there then a contradiction between the competitive advantages bestowed by a strong corporate culture and the highly competitive benefits to be achieved in time of change through interim management? While a truly professional interim management company should make allowances for maintaining corporate culture, the question is bound to arise whether interim management as a technique inevitably endangers the culture's very preservation.

When interim management becomes necessary, change is usually desirable. Interim management, by its very nature, is *supposed* to produce changes. Indeed, the worldwide business community has come to expect changes and new developments at an ever-increasing pace, particularly in those circumstances where interim managers operate. To many, therefore, the preservation of corporate culture in itself seems to have no great merit. Before the creative tension between preservation and change can be fully appreciated, though, it is necessary to delve a little further into the realities of corporate culture. It cannot be viewed in an abstract way. It has to be seen in the light of the economic success of the company. There is always, understandably, a tendency to retain a corporate culture which has produced sustained success, to keep it unchanged and to consolidate.

The dividing line between the benefits this brings and the dangers it reveals is narrow. The specific culture of a company, sustained unchanged for a long period of time, can in the long run also lead to the company and its management cutting off from outside influences. Staff who have joined the management team from outside, and are supposed to bring in new ideas and improve responsiveness to different commercial conditions, often find themselves isolated and rejected. Identification with the previously very successful management, its image and products can be so strong that it leads to stagnation. This situation is very often faced by the interim manager, who comes up against a corporate culture which refuses to change and refuses to be changed.

His position is clear. He will be there only a short length of time. He is under no obligation to conform to the existing cultural structure. He is free of pressure and can effect changes more quickly and consistently than a permanently employed manager. For him, the necessary changes are not uncomfortable, but a fundamental part of the job. To this degree, he can operate outside the corporate culture. But at the same time he has to persuade broad sections of the management of the necessity of the changes he is planning. He can do so because of his personal experience of several different organisations. In a very short time, he should be able to assess the specific circumstances of the company and work with it, while remaining outside it. It is a skilled and difficult task, but one which, if successful, can bring the benefits of real, necessary change, without destroying the very fabric of the company itself.

Bringing cultures together

If this can be achieved within one company which is facing change, then greater benefits are there to be gained in the most difficult of situations – where two or more organisations (companies, partners, divisions or subsidiaries) face changes together. In the case of mergers, for example, the interim manager's experience of different organisations and their cultures puts him in a position where he can mediate between companies which begin from quite different stances. What is more, he can do so without being perceived as partisan toward either camp. His position is one where he has no personal axe to grind, and where he will be believed to be taking decisions in the proper interests of the joint organisation.

The tensions between coping with change through culture shock and safeguarding what is already good is the inevitable dilemma between baby and bath-water. But in hard, recessionary times it has to be recognised that keeping the status quo – safeguarding the bath-water – is just not enough. Brave management decisions *must* be taken, whether they are

THE CONFLICTS OF CORPORATE CULTURE

comfortable or not, and the most effective brave decisions manage to keep the good, and add to it.

Klaus Leciejewski is an associate of Executive Interim Management.

THE QUESTIONS OF MOTIVATION

David Evans

Human resources are invaluable to any business. Managers must be able to effectively attract, retain and motivate their staff in order to achieve optimum productivity.

The subject of motivation is often an intimate corporate concern. As with advertising, everyone is an expert. I have been writing about the subject matter for a decade or more; over that time what has changed? As a starting point, I choose the words of Kipling, like many Victorians a student of behaviour. I have corrupted the order, but not the sense, of his simple thought: 'I kept six honest serving men, they taught me all l know, their names are why and when and how and when and who and what'. The order of these questioning words is not as crucial as providing a reasonable answer to all of them.

In practical terms, the management attitudes of the previous 70 years, the period since Taylor created scientific management, have only just started to give way to an understanding that the human beings in businesses are assets – the most flexible assets and the only ones in the business mix that are able to be infinitely responsive.

Tradition in the formalised motivational incentive business is not ancient. In real terms, it dates back only to the 1930s recession when suppliers of goods turned to supplying incentives to stimulate sales. The formality of sales-led incentive plans was the staff of life for the industry, which burgeoned in the USA and made camps in Europe and other parts of the world via English-speaking locations. The forms of incentives have been many and varied, but all have included the notion of recognition as an important ingredient.

The 'why' of the late 1980s and into the 1990s has not changed a great deal. The target group has broadened and to some degree is a function of the general agreement that there is more to life than a transaction sale. There always has been, but when the general business trend is rising and the level of competition is not so fierce, why worry about customers when another is always coming through your door?

'Why' has become more important and broader in context. More important because customers are stronger and more aware of their power, broader because all writers on the subjects associated with business success have acknowledged the power and energy of all human spirits within the business, not simply those of managers and sellers.

Alongside the 'why' of motivation has been a fundamental change in the 'when' of doing it. Again, by tradition, the issue was dealt with by management only *in extremis,* when sales or profits were down: what can we do to get back on target? 'When' was then a function of isolating the period in which one technique or another, one plan or another, might be applied to a tight group who could make a rapid difference to the results. Today it seems that more and more managers recognise that the motivation of employees lasts for their entire life within the employed relationship.

In simple terms, the value of human assets has been acknowledged through their costs to the organisation. For while all Western businesses have been right-sizing, there comes a point where the people left in the business must receive investment made with some degree of consistency.

The next of Kipling's questions is 'how'. This is the Holy Grail of the subject matter. Here, everyone has an opinion and you pay your money and take your choice. In the parlance of the 1990s, it is my view that this is an environmental question. There is an old Harvard saying: 'in perfect conditions of temperature, humidity, light and all other variables, the organism will do as it damn well pleases'. So what can motivation environmentalists do to solve the riddle of 'how'?

Schools of thought

To some degree managers were tempted into the predominant schools of thought. Two pre- eminent schools were those of Abram Maslow and Frederick Herzberg. Maslow might well be described as a fundamentalist. He observed that rationally or instinctively, people seek a range of needs that start with physical comfort and ascend through stages of security, social acceptance, personal esteem and the nobler virtues of self-realisation. That can be accepted by most reasoning managers. However, it does not follow that, in modern environmental motivation, managers have to offer a pyramid analysis to find the routes they need for their people.

European perspective

Like many British businesses, Grass Roots has turned toward Europe for further expansion. To do so we commissioned a young, bright but experienced executive to do a European tour. The brief was to see the state of attitudes toward motivation and to seek out partners. The results were fascinating, if not encouraging. After a year of study, we had to conclude that Europe on the subject of staff motivation does not exist. In most countries, the processes undertaken were not very enlightened and the supply of sources for assistance were largely in a state which compared with the UK before the 1980s.

It sounded like an ideal opportunity, and some partnerships within various countries are in place or are in the process of being put in place. But in the usual tradition of this management services sector, it is being driven by economic short-termism, and we have come to the conclusion that progress will be slower than expected. Europe has started to embrace the fact that the quality issues are crucial and there is no shortage of management consultancy on offer. But we have yet to find firms that have taken a holistic view of the subject matter, whether they are clients, advisors and suppliers.

Each and every member of the EU is different, and the cultural questions have to be tackled at the outset. But the whole history of man bears witness that people need motivation, and thus we are certain, that if Europe is to succeed in the face of lower labour cost areas around the Pacific rim and beyond, its working population needs to be sharper, more focussed, better coached and more meaningfully incentivised.

The recent protracted recession was interesting for observers of the subject. It was sad to see how quickly management used the need for security to promote an environment of fear as a motivator. For the Herzberg school, however, the role of the manager is potentially very positive. Creating an environment of positive opportunity was at the heart of Herzberg's work.

'Where' do we apply this thing called motivation? Again, the idea rests on the cultural acceptance that all business functions impact on customers, and that in impacting on customers they impact on shareholders (public or private). The truth is that few ever did much about that acceptance. Possibly control-based corporate structures were to blame. The application of 'where' can be best illustrated through a sporting metaphor. Commercial life is a continuous relay race in which customers are the baton. They are handed from one part of the organisation to another. On too many occasions that baton is dropped or handled badly. In the new environment of customer retention, it is commercially suicidal to fail to recognise that every baton change matters.

If every little action matters, then the answer to the question of who should be motivated, must be: everyone who impacts upon the performance of business. Finding the money to fund this realisation is not the problem: it is there now, but it has not been applied in ways that allow measurement of its effectiveness. Since people spend the bulk of their lives working, management has a duty to inspire interest in the task.

What, then has to be done? The Mahatma Gandhi, not noted as a management guru, wrote 'if you take care of the means the end will take care of itself'. So what are the means to the end-game of happy customers, happy shareholders and happy staff? Here is a simple framework; each and every situation will provide its own complications, but there are always three basic ingredients.

Item one on the agenda is awareness. Management has the duty and right to communicate what may be required to succeed. Equally, staff have the right to know what that is. Those who have indulged in corporate newspapers, videos, and so on, will feel they have carried out this task. But it is a two-way street and relies on regular interaction. All people value direction, but not always through direct instruction. They appreciate knowing what is expected of them and receiving regular feedback on those issues. They also expect to know why they should be involved. Their ability to apply rational thought is as powerful as their manager's – they rarely choose to apply it because they lack a reason to do so – that is motivation.

The second great cause is that of ability. Education is a life-time necessity, and in traditional management terms means training programmes. We learn, however, by diverse means. A piece of Chinese wisdom, written more than 2000 years ago, holds that 'what I hear I forget, what I read I remember, what I experience I understand'. Taking these principles and applying them to business life is not onerous. It means that all actions need feedback, making managers and co-workers part of the coaching educational team. It also means that traditional appraisal must be supplemented, if not replaced, with more meaningful performance measurement – measuring the quality of actions, not simply the financial outcomes.

The final step involves that much-abused word 'incentive'. Writing in 1981, I made the insulting suggestion that the first profession was not what you might expect. It was after all a serpent in Eden that persuaded Eve that a certain fruit might change her lifestyle. Ever since she apparently swapped innocence and the rural lifestyle for the historic march to a consumer society, the incentive fruit has been viewed with suspicion.

The question of whether you need to reward right actions by employees or simply prompt more of these right actions is fundamental. Everybody needs goals. Prompting action is partly the role of setting objectives and also the tangible recognition of success in reaching them.

People in work are consumers of management decisions. Like the buying public, they can decide not to buy. If that happens, management has failed in its task. No matter who your stakeholders are, success depend on getting mutual goals. Perhaps the god of motivation is attitude and the Holy Trinity is awareness, ability and right activity. I will leave the last word with the Henley Centre. Its recent survey of chief executives asked what are the most important attributes for successful companies to have in the next five years? The answers were the ability to manage change; the ability to react quickly to changing customer needs; and the ability to attract, retain and motivate employees. If the last is not achieved the first two efforts will certainly fail.

David Evans is chairman and chief executive of Grass Roots Group plc

TECHNOLOGY'S HUMAN FUTURE

Peter Berners-Price

As managements face up to the technological challenge, few may recognise the human challenge that goes with it. Motivation and inspiration must be nurtured and looked after.

Over the past decade, the personal computer has made the transition from office rarity to business necessity. And over the next 10 years, the PC will become so much a part of business life that people will barely notice its presence. It will become as common as a telephone on a desk. It will also become small enough to fit into the palm of your hand, and will be an even more flexible tool than it is today.

Hewlett-Packard, for example, is looking to develop what they describe as a 'Swiss Army Knife' peripheral product, which combines cellular infrared serial technology with scanning, printing and network computing technologies. So with one hand-held device, you will be able to retrieve, manipulate, duplicate, create, store, distribute and print information. It is already possible to buy a computer, with hard disk and fax-modem, that fits easily into a jacket pocket. But whether management techniques will adapt as rapidly to take advantage of the new opportunities presented by this amazing equipment is a very different matter.

The changes in managing the information flow that this new technology will introduce present remarkable new opportunities. For example, it is already possible for people to take part in a meeting by using digital

PC networks without leaving their offices. In time, a manager sitting in an office in Bracknell will use a lightweight headset to take part in the meeting. As individual managers look around, they will see each colleague as if they were all in the same room, even though they are in their own offices in Dallas, Hong Kong and Rome. And the whole meeting will be set up within minutes.

When it is over, the computer will be capable of producing a verbatim record of the complete meeting on screen. If a précis or minutes are needed, the computer will offer a first draft, which, if necessary, will be printed out anywhere in the world, in the local language. This is just one example of the way exchanges of information will speed up. For example, instead of having to wait 10 days for sales and market share information, car manufacturers will be able to see what happened yesterday – or even today, as it happens.

Whether or not all these developments help or hinder companies will depend on the willingness of people to adapt to the technology, use it and, even more important, introduce the management processes that take account of it. This is the real challenge, because existing management systems are not designed for the level of entrepreneurial flexibility or decentralisation that will become possible.

Traditional corporate management structures tend to be based on the idea of a communal place of work, clearly defined roles, teams that rarely change and a set of functional priorities that were fixed years ago. The result is that a finance person goes to the office every day, reports to a single manager, and works alongside colleagues who have been in the finance department for years, with the sole objective of analysing and controlling company budgets.

In some cases, existing structures are actually counter-productive, because they control functions so tightly. For example, why should finance people not be confined to the finance department, just keeping track of budgets? Why should they be moved around, to get closer to the operational departments? Financial skills and knowledge can be invaluable in project management. This fact has already been recognised in many companies, but few have yet made the final, logical change and moved finance people out of the physical confines of the finance department into operational teams.

It is perfectly practical to do this, and there are clear benefits in doing so. Now that information can be moved around quickly and easily, even to a location where there is no telephone, by using cellular technology, there is no functional barrier to where any one individual can work. In the future, therefore, it will not be necessary for members of staff to go to work in the same office every day. They will be able to work on a much more decentralised basis.

Personal contact

The very fact that staff will not need to be in the same office every day to fulfil their functions may have practical benefits, but it also carries a risk. Senior managers may think it is less important to bring their people together at all. To some extent this will be true. If people can communicate by using digital highways, the Internet and all the associated new technology, in theory they should not need to come together to deliver or receive information face-to-face. The key fact that this theory overlooks is that most people need personal contact in order to function effectively.

For example, if teams are not brought together on a regular basis, people may run off in different directions like a cluster of unguided missiles. Managers will have to work harder to ensure that people understand and are working consistently toward common goals – even though those goals could be quite short-lived. In the future, everybody's business objectives will change very quickly, and the members of business teams will be changed very quickly, too.

Cross-functional teams will become a reality as the PC revolution allows companies to network more information. The increasing pace of business will mean that companies will be realigned more swiftly to reflect changing market situations. Some people will find all these developments easy to cope with because they are comfortable with the technology. Others will find it frightening. But as today's children make their way into employment, the proportion who see computers as a normal part of the environment will increase.

The vital factor that must not be overlooked is that information technology can never be a substitute for inspiration, motivation or imagination. These are the human qualities that companies will have to work hard to protect and nurture. Equally, it will be necessary to devote a great deal of energy toward ensuring that decentralised workforces are communicating both ways. Each person must be encouraged to give more information about what he or she is doing.

But the sheer volume of information processed could also cause problems. Companies will have to introduce disciplines to ensure that information is filtered, to avoid clogging PCs with data that is of no interest or practical importance. A process will also be needed to ensure that networked information is both understood, and can be acted on. This can be handled through an interactive process with the PC, making the recipient respond in a way which demonstrates that information has been received and understood, and that the recipient knows what to do with it. Diligent feedback, and intelligent monitoring must both become a fundamental part of the new management processes.

This reaches into the heart of the problem facing managers of the future; it will become increasingly easy to provide huge volumes of information very quickly, but the ability to turn that information into competitive advantage is what will really count. Leaders will have to spend more time finding ways to inspire people to use their imaginations, to look at things differently. They will have to find ways to help employees turn information, however creatively presented, into worthwhile new initiatives, worthwhile new actions and worthwhile new products.

269

Systems provide a management structure, people lead. In the new environment designed to help people to think and act freely, PC- driven systems will provide the management structure. Then, the synergistic interaction of management systems with human motivation activities will take businesses confidently into the new century. Yet as managements face up to the technological challenge, few may recognise the human challenge that goes with it.

In some companies, basic structures are already changing. But if they are to take full advantage of the benefits of the new technology, these structures will have to go on changing. This does not mean that office complexes can be closed down wholesale, because it is important to recognise that different people need different working environments – it is not given to everyone to be comfortable working from home.

Flexibility

Most companies will have a mix of people. Some are happy to work as a decentralised team; while others need the reassurance of the professional 'tribe' structure. So employers will have to be flexible. To start with, instead of saying that everyone must work from home, they may have to offer the choice. Then it may come to revolution. When the majority of employees are working on a decentralised basis, they will have to be brought together, and coached to network together, irrespective of where they are.

The brilliant technological era now beginning has come just at a time when people are realising that the smaller the unit, the more productive it is, no matter how big the whole company is. Ten to 20 people working together creatively can probably achieve more than 100 to 150, certainly more than 3000 or 4000. Indeed, businesses are realising that more can be achieved by empowering smaller groups to work together.

These do not have to be empowered on a geographical basis, or even close organisationally to each other. More and more companies are trying to lay the vertical management structures (what Jan Leschly of SmithKline Beecham recently called the functional companies 'silos') on their sides so that they become truly cross-functional. Firms are trying to get teams working together across activities in different parts of the world. So there may be a team working on one project with people contributing from London, Tokyo and Los Angeles.

This is an exciting shift. Individuals may remain part of a vertical management team whether they are in marketing, finance, sales or running a business – but at the same time, they may have responsibilities within a horizontal structure. In Spectrum Communications, for example, we have eight vertical operating businesses, but the individual who heads up our German operating business in Stuttgart, a part of the vertical management structure, also heads up a horizontal client account team globally. Through that team, he interfaces with five or six of our operating businesses. And our creative directors also network horizontally, ensuring consistent creative quality across the business.

270

The multi-faceted method of working that is the future cannot easily be reproduced as a traditional organisation chart. Through its networking capability, PC technology opens the door on new thinking. It allows firms to throw organisational charts away, pulling appropriate teams together very quickly to address new, given situations as they arise. Without doubt, the new communication technology is creating tremendous new opportunities. At the same time, nobody should allow the new equipment to dazzle them so much that they forget the human element. After all, without the people, it is all just plastic, metal and information.

Peter Berners-Price is chairman of Spectrum Communications.

INTO THE TWENTY-FIRST CENTURY

Peter Gardiner-Hill and Ivan Fallon

The art of corporate survival is increasingly going to be learning to live with change. What will life be like for senior managers 10 or 15 years from now?

Senior managers will have to learn to live with change. What new pressures, conditions, circumstances and opportunities will shape their working lives? How should they begin to prepare themselves now? And how can the leaders of the big corporations attract and train the next generation of managers to ensure their business goes on? Some things will stay the same of course: strategic vision, leadership skills and entrepreneurial drive will be – at the very least – as important as they are today. But they will be applied in a different way and in a different world.

Even today, there are many senior executives who have not fully understood the significance of global markets which have really only emerged in the past 10 years and mostly in the past five. Global does not mean international. Essentially it means one giant world market, with competitors in countries as diverse as China, India, Mexico and those of the old Eastern Bloc. It means wage differentials which run on a scale from five to 100 – the cost of manufacturing man-days in parts of China, Vietnam and Indonesia is 5 per cent of the wage rates in Germany, and less than 10 per cent of wage rates in Britain.

In the past that did not much matter, since these countries were mostly isolated and enjoyed neither the capital nor the technology needed to compete seriously. But that is no longer true. Today there are no boundaries on either capital or technology transfer – it is instantaneous. And with the entry of China, India, Bangladesh and so many other countries into the world economy, the size of the global market has grown from less than a billion to more than four billion people in a decade. It will almost double again over the next 25 years.

The industrialised and the developing worlds, which in the past lived off each other, are now meeting in head-on competition. US management is facing up to that, and discovering, as everyone is going to have to do, that the nature of competition today makes it impossible to survive on good operational management alone. Even 10 years ago, you could have done that, but not any more. In the future the chances of surviving on good operational skills will become even less. Managers will have to have a special kind of vision and leadership.

The life-cycles of many of the more recent products, in computers or telecommunications for instance, are getting shorter and shorter. There is an incredible difficulty in getting enough volume with a good enough margin to recover the research and development costs before the idea has been taken on by somebody else and it has become a price-competitive commodity. The high-tech companies are wrestling with this all the time, and that is a trend which can only get worse in the years ahead.

Again and again, when one considers the type of conditions and problems with which the senior manager of the future will have to cope with, one comes back to the same point: the need for ever greater flexibility and adaptability on the part, not just of the managers themselves, but of management structures. The prevailing mind-set will have to be: are we sustaining the nature of change within the business? Are we confident that we are changing fast enough? Are we enjoying change and being successful at changing? Change has to become a lifestyle, as opposed to being comfortable with what you have got.

Everyone at any level in business knows how easily bureaucracies create or recreate themselves. New managers entering businesses set up in the past five years have been astonished to find how quickly they have grown bureaucratic styles of doing things, simply because it is less challenging. The fundamental skill that the new leaders of the world will require is 'learnership'.

Even for the perpetual learner, one of the principal problems in the next generation will be distinguishing between the issues which need to be dealt with fast, those issues where a certain amount of intelligence-gathering will make for a better decision, and those which are longer-term. This will become an increasingly necessary skill for a top manager. It will be more and more difficult to read where the competition is coming from. So the question of speed of decision-making becomes all the more vital. People will develop a much better scanning mechanism for what is going to happen.

Scanning mechanism

The mechanics of that scanning system are already becoming available: but so far few organisations are good at using it. Today's older generation of managers may never learn to grapple with the issue, at least with any confidence or finesse. But their juniors will, and 15 years from now it is they who will be occupying the senior roles. The managers of tomorrow will have much more intuition into how to use this fantastic technology – turning a business upside down with it. There are dangers in that too, of course, but the opportunities far outweigh them.

There will be other fundamental differences. Flexibility of the kind required cannot be learned simply by working for just one company. Few managers will remain with one company, or at least one division of a company, for long, but they will gain experience by moving from job to job and between countries and cultures. It will be absolutely inappropriate for potentially successful senior people to be with one company all their lives.

Potential high-flyers will spend three to five years with one business in the early stages, learning what it feels like at the coalface – which means running a substantial operation inside a large group – and working in at least two of the three major markets of the world. The successful chief executive in the year 2020 will almost certainly have run an operation within more than one national culture – maybe American, European or Asian. He must also have played a significant part at the centre of a corporate conglomerate. Otherwise, he will not have seen the difference between the management style required by the leaders and the influencers, as distinct from the drivers and the operators. He will probably have worked for at least two or three different companies by the time he reaches his mid-40s and is ready for his move to the top.

To a large extent that trend of mobility makes loyalty a thing of the past. There has already been a massive shift. Employers simply are no longer able to offer lifetime contracts and therefore demand lifetime loyalty from employees. In the past, loyalty normally exerted at least 80 per cent of its pull on the employee in favour of the employer, and only 20 per cent in reverse. In the next century it will become 50/50 at best.

The successful senior manager 10 or 15 years from now will therefore not only be much more flexible and adaptable, but also more self-disciplined and self-driven. He will have to walk the fine tight-rope between looking for loyalty on the one hand, and offering less of it in return. Management will be critically dependent on strategic vision, and the skill to evaluate the talents of senior people. The successful manager will need to be able to encourage and motivate good people, as well as recruit and retain them. At the end of the day, it is the vision of the business, in terms of its markets, its technology and its people – who are going to be there to drive the vision – which will make the difference between success and failure.

Management structures will probably be very different, too, reflecting the changed relationship between employer and employee. In the future, the formal organisational chart, based on the old army concept of no more than eight people reporting to one, will increasingly break down into a much more amoeba-like structure (in fact, often the reality today when a person's reporting lines are drawn). People will understand what their objectives are in the context of particular projects or assignments. They will be planning, monitoring and acting in a number of different areas, probably with different reporting lines, and different teams. People will be much less threatened by the boss talking to someone below them on the structure; but equally the boss's sensitivity will need to be greater.

Organisational structures

Organisational structures will become flatter (they already are), with more outside specialists used. Management teams will no longer consist solely of full-time employees: consultants or specialists will be brought in on short-term assignments or for specific projects, as will regular advisors to deal with different areas. The nature of the organisation structure will be a mix of individual talents pulled together on different sorts of contracts and with different sorts of working relationships – some working part-time from home, some plugged into the computer system from their offices. There will be much more sensitivity among senior managers to the way individuals perform, work, operate, and to the way groups are relating and interacting.

In the past, too much attention has been paid to the traditional scoring skills of accountants and not enough to the soft skills, which are rather more difficult to measure. Accountants are very bad at measuring people assets, customer relationship assets, supplier relationship assets, technology assets and community interest assets. And yet all the commentators on management in big international organisations are saying that there are at least four basic stakeholders – customers, employees, suppliers and investors. If that is so, they all have to be cosseted, grown and managed.

Corporate culture, which has already changed out of all recognition in many companies in the past decade, will need to be much more open, because of the different ways in which people will be reporting. Training will be different as well: the nature of business school training is already changing. Even Harvard, which developed its reputation on the case study method, is beginning to realise that case studies by definition are historical, and are not necessarily applicable to future scenarios. Training is becoming a more practical mix between actual situations and academic thinking, with more and more academics becoming actively involved in business.

The new style of training will be aimed largely at helping people to learn more about themselves, to become more conscious of the influences on their careers, to think through their career ambitions and aspirations, both financial, personal and so forth. The mix of success and satisfaction will be directly proportionate to the skill that individuals show in planning and managing their personal careers and development.

OPTIMISING PEOPLE PERFORMANCE

At the end of the day, the feature that will count for more than anything else is good old-fashioned passion. The whole essence of career management is that individuals should understand themselves and their talents and their personality well enough and early enough in their lives to feel where their passionate commitment may be best applied. Ideally by the age of 25, and certainly by the age of 30, there should be some focus. But if they have not found it by then, they must not stop looking.

Peter Gardiner-Hill is co-founder of the career management consultancy Gardiner-Hill Needham. He wrote this article with financial columnist and biographer Ivan Fallon.

THE BASICS OF BUSINESS

THE INTERIM SOLUTION

Nicky Cutts

Companies can now have knowledge and expertise only when it is needed, without the financial commitment of a permanent position. Interim managers are a cost-effective solution.

For the first time in many years, a totally new concept has begun to take a hold on British management style. One of the results of the recession, and the concomitant downsizing that many companies have undergone, should be to accelerate and to deepen this hold. Companies must ask themselves, before making any long-term appointment, whether such an appointment is necessary, appropriate or, indeed, possible. If it is none of these, yet a task remains to be done, that task will not be performed, and the competition may well steal a march. Interim management could be the way out of this cleft stick.

Take a look at what has happened to management during the recession: note that far more than ever before of the three million or so unemployed represent that sector. For obvious, if short-term, reasons companies facing a squeeze have made their more senior employees redundant. These decisions were shortly followed in some cases (of perceived necessity) by removing any middle management with nous and backbone. Anybody who stuck a head above the parapet got shot, leaving the nicely middle managers in middle place. Finally, there has been comparatively scanty graduate recruitment for three to four years.

So what are companies going to be faced with in five years? Few grey hairs at the top, average middle managers promoted, possibly above their natural ceiling, and few bright sparks beneath. What could, and should, companies be doing to prepare themselves? In its simplest form the answer

279

could well be to hire back talent, knowledge and expertise when and only when it is needed, possibly in the form of an interim manager. He would be paid when, and only when, he worked, and be expected to complete the job and would immediately afterwards go away. No PAYE, no holiday pay, no redundancy compensation.

This all sounds ideal, not only for the company but for the individual who, only recently, may have had his whole life changed through redundancy. But there is a catch. Not everyone makes a good interim manager. There are many early retired, or newly redundant, people who anticipate taking on interim management assignments to have something to do, and pay the mortgage/school fees. What is often not fully comprehended is that an interim manager's life is far more exacting during periods of activity than most usual jobs; and that assignments do not naturally convert into full-time positions. Most individuals who think about interim management do so as a means to an end – that of securing a permanent job. Anyone considering hiring a genuine interim manager should be aware that:

- They are committed to the way of life and sincerely do not want a full-time position
- They are over-qualified for anything they are asked to tackle, and therefore have a minimal job learning curve in any particular environment
- They will be outstanding people-managers...
- And outstanding salespeople...
- Generalist by background...and
- Task-orientated by nature.

For example, the managing director of a sawmill machinery manufacturer wanted to restructure radically. 'Strategically, the focus of the company had evolved into feeding the machine shop,' he explains, and away from the design and production of finished equipment. The emphasis was in the wrong place – it was time for a change.

'We knew what we wanted to do, but wanted to buy in someone who had done it before.' Although the metaphorical axe had to be wielded on the manufacturing side of the company, whole new skills had to be developed in areas such as sub-contractor assessment, contract negotiation and planning. The goal was clear: a flow of parts that would come not from one machine shop but nine, and a better factory layout that would yield an assembly flow to turn the parts into finished products more quickly.

Cultural shock

The interim manager brought in had the requisite skills. By working alongside the workforce, he helped the company to select suppliers and establish component flows. The cultural shock was immense: in many cases, people had been with the company for 30 years or so, and suddenly the old ways, and faces, were gone. Fresh doubts and worries surfaced constantly as the project evolved: constant communication was vital. 'You have to be absolutely inured,' says the interim manager, 'to answering the same questions over and over again before people actually assimilate what it's all about.' And you have to structure and present it in such a way that the employees believe that they came up with the solutions; otherwise, as soon as your back is turned, they will revert to their old working practices.

With a better layout and more efficient product flow, both leadtimes and inventory levels have shrunk. Capacity has actually increased, despite shrinking the workforce by two-thirds: the old machine-shop constraints can no longer hold back output. It was obviously an uncomfortable time: restructuring is never painless, and cuts on this scale can cause deep wounds. But both the managing director and the interim manager emphasise the latter's role in the change process: not as a hired 'Dr Death', but a short-term additional member of the management team, who possessed particular skills – and who indeed anticipated, provoked and controlled the change while the company profited from it.

But it is the remark made at the end by the managing director which underlies the skill of a professional interim manager. 'We did it ourselves. The interim manager helped us – guided us at times – but *we* did it. *We* own it. He was just a consultant.'

But there is an important distinction between consultants and interim managers. They form a continuum of a sort, the extremes of that continuum being that consultants advise while interim managers do. Put another way, when consultants have completed their given task, handed over their report and left, companies frequently need to bring an interim manager into implement their recommendations. This is usually because the companies lack the expertise and the time to carry out the exercise themselves, which is precisely why they brought in a firm of consultants originally.

In fact, the consultants have just done what any interim manager would do as a natural, initial, stage of *his* job – find out exactly what is wrong, in particular areas where reality differs from what is perceived. Used wisely, interim managers can be all that anyone ever wished consultants would be, but somehow never were. This is not to knock consultancy. There are many scenarios when advice is what is needed, and the implementation can be done in-house, and when teams of consultants can brainstorm ideas through. Furthermore, there are many occasions where consultants and interim managers can work effectively together, an avenue that some major consultancy firms are beginning to explore.

However, on many other occasions, hiring an interim manager would be appropriate where a consultant would be completely out of place. An example is the stop-gap – whether caused by short-term pregnancy leave or longer-term factors, sudden death or dismissal. For the small- and medium-sized enterprises, as they grow, there is frequently a need for in-house expertise at a level which is neither affordable nor indeed necessary on a full-time basis. A small firm can recruit a senior FCA as its interim finance director perhaps just for one day a week and will have access to all his or her experience at a reasonable cost. For the interim managers, this offers an alternative approach; instead of working on short-term assignments, they can work on a continuous basis as FD, human resources director and personnel director, for a number of clients on a part-week basis.

Other appropriate roles for interim managers are as members of buy-outs and buy-ins, acting as company doctors, when a new department needs to be established, or European distributors appointed for the first time – at any time, to recap, when a permanent appointment is either unnecessary or inappropriate. In the UK, furthermore, interim managers are relatively inexpensive; coupled with the fact that they carry no overheads, this makes them extremely cost-effective.

Hands-on experience

Another more subtle, but nevertheless significant difference between consultants and interim managers is their average age. Interim managers are not recruited straight after their degree/MBA courses. They tend to be well into their 40s, sometimes over 60, and are recruited for their hands-on experience and management skills rather than strategic thinking. Interim managers are concerned with getting the task done, not with company politics or individual stardom. They come in at a fairly senior level in organisations, carrying considerable clout.

Frequently they operate at a level beneath that which they had reached in the corporate world; as one who had flirted with interim management put it, 'It's a rather ego-bashing experience.'

Finally, interim managers are interviewed and selected on the basis of who they are and what they themselves have achieved, not on which firm of consultants they work for. Despite the opening remark, interim management is not new – it has just acquired a name. It is still, however, in its infancy in the UK. In The Netherlands, where its cost-effectiveness has long been understood, it is now automatically on management's shopping list.

British managements have been slow to capitalise on this asset for reasons that are unclear. It may be the underlying British attitude that not going out to work to earn a salary but rather working self-employed from home, is somehow not serious, that such people must therefore be second-rate: the 'if he were any good, he'd have a job' syndrome. It seems an innovative approach, and companies during and coming out of recession have been very risk-averse – added value has been lost in the mist of misconceived safety.

On permanent positions, companies have recently been tremendously, possibly dangerously conservative – gone are the days when companies would take the chance on someone who did not exactly fit the brief but possessed a certain something, a certain *je ne sais quoi*. Interim management is a way to bring back into the company other experiences and knowledge, added value without the financial commitment involved in a permanent placement. The risk/reward ratio works in the employer's favour.

Interim management is akin to outsourcing. The rationale is the same, but the rewards are potentially far greater. It is strange, therefore, that, while UK companies have embraced outsourcing, they have not embraced something so fundamentally similar and which, handled correctly, is a powerful tool in achieving the vital competitive edge.

Nicky Cutts is managing director of Barton Interim Management.

FACILITIES FOR COMPETITIVE EDGE

Keith Alexander

As competition intensifies, and as change accelerates, many leading organisations are re-evaluating the contribution that facilities make to business success.

Managements are beginning to recognise the business consequences of poorly managed facilities, and are searching for value that can be added through effective planning and management. Yet an organisation's facilities are often overlooked as a source of competitive advantage.

Few organisations fully recognise the contribution that facilities can make to business performance, or can identify the opportunities they provide for new business. Effective facilities management can impact on cost/income ratios, product lead-time, process improvement and other business indicators. Corporate attitudes toward facilities must therefore change toward managing them either as a business service or as a company asset. Facilities must be managed to offer service quality in support of key business operations. Managed together, to a strategic plan, facilities can offer a significant business advantage.

Surveys for the Responsible Workplace Study have identified pressures for change, workplace issues and decisions that organisations considered most important for the future. Key pressures concerned information technology/telecommunications and organisational structure. Workplace decisions reported to be most important concerned location, servicing the workplace, layout (for example, open or closed offices) and security/access. Organisations said that their most important future decisions will concern adapting the workplace to changing organisational needs while making it more responsive to users' requirements.

The study focused on organisations attempting innovation – introducing advanced information technology, devising organisational structures that can cope with change, searching for ways of increasing productivity and using time more effectively, responding to expectations for a safer working environment, and taking environmental responsibilities seriously.

The role of facilities management is thus broader than provision of the physical workspace. It entails integration of people, technology and support services to achieve an organisation's mission. It is concerned primarily with the quality of service to all stakeholders. The concept of workplace ecology includes considering the physical, social, environmental and administrative setting for productive activity. Design and management must consider the broad dimensions of workplace ecology to create conditions in which all needs can be satisfied and objectives fulfiled.

The starting-point of effectiveness is a clear understanding of the organisation's culture, in one definition 'the collection of traditions, values, policies, beliefs and attitudes that constitute the pervasive context for everything we do and think in an organisation'. In many ways facilities reflect an organisation's culture and are a clear expression of its values.

For example, a study in the early 1980s, Premises of Excellence, investigated how successful companies manage their offices. A survey of senior premises managers in these organisations identified a hierarchy of roles according to how central their premises were seen to be as a support to company operations. The results showed that, as the rate of change increases and the pattern of work responds to the increased take-up of IT, new concepts evolve from the view of buildings as mere containers, while mechanisms for managing them become more sophisticated.

The research showed that, with increasing pressure from users and technology, corporate attitudes change from treating premises as accommodation to stressing their role as a corporate symbol, with the emphasis on dominant location and impressive exterior image. After further pressure, organisations begin to consider the building as a tool of personnel relations and as an instrument of efficiency, with layouts and services designed consciously to aid productivity and support internal communications.

Levels of importance

The highest level in the hierarchy is something of an ideal. The building becomes an inspirational force, which overtly expresses the high standards of attainment sought from all staff – in particular, a commitment to excellence. The report identifies this as the goal of excellence in the design and management of premises. The realisation of this idea, in the view of the authors, implies:

- Harnessing the full potential of buildings for function and expression
- Realising and following through the building's implications for a company's culture
- Providing the management back-up necessary to achieve these requirements.

There is a link between the layout of the workplace and the management style of the organisation. Open-plan offices, with plenty of meeting spaces and round, rather than square, conference tables, suggest a democratic culture, but separate rooms are a sign of bureaucracy at work. Imagination, the London-based communications business, has created an attractive atrium, visible to everyone, to foster social and professional interaction.

Even the parking area carries its own cultural message. If there are no reserved places for senior managers, what counts is who gets to work first, not your title. What you see in your first impression of an organisation is what you get if you do business with them or go to work there. If the impression created in the first five minutes is lasting, issues like car parking, security and reception are much more important than generally recognised.

Cultural message

If the general appearance of the workplace is an indication of the way it is run, it follows that to alter the culture, you need to change the look of things. Microsoft, for instance, is coming to grips with the cultural implications of turning from a company of 'techies' into the world's leading provider of software in a market that is expanding far beyond its computer-industry base of a few years ago.

A weak or poor corporate image can have a powerful negative effect – dispiriting decor, or lavish and conspicuous spending, can convey the wrong meanings. An image survey can be revealing, and should lead the organisation to question how it wants to be perceived by others. Image consultants are now beginning to address the ways in which facilities convey an appropriate identity. The environments that companies create for themselves reveal the message.

Individual and group demands for quality of working life have, of course, to be balanced against corporate demands for added value and cost control. Conflicting requirements need to be resolved. A study by the University of Surrey differentiated between extrinsic and intrinsic factors in the workplace decisions, and showed a tendency among facilities managers to give corporate requirements priority over those of individual workers. There is, however, a big difference between taking account of users' perceived needs on the basis of current working practices, and taking a strategic overview of working practices and company culture and what can be done to change them.

The physical environment in which people work is one of the most

profound factors in *how* they work; organisational design affects building design and *vice versa*, and a change of location is often seen as an opportunity for profound cultural change. However, the personnel function is rarely at the heart of decision-making when it comes to the design of a new building or the redesign of an existing one.

A number of leading European organisations, though, do understand the importance of human resources to the health of the organisation and have developed appropriate approaches to building a better workplace by design. Standard Life, based in Edinburgh, has developed two new buildings, designed from the inside out in response to questions of organisational design and to user requirements. In another example, Vickers has shown that it is also possible to achieve 'greenfield performance without a greenfield'.

Health problems at work are also now recognised as a major factor in lost productivity through illness, absenteeism and poor performance. Considerable attention has been given to the role of the physical environment, and to the incidence of 'sick building syndrome' and building-related illnesses. But causes of health problems in the workplace cannot easily be attributed. Rather, organisations should provide an appropriate balance of facilities to support the needs of individuals and groups and promote the philosophy of the organisation, for example, providing an appropriate balance of space, leisure and recreation facilities – a working environment in which people can be effective.

Facilities are rarely treated in this way, as an expression of corporate values, a factor of production and a positive source of competitive advantage. Few management texts refer to their role in the search for excellence. However, there is increasing evidence that facilities can be tuned to organisational objectives, providing competitive advantage by improving corporate identity and staff morale, facilitating change, reducing the on-costs of business, and promoting overall effectiveness. Some basic business questions must first be addressed:

- What facilities are required to support the business operation?
- What are the most effective ways of providing them?
- Where are we now and where do we want to be?
- How do facilities perform now?
- What steps should be taken to improve that performance in support of the key business objectives?

Company policies for production, marketing, human resource management and finance all have implications for facilities management. These business decisions create the conditions for organising the provision of facilities. In turn, the extent to which facilities support business objectives will be determined by the opportunities of the facilities team to develop their full potential. The level of responsibility and degree of autonomy provided, and the commitment and encouragement given to improvement of quality, will determine the value that facilities management can add.

Facilities management

Appropriate relationships should be established within which people are empowered and decisions about the use of facilities are taken closer to the customers. The facilities team must be organised to achieve strategic control. The model of an enabling organisation, in which responsibilities for policy formulation and service delivery are separated, will promote more effective and business-like management, which pays more attention to customer requirements and value for money. Improving the quality of the environment and providing quality support services will be the result, and there is an extra bonus. It does not necessarily involve heavy investment.

Keith Alexander is academic director of the Centre for Facilities Management at the University of Strathclyde.

THE STRATEGY OF CLEANING UP

Waldemar Schmidt

Efficient cleaning is vital to the running of any business. Cutting costs while retaining value for money is the key to success; senior management must choose how to achieve this.

As European companies drive to cut overheads and contract out their non-core activities, the market for bought-in cleaning and allied business support services has continued to grow. If purchasing decisions are made sensibly, the scope for savings in large companies is significant. The secret is to cut costs while retaining value for money – something not always easily accomplished in the cleaning industry – and the decision should be a strategic one made at top management level, particularly where large budgets are involved.

The market for contracted-out industrial cleaning services in the European Union is worth 21 billion ECU, and is growing by around 5 per cent a year. This represents half of the total market for cleaning services, with the other half remaining in-house. While office cleaning is by far the largest market, there are specialised niches in healthcare and the transport and food industries in various stages of development.

Penetration varies from country to country, ranging from 65 per cent in Germany to 30 per cent in Denmark. Use of contract cleaners is sometimes higher in the public sector than in the private sector; in Spain, for example, 70 per cent of public sector cleaning is contracted out, compared with 60 per cent in the private sector (according to the European Commission's *Panorama of Industries*).

Why buy in these services from outside? In common with other outsourced activities, the principal reason is cost. Depending on the outsourcing route chosen, savings should be generated directly or indirectly by improved productivity, reduced headcount, reduced cost of materials and equipment through purchasing power, and administrative efficiencies. By switching from in-house cleaning to several competing contractors, a large company can cut costs by 15—20 per cent.

One major German property management company that wished to move from in-house to contracting-out awarded contracts to four separate contractors, including one worth $20 million to ISS. It estimates cost savings of 30 per cent on this contract alone. These were achieved in various ways. Headcount was rationalised dramatically and productivity in staircase cleaning was improved by 50 per cent. ISS purchased the customer's waste-collection trucks and invested in modern collection equipment. It also achieved 20—40 per cent savings by using its purchasing power to buy new snow- and ice-clearing equipment, while a single, monthly, itemised invoice resulted in administrative efficiencies.

Managing multiple suppliers can be expensive, moreover. We carried out a survey of a large Belgian bank, for example, only to find that it employed 160 different cleaning companies. By switching from several competing contractors to a single, long-term source, on a national basis, the cleaning budget can be cut by a further 10—15 per cent.

One of the UK's most famous historical landmarks wanted to rationalise 10 existing cleaning contractors as well as contract out certain in-house activities. It is now benefiting from 10—15 per cent in savings. ISS purchasing power is reducing costs in laundry and feminine hygiene consumables. Competitive rates in productivity, wages, and terms and conditions are now being applied to in-house activities, and the customer has flexibility in staffing coupled with a dedicated management resource.

Yet another 15—20 per cent in savings is possible by changing from input specification (such as required manning levels and cleaning frequencies) to output specification; that is, focusing on the end rather than on the means. I shall return to this point later.

These savings can be substantial. A building's operating costs for a given unit of area can be broken down into utilities, maintenance, security and cleaning. Cleaning, on average, accounts for 20 per cent of the total. We are currently negotiating an international arrangement with a large Swiss-based multinational which estimates that its annual cleaning costs are $150 million. We believe that we can take out 15 per cent of that figure, which represents more than $22 million.

Value for money

Sums of this order suggest that strategic decisions on sourcing of cleaning services do indeed deserve the attention of senior management.

Unfortunately, this is the exception rather than the rule. Cost, however, is not the only consideration. In the cleaning industry, it is easy to find someone to do it for less – quotes from the cheapest contractors can be as little as one-third of those from the most expensive.

But, at that level, service delivery and performance tend to mirror prices. Given that labour accounts for 60 per cent of total cleaning costs, low prices invariably go hand-in-hand with low quality and high turnover of staff. And, as cleaning quality is integral to external image and internal morale, poor quality can be more expensive than at first appears.

Value for money is ultimately more important than price, and savings can be allied to improved performance by changing the way in which the business is put out to tender. Cleaning contracts are traditionally awarded against tight specifications on manning levels and hours worked. This is understandable – the industry, worldwide, does not have a particularly good image, and customers feel that tight input specifications will ensure that they get value for money.

But issuing tenders based purely on input specifications merely ensures that contractors will compete on price alone. They may not necessarily be solving the customer's problems. Customers are often aware of this. Their attitude is: 'Oh well, all cleaning companies are bad so we might as well take the cheapest one.' And two years later, dissatisfied, they fire the old contractor and hire a new one. This is not the way to achieve high standards at a competitive price.

A more effective approach, which cuts costs as well as delivering quality, is for the customer to tell the contractor what he expects, not how to do it; that is, to emphasise output, not input. This does, however, require confidence in the contractor and a willingness to enter into a long-term partnership.

A good example is the cleaning contract for BAA's Terminal 1 at Heathrow Airport. Starting with output specifications determined in partnership with the customer, we designed a contract based on BAA's needs and on jointly defined quality standards. In the past, individual cleaners were assigned to do regular tasks, not in response to a need, but in response to a specification. The toilets, for example, were attended for 16 hours a day. That was the specification. But the customer's actual requirement is to have clean toilets. We now have a properly trained team which attends to them, among other tasks, on a needs basis only. This allows more flexibility and better resource allocation and is more motivating for staff than being assigned to clean lavatories for 16 hours a day.

Properly trained cleaners can now provide guidance to passengers, and audits already show a 20 per cent improvement in public perceptions of cleaning quality. The agreement between BAA and ISS embodies Total Quality Management principles, including close partnership between customer and supplier, a fundamental commitment to quality, the deployment of human resources of the highest calibre, and the ongoing pursuit of added value.

BAA had been concerned about the quality of cleaning in general and, in particular, that cleaning should not disrupt the environment for retailing operations, which generate more revenue than aircraft-landing fees. The contract specification was agreed between BAA and ISS to cover cleaning, waste collection and passenger guidance. Work goes on 24 hours a day, seven days a week, involving more than 100 workers.

New uniforms and equipment

Cleaning supervisors have full discretion to decide from day to day what needs to be done to achieve the standards agreed with the customer. This type of flexibility is critical in servicing areas that have heavy but varying passenger flows. The staff themselves were specially recruited and trained, and most have no previous connection with the cleaning industry. With the retail environment in mind, a special range of livery uniforms was commissioned for the employees, and equipment and rubbish trolleys were redesigned, with stainless-steel surroundings to hide unsightly bins. ISS invested £300 a head on training and uniforms.

In-depth cleaning takes place at night when crowds are minimal, and the day is given over to maintenance cleaning. Together with BAA, the customer, various cleanliness problems have been documented, and a rating system for the quality of cleaning has been developed with the help of the ISS Quality Institute. This system is implemented by both ISS and BAA, and leaves very little scope for disagreement or misunderstanding over expected performance levels.

In the first year of this two-year contract, BAA will pay slightly more than before for cleaning at Terminal 1. Productivity has increased by 30 per cent, but this is offset by the fact that cleaners' wages have been raised by a similar amount. Within that context, however, ISS is always searching for ways of improving productivity, minimising costs and continuously improving service levels.

As in all other businesses, image is important to BAA. It wants its customers to feel they are in a clean, orderly environment. One innovative twist in the Terminal 1 contract is the way, or ways, in which quality is monitored. Not only is cleaning assessed by ISS and BAA against clearly defined standards, but BAA also conducts monthly passenger surveys on a range of issues, including cleaning. So each month the company is able to measure cleanliness as perceived by its own customers.

Flexibility and attention to needs rather than specifications are features of another new approach being adopted in Scandinavia – day-cleaning of offices. Originally suggested by one of our customers, this provides bene-fits in both cost and quality. The idea behind it is that, while the office is busy, cleaners are better able to see where cleaning is needed. If the sales manager is away for three days, there is no need to vacuum his floor just because the specification says so. The result is increased productivity and more effective use of the cleaning budget.

Companies which contemplate contracting out for the first time are often put off by the human resources aspects of such a decision. Unions often resist outsourcing of any kind, not least because it may result in membership losses. Employees themselves do not welcome it because of perceived job insecurity. But it is standard practice – indeed, in some countries it is the law – for large contractors to take over many or all cleaning staff when an outsourcing contract is first awarded. When ISS took on the cleaning contract for Philips in Eindhoven, it also took on some 300 Philips cleaners, together with their pensions and other liabilities.

Employees who are subject to such a move soon become very positive about the change. Suddenly they are part of a large international service company where they are the core business, not just an overhead department subject to cost-cutting. They are properly trained and motivated. They can progress within the company, and we care about them, because they are important to our business.

Waldemar Schmidt is managing director of International Service System Europe.

THE WORKFLOW OF COMPUTING

Colin Starr

Workflow software minimises communication lead-times by creating a cultural shift — from dependence on a piece of paper to partnership with personal computers business-wide.

Most information systems automate paper techniques that evolved with the growth of the classic 1950s organisation structure. To date, most information systems have merely attempted to automate the path that paper takes and have therefore replicated existing structures. However, with the advent of business process re-engineering, and the attempted restructuring of businesses, managers are looking to IT to facilitate and speed their re-engineering. New technologies such as client-server architecture, relational databases, document image processing, graphical user interfaces (GUIs), decision support systems and workflow technology are being examined in more detail to see if they can help to implement new business strategies.

In essence, the goal is to allow people in the workplace to spend less time gathering data, to spend more time analysing data, and to plan more effectively to address the needs of the market-place now and in the future. However, all too often technology becomes an end in itself. Managers actually spend more time learning about the systems which gather and distribute information, than actually using them. Technology companies are now realising that access to technology must not be retained by specialist personnel, but that all staff must have access to systems capabilities and the analytical power they can provide with the minimum of training.

The combination of the GUI with client-server architecture has been the single most important step in distributing and providing access to information throughout the workplace, rather than centring information in an inaccessible data processing department.

A client-server system enables you to request a bar chart from the PC (the client) simply by pointing the mouse at the correct icon. Typing in commands or conferring with IT staff is unnecessary. The PC then passes the request to the departmental computer (the server). The server finds the figures needed, whether they are in its own database, in computers in other departments, in the company mainframe, or even on someone else's PC. It does not matter whether these computers are next door or scattered across five continents; the server and PC work together to sift through the data and pinpoint the information you need. Your PC then draws the bar chart. Intelligent networking conceals this entire data transport and collation process, so that after the original request the next thing to appear on the screen is the bar chart.

The need for better reports is just one of many factors that have fuelled the development of client-server computing. The underlying need has been to imbue systems with flexibility, so that users have the freedom to view data in different ways, to combine information from different sources, and to exchange it with colleagues. The arrival of client-server architecture coupled with GUIs has provided the stepping-stone for the birth of decision support systems (DSSs) and Workflow. Employees can now be empowered with information to support decentralised decision-making with a more flexible and proactive approach to conducting business, fostering flatter and more effective company structures and reducing traditional hierarchies, which are often propped up by the limitations of access to information.

Because most organisations over the past decade built up their applications library on a variety of databases, their corporate data structure has become both physically and locally fragmented. Take an organisation which maintains the payroll system centrally, but has distributed the personnel systems to individual sites, which are, say, geographically as well as functionally dispersed. DSSs, which include both applications and tools, offer a way to collect data from each of these applications and sites through client-server architecture.

Workflow technology

The distribution of information, automatically throughout an organisation, reaches its zenith with Workflow technology, which enables applications to automate the business process by facilitating the flow of information among related business activities and users. Workflow computing was introduced less than 10 years ago into project management areas to facilitate interdependent relationships among workers. In projects with critical interdependencies, such as software development, people continually assessed a project's status and had to alert downstream operations so that the next steps in the project could be initiated at the correct moment. Workflow provides the means to identify these interrelationships and build initial bridges between activities. The benefits of the application of Workflow computing were in abeyance until the emergence of client-server technology.

Workflow truly enables companies to take advantage of the investment in client-server technology. Effectively it minimises communication lead-times by creating a cultural shift – from dependence on a piece of paper to partnership with computers. The machine therefore notifies the users instead of the other way round. Before a detailed examination of Workflow begins, the following scenarios illustrate how the technology facilitates accounting events in a faster and more reliable manner.

Improved accounting

An accounting clerk receives an invoice for a desk bought by a regional department and captures the invoice document for filing. Many tasks ensue: accounting entries are automatically created, general accounting is notified that entries exist, to be posted at any time; the regional manager receives a message in his 'to do' list to approve the invoice, based upon pre-approved rules. When the manager selects the message, the invoice is displayed. The manager then issues approval, verifying that the desk arrived in good condition and that the invoice is correct. A message can then be sent to the next defined approver, such as the asset manager, noting that the organisation has a new asset.

The skeleton asset is added and the manager can select the item from his 'to do' list, triggering the asset maintenance activity. By adding asset-specific information for classification and depreciation, the asset is ready to depreciate. Meanwhile, the accounts payable supervisor can select the approval task from the 'to do' list, look at the information captured about the invoice and issue final approval. Payment is then scheduled. Approval and asset activities would normally be triggered by sending a hard copy of the invoice to the appropriate manager. In this example, Workflow capabilities facilitate the account recording and ensure that it is managed more efficiently and reliably.

The term 'flow' can refer to two things when discussing Workflow. Depending on context, it can refer to the flow of information from person to person, or to the flow of activities to be done, each of which is assigned to a specific user within the Workflow. In some situations, it can refer to sending both the task and associated information to the worker. The software enables the automatic routing of tasks and information based upon pre-defined sequences (such as the tasks involved in issuing a purchase order), or conditional situations, that may be ad hoc (while John is on holiday, all purchase orders are forwarded to his manager). This can be accomplished through a Workflow definition facility or 'agents' (automated task-handlers), or both.

The automation of these processes can improve business efficiency beyond anything yet seen. In most organisations, paper information moves from desk to desk awaiting approval and it is not uncommon for a document to be delayed for days. According to Delphi Consulting Group, the transfer of paper-based information may take up to 90 per cent of the time in the entire process. Workflow makes the movement of documents or tasks from desk to desk automatic, correctly routing the information to the next person without human intervention. Because delays are minimised, processes speed up. If a new market opportunity arises or a business restructures, the organisation can use Workflow to respond quickly and redesign its business process. Workflow can be categorised, divided according to the level of complexity, flexibility, purpose and structure. There are three types: production, administrative and ad hoc.

The *production* type involves complex, highly structured processing activities, such as loan applications, engineering change orders, product development and insurance claims. Many applications in this category involve tasks that fit a standard pattern common to a particular document type, such as insurance claims or invoices. Production Workflow is task-driven. Activity-driven Workflow can involve the same people, who repeatedly perform the same tasks, sending work to the next person in the flow for approval or processing. Production Workflow is enterprise-wide; that is, driven by repeated customer interaction. It must continually be refined and updated as new needs arise.

Administrative Workflow involves simple, form-intensive tasks like cheque requests, purchase orders and personnel procedures. A typical administrative procedure might be hiring new employees and providing them with a computer, phone, E-mail and user ID. Workflow typically uses E-mail as a conduit because it can be distributed across multiple locations. Its main purpose is to automate the approval cycle and route forms to the appropriate person. Because of its relative simplicity, an administrative Workflow system does not require frequent modifications. It is also typically used to process in-house work, rarely interacting with customers or other companies.

Ad hoc Workflow consists of repetitive, unstructured processes that may involve a different manager with each transaction – typically product documentation, sales proposals and product evaluations. For example, an ad hoc team may be set up across departments to assess company-wide downsizing.

As Workflow is such a new technology, there is much debate within the IT industry about its exact nature – with, for example, some confusion between groupware and ad hoc Workflow. In fact, the following technologies are incorporated in Workflow, but are not, of themselves, true Workflow.

E-mail

E-mail is often used as a conduit for Workflow processes, and people can confuse sophisticated E-mail products with Workflow. But E-mail simply moves messages across a network, without sophisticated data management tools for storing data, nor the intelligence to route an activity to the appropriate next person in the flow.

Groupware also allows users to share information within a group, with the aim of improving efficiency through a common database. Again these applications lack the ability to route activities and documents within the Workflow process intelligently. Also, Workflow is closely linked to the enterprise-wide business process, not just isolated collaborative groups.

Image systems capture, store and retrieve digital representations of hard copy images. While some of these systems can route their images across networks, they are often closed and proprietary. Typical image systems have been associated with document management systems. For example, some image systems can link an accounts payable form to a scanned invoice residing on a optical disk. The accounts payable clerk processes the invoice, then sends the now linked documents to the next person in the flow.

Although Workflow products are still new in the market-place, many organisations have clearly stated what they expect and are looking to this type of technology to show a significant return on their IT investments. However, a great deal of thought and planning goes into successfully implementing Workflow. An organisation must have a clear understanding of its business processes, and during the development of that understanding may choose to redesign or re-engineer them.

Re-engineering

Business re-engineering involves analysing how an organisation works and how it can work better. This radical process forces managers to ask fundamental questions about their business, such as why it performs particular activities in a certain way. When fully implemented, re-engineering strips away previously implemented processes and restarts the business from a clean slate. Re-engineering a business Workflow is problematic, because as the re-engineering takes place, procedures and structures are ever-changing, so the Workflow has to be constantly modified. However, as the company evolves its new structures, Workflow can be quickly and effectively applied to speed processes.

New or existing business structures need to be thoroughly mapped for Workflow to be applied. Every current business process can be defined, and steps can be eliminated to make the organisation more efficient. The interaction between cross-functional departments, such as sales, marketing and development can be fully explored and linked together through this emerging technology.

What characteristics are required by users in a Workflow enabled system? The most common are as follows:

• Rules-based reporting – an application should be able to route information, in many forms, to a predefined list of individuals or groups. There may or may not be rules associated with the contents of the information which determine who gets what. There will also be times when information is routed to two or more people who intend to take different actions.

- Tracking, notifications and priority – an application should be able to track the progress of any task, while providing an address with some form of notification as to the actions that may be required. Typically, the notification should include some form of deadline which will trigger a report or another action when it is exceeded. This would normally be proactive, giving each user a 'to do' list which is automatically monitored and maintained by the application. It should also be possible to place a priority on any task as it passes through the system. When an action creates a next step the user should be able to specify the priority.
- User-defined – it should be possible for the system users to modify the applications and change addressees and routes for any actions or next steps.
- Provision of the right tool for the job – where a specific package or screen is required to complete a task, the system should provide it without further prompting. An example might be a spreadsheet loaded with the appropriate data.
- External links – Workflow-enabled applications should provide seamless links to electronic mail and document management systems.

Users also demand that the Workflow software should allow exceptions to be programmed into the flow. The a fear is that Workflow is too much of an autocratic tool and may prevent on-going redesign of business processes, as procedures get set in computer concrete. What happens if a crucial member of the flow is on two-week vacation? Sophisticated exception handling should allow the administrator to program an alternate recipient while the employee is away.

Exception handling could also allow users to program their own exceptions in the middle of the Workflow – ones that may have not been anticipated by the application development. The ability to add processing steps with intricate branching will clearly distinguish a robust Workflow product from a less flexible one. Finally Workflow must be integrated with the tools that users are already running in their organisations. If users' needs are fully addressed and implementation is successful then the benefits of Workflow technology and therefore of the whole IT investment can begin to be realised.

Applications built using Workflow Technology, are task and event-driven. They eliminate non-productive activities and efficiently process others. At a very simplistic level, documents do not have to be physically transported from person to person, minimising delays resulting from the transport procedures and minimising internal postage costs. Documents are always traceable and available, allowing instant response to enquiries, especially from external customers. This automation of the information flow throughout the entire enterprise can result in greater speed in taking action or making decisions.

Individuals and their roles and functions can also be fully integrated. Control over tasks and procedures means that work effort can be better managed. Tasks are automatically routed to the appropriate individual, with notification of what work is expected of them. Individuals can also, using exception reporting, model the flow around their own work-style and decision-making processes, acquiring the right information at the right time.

Business procedures can also be formalised and monitored more easily. Work can be tracked around the organisation, making possible the auditing of bottlenecks and ending inefficient procedures such as replication of work in different departments.

Colin Starr is engagement director of Dun & Bradstreet Software.

SELECTING SITES IN EUROPE

Jan E Scheers

Increasing integration of the European Union's markets has caused major shifts in corporate location strategy. Assessing location options involves a series of judgments.

Many companies are starting to rethink the positioning of their production, distribution and research and development operations in Europe. But they are running into two complications. First, the gradual emergence of new markets in Central and Eastern Europe is encouraging some companies to shift their European centre of gravity eastward. Second, there is the overall trend toward the globalisation of both markets and corporate operations.

These factors are accelerated by the current economic realities of reduced demand and profits increased competition, and changes in comparative cost levels. All this results in opening new operating sites, enlarging existing ones and, inevitably, closing old ones.

Evaluating the location options involves a series of judgments. The first step is to determine which sites, if any, are appropriate to the new European order. Then comes the question of how to withdraw gracefully from sites that are no longer relevant. Finally, should you establish a new facility or acquire an existing operation?

The pharmaceutical and food industries are currently going through this process, as are electronics wholesaling and distribution. Their aim is to maintain market presence, sometimes in a more remote but more cost-effective location.

The process of making decisions on locations varies according to activity and industry. In high-technology activities, production companies are consolidating in areas where they can benefit from the availability of human resources offering the appropriate skills.

Distribution operations are also consolidating, as shown by the number of centralised distribution facilities appearing in Europe, particularly in The Netherlands where the government's Nederland Distributieland programme has been successful.

The corporate headquarters and administrative operations of many companies are also being reorganised. Improved telecommunications facilities are eliminating the need for duplication of supervisory operations at the centre and in individual markets. The Nike sportswear company, for example, in addition to consolidating a major part of its warehousing and distribution activities at a site in the Antwerp province of Belgium, has centralised all European management and administrative functions in a single unit based in The Netherlands.

In the case of marketing and sales centres, there is a marked trend toward the establishment of a central office that supports local offices. The central office performs administrative and planning tasks such as billing, credit collection, tax reporting, control of import and export across the external frontiers of the EU, and the preparation of a European marketing plan. Local offices are responsible for identifying new opportunities, customer service and order entry.

Choosing the right location now for future R&D is also important. Multinationals – such as Toyota, which has established its European product marketing development centre in Brussels – need to be in the right place to track the norms, tastes and demands that set European markets apart from those of the USA or Asia.

If a corporation concludes that one or more of its facilities is redundant, then the objective can be expressed in two words: damage limitation. As consultants, we strongly urge clients planning a facility closure to respect obligations to the community, in such matters as reimbursement of investment grants received, so as to avoid lasting damage to the company's goodwill and future status in the national market.

Few companies today can afford simply to walk away from an unsatisfactory location. Some US corporations tried it in the past, but the international arm of the law gets longer as the years go by. The costs of closure can be very high, especially because of the legally required compensation payments to laid-off employees. (Even with EU integration, the potential for relocating redundant employees to other company facilities in Europe is severely limited). The alternative, in the words of a Dutch development agency executive, may be to let the operation die on the vine.

Closing a plant involves a certain kind of discipline that falls well outside the experience of many business people. It is a painful process for all involved. So if the facility has some economic value and is not hopelessly out of date, like some of the old 'smokestack' sites, a simple closure is not necessarily the best answer. The property's reuse potential should be thoroughly explored.

One case handled by our company was that of a pharmaceutical manufacturer who had taken an option on a site in north-western France. The company had negotiated a generous incentive package from the regional development authority. But an unforeseen change in business conditions forced the project to be postponed indefinitely just before construction. So this was a case of a site that was never actually occupied.

French authorities were inclined to hold the company to its commitments, while we (as consultants to the company) were concerned about the effect that a sudden withdrawal would have, even if no jobs were at stake. With the high degree of government regulation and control in the European pharmaceutical industry, any loss of goodwill or credibility with public authorities can have serious repercussions on a company's business prospects.

So we proposed a site conversion formula to our client, with the aim of finding somebody else who would take over the property. With the client's agreement, we made a site and environmental analysis, and persuaded the development authority that preserving job potential was the key issue. Then we drew up a short list of potential acquirers and established contact with those companies. The result was that, within seven months, the site was occupied by a chocolate manufacturer in need of additional production capacity.

There are signs that European mergers and acquisitions activity is on an upward trend again, after a two-year dry spell prompted in part by the emergence of the Single Market. For companies rethinking their European strategy or moving into new markets, a viable alternative to a greenfield investment is the acquisition of a going concern. But there is one vital difference. In a site search the area targeted can be unlimited; for example, anywhere in the EU. But in an acquisition, the choice of target almost inevitably implies some degree of geographic orientation or compromise.

Typically, a merger or acquisition is a time-consuming process. Bringing two unrelated living organisms together is a risky business. The ideal acquisition is one where the interests in a deal are the same for both parties and where the markets, technologies and product lines are closely related. In fact, in most cases where acquisition is contemplated as an alternative to a greenfield investment, the underlying motive will be the opportunity to increase market share or to take advantage of the target company's existing market relationships and infrastructures, as much as its exist-ing technologies.

In such situations, acquisitions can be an attractive alternative. You can buy market share and presence, you can buy know-how, and you can also buy time. In the best of circumstances, a greenfield start-up will take at least 19 months from initiating the search to turning the key on the completed facility. Moreover, it may take years for a greenfield project to achieve full integration in the host market.

Of course, there is no right approach that applies to all companies. Both greenfield and acquisition opportunities should be considered by any company seeking to be a player in the Single Market. Despite the European recession of the early 1990s, these opportunities will grow as market integration proceeds and as the Single Market expands to include the Nordic and Alpine nations of the European Free Trade Area, and ultimately, Eastern Europe.

Jan E Scheers is a partner of Plant Location International (PLI), a subsidiary of Price Waterhouse headquartered in Brussels.

THE FUTURE OF THE OFFICE

Kathy Tilney

New technologies mean that companies are no longer bound by the rigid constraints of the traditional office. The alternative office will be the only competitive and efficient way to work.

New technologies have made it possible to work anywhere, and at any time. Everybody may still be talking, reading and writing, but the mouse and keyboard have in part replaced the pen and paper. The person-to-person meeting is increasingly under threat as voice and E-mail flash answers around the organisation before you have had time to walk down the corridor and consult with your colleagues. And this is all having a profound effect on how people carry out their work.

The company, for so long embodied by its physical being, is no longer bound by the rigid constraints of the office. A handful of companies have auctioned off the office furniture. In its place they have created what has become known as the non-traditional office; an integrated group of settings – such as home, car, hotel, central or satellite office – linked together by no more than the people who use it and the information which travels electronically around the 'office'.

This alternative office is at last delivering the gains in office efficiencies which were predicted long ago as computers democratised the workplace. It has also given birth to some fiercely competitive organisations which can muster resources instantly, leaping ahead of competitors still burdened by the expensive strait-jacket of a traditional workplace. Given its superiority, we believe that the non-traditional or alternative office is destined to become one of the norms.

Much of the research and development of ideas on non-traditional offices has been carried out at Cornell University's College of Human Ecology. In 1989, the college set up the International Facilities Management Programme (IFMP). Working with a consortium of private and public sector organisations, the programme is studying the ecology of new ways of working.

Currently its focus is on workplace innovations, introduced by companies around the world, which aim either to reduce costs or, more ambitiously, to enhance the organisation's effectiveness. There have been two broad approaches to establishing the non-traditional office. The first is driven by the need to reduce overhead costs. Not surprisingly, given worldwide recession, this approach became the preferred option for several companies. The second route entails property becoming an intrinsic part of managing the company's development. The goal is broadly one of achieving a sustainable improvement in the organisation's competitiveness.

Linking both the cost-driven and the strategic approach is the realisation that occupancy rates in the traditional office are extremely low. IFMP research has shown that across some job functions about 70 per cent of desks, offices or workstations are unoccupied. This figure remains fairly constant across industry sectors and geographic locations. If one accepts that offices can be managed on a non-territorial basis, so that employees no longer have a personal desk or workstation assigned to them full-time, then there is considerable potential to reduce facility costs and to use workspace to meet strategic objectives. In reality, though, our research among UK companies shows that most businesses do not know exactly how work time is spent, meaning that their ability to benefit from non-traditional offices is impaired.

Andersen Consulting's San Francisco office in California provides an early example of the alternative office. The consultancy was fast outgrowing its floor within a high-rise tower in San Francisco's financial district. Renting another floor to contain more consultants was the obvious option, but this would work directly against the desire to constrain costs.

Just-in-time approach

Based on an informal assessment of actual occupancy rates, the Andersen partner responsible for facility planning decided that he could either allocate about five managers to one office or move to a non-territorial office policy. Andersen named the latter its just-in-time (JIT) approach. Managers and consultants opted for JIT offices which promised more intensive use of space, reduced facility costs and lower space requirements.

In the new plan, 13 offices were provided for Andersen's 70 consultants, generating an annual cost- saving of $114 000, and a first-year total economy of \$505 000, which stemmed largely from reduced furniture costs. Consultants make advance reservations for their use of JIT offices, which only differ in appearance from previous facilities by having no personalised memorabilia. Managers have centralised storage and an individual telephone number, which transfers to any office they occupy.

Response among employees to the new system has been almost wholly positive. In post-occupancy evaluation tests, 90 per cent of respondents reported that the quality of work done matched up to previous performance; 70 per cent considered that the same or more work was completed; 75 per cent thought their accommodation to be as good as, or better than before. One significant complaint, however, concerned access to files. Three-quarters of the consultants felt this had suffered.

Variations on Andersen's San Francisco experience have been successfully applied in several organisations, including IBM, Ernst & Young and the Shimuzi Institute of Technology. While these companies have proved that significant one-off financial savings can be made, the innovations have not necessarily had an impact on long-term competitiveness. The business-driven approach, to use the term used by IFMP director Prof Franklin Becker, does exactly this. Non-traditional offices which are part of a competitive management strategy require nothing short of the rebirth of the organisation. The concept of the office moves from being a single site to that of a series of places, linked by information resources that work across time and place to bring the workforce together.

Status under attack

Real estate is no longer the inflexible strait-jacket for work. Nor is it the means by which a company manifests its hierarchies. 'Status is under attack. Companies are realising that it is far too expensive to use office space, furniture and fittings to reflect the individual's ranking within the organisation,' says Becker. Of 80 leading UK companies we spoke to, 83 per cent said that functions were no longer visually identified by the work environment and 53 per cent said that staff hierarchies were not evident from office design or layout.

The business-driven alternative office requires a fundamental shift in design. This is in contrast to the cost-driven approach; the latter can be regarded as a mathematical puzzle in which existing components are reformulated. For years, the driving-force behind the development of the office has been the desire to provide everything as closely as possible to the individual. Occupying his own workstation, the employee likens himself to an airline pilot sitting in his cockpit with everything at his fingertips. This goes against the real ergonomics of work, as Becker's research supports. People carry out different tasks best if they are given the flexibility of different settings. Rather than creating everything to meet the individual's need, the design of the alternative office seeks to create a group environment with different, integrated experiences for a more mobile workforce. By supporting the team as opposed to the individual, the alternative office becomes an important tool in changing the way in which people work.

Oticon, the Dutch hearing aid manufacturer, introduced an alternative office in 1991 as part of its drive to become far more competitive. Lars Kolind, Oticon's president, replaced the company's structure, culture and physical setting, and the very nature of work itself, all in one go. He regarded the office as the thing which expressed the organisation in its visible physical form, and as the factor that most effectively prevented people from doing a better job. Individual offices located off long corridors were replaced by a non-territorial office of unassigned workstations.

With all job titles removed, employees are part of one entity which forms itself into teams assigned to projects that evolve on a continual basis. People locate themselves according to their team, taking their mobile work-cabinets with them. To encourage communication between teams, all staff use the stairs. Coffee shelves located on each landing encourage chance meetings, while the lift is used only to transport goods.

The personal storage problems associated with non-territorial offices have been avoided by a move to a near paper-free environment. Almost 80 per cent of all paper has been eliminated. Incoming post is optically scanned into the computer network, shredded and thrown into a symbolic clear tube which runs through the building enabling employees to watch as the company gives up its paper dependency. Most documents exist in electronic form only. Oticon's staff describe this unconventional way of working as the ideal working environment. Kolind believes it has made the company's recent success possible. Profits and market share are both rising, and a new product has been launched in half the normal time to fill a gap in the market which none of Oticon's larger competitors have been able to match.

Computer company Digital Equipment has introduced alternative offices at several of its locations. Digital's dual goal was to increase the time that its sales people spent with customers and to improve teamwork and communication within the teams. The Stockholm office was one of the first to change its work environment. While personally owned space has been taken away, a range of incentives has been introduced. These include a kitchen, reclining chairs, sofas, cordless telephones and a conference room in the form of a porch swing.

Growing social function

In increasing its meeting and leisure facilities, Digital is recognising the office's growing social function. This reflects the trend among most companies which have moved aspects of the work process out of the office. Our research shows that 67 per cent of UK companies now regard their leisure facilities as inadequate for their long-term requirements. Has the Digital model worked? Management point to last year's sales figures which exceeded the 20 per cent target by a massive 60 per cent. Facility costs have also been reduced. Space has been halved, paper consumption is down by

70 per cent and cleaning costs have been cut by 60 per cent, while sickness rates dropped to zero during the first six months.

We believe that in time more and more companies will consider some form of alternative office in order to stay in business. Given the experiences outlined above, our argument becomes stronger by the day. Our role in developing the office will be less and less about creating a fixed workplace. Increasingly, we will help organisations to distribute their resources so they are as flexible and as close to the customer as possible. This will be the only competitive, efficient way to work.

Kathy Tilney is CEO of Tilney Lumsden Shane.

HOW TO FINANCE THE FLEET

Meryl Cumber

**Various methods of fleet funding are available —
hire purchase, contract purchase, contract hire and
finance leases — as well as outright purchase.
Which one is right for you?**

Purchasing vehicles, either with or without a buy-back or trade-in arrangement, remains one of the two most popular means of car acquisition used by companies (the other being contract hire). There are, of course, both advantages and disadvantages to outright purchase of fleet cars, not least the opportunity cost (which may be either positive or negative) of using financial resources for car acquisition rather than investment in the operation's core business.

Another tried and tested method of ultimately achieving vehicle ownership is hire purchase, sometimes referred to as lease purchase. Its prevalence, however, is declining as other, more sophisticated funding arrangements have been introduced to the market. The arrangement may require a three- or six- month deposit at the start of the contract and terminate with a larger balloon payment which need not necessarily be equivalent to the residual value of the car. Furthermore, while the agreement includes an option to purchase the vehicle at the end of the period (during which time the asset is hired), the vehicle user can choose whether or not to exercise that option.

The finance lease, a long-standing source of fleet finance is sometimes referred to as an open-ended lease. The lease generally conforms to one of two standard formats; the residual value lease or the fully amortised lease. In the former, the diminishing value of the asset is reflected in and determines the monthly rental, with a final balloon payment covering the anticipated residual value, thus offering lower monthly rentals than repayments on a bank loan for the full capital amount. In the fully amortised lease, the full value of the vehicle is accounted for over the primary lease period by the monthly payments. Under these circumstances, the lessee may often contract to lease the vehicle for a secondary period at a nominal rental. As with HP, the popularity of finance leases has been waning, but its fortunes may improve with the introduction on 1 August 1995 of new regulations governing VAT recovery which will adversely affect the viability of contract purchase.

Contract hire

Research undertaken by the British Vehicle Rental and Leasing Association among its members found that, of the various fleet funding methods excluding outright purchase, contract hire has consistently experienced high rates of demand over the past few years.

Recent popularity has been based on an intrinsic ability to shield the fleet user from all the risks of ownership, augmented by the option to hand over a proportion or 100 per cent (as in outsourcing) of the administrative burden to the contract hire company.

Future market penetration is anticipated due to the revised regulations governing reclamation of VAT, scheduled for introduction on 1 August 1995. In short, only organisations purchasing cars which will be wholly dedicated to business use will be able to reclaim the VAT paid on the purchase price, and since travel to and from work qualifies as private usage the new rules will be restricted to organisations for whom cars are the stock in trade, i.e. leasing operations.

Although the Chancellor muted the windfall by declaring that VAT would have to be added to the price of the cars when resold at lease termination, there will still be a net saving which leasing companies intend to pass on to their customers, thereby reducing monthly rates and enhancing the cost-effectiveness of contract hire and, indeed, straight finance leasing compared with other means of vehicle acquisition. The changes will also make contract hire a more attractive proposition for for fleet users which are partially or fully VAT exempt and so, in the past, have found contract hire a tax-inefficient option.

Contract hire, based on a legal lease instrument called an operating lease, is sometimes referred to as long-term rental, because, when stripped down to its core, the lessee hires the car for a predetermined period and monthly rental rate from the lessor. As noted, ownership, and all risks, rewards and responsibilities associated with it, are retained by the lessor; the arrangement does not embody a purchase option.

The monthly rental charge is not only derived from the cost of the car,

311

period of use, rate of depreciation and anticipated residual value, but also on expected maintenance and service requirements (on which the lessor takes a view based on detailed historic and manufacturer's data), annual mileage and what, if any, additional services the lessee decides to take.

Total annual mileage has implications for both the service requirements and the resale value of the car. Consequently, the lessor needs to have some idea of the forecast mileage before calculating the monthly rental charge. Underestimation may reduce the monthly rental rate but could also result in excess mileage charges over and above the agreed rental. Just under 40 per cent of BVRLA members offering long-term rental (contract hire) and leasing increased their excess mileage charges by up to 20 per cent during 1994, with a further 7 per cent of members raising them by more than 20 per cent. By contracting to keep the car for a longer period, a lessee can benefit from decreased rental rates. The harsher economic climate has served to pressure fleet users into opting for longer contract periods and lower monthly rentals.

In its barest form, contract hire covers car rental alone, though more commonly the agreement incorporates at least a standard maintenance package. Beyond that, most lessors offer a range of additional services which, depending on how many are written into the contract, can transfer varying degrees of the fleet administration burden from the vehicle user to the vehicle owner. Examples include relief vehicles to replace broken-down or damaged cars, insurance and claims management, fitting car telephones and fuel management. In 1994, 54 per cent of BVRLA members offered fuel cards and 46 per cent service cards as a means of reducing administration and increasing control over expenditure.

Lessees can choose from a menu of options to meet individual factors, such as the available budget and the existing level of in-house fleet support resources. Nearly three-quarters of BVRLA long-term rental members offer a claims handling service, 27 per cent can arrange insurance policies, and 54 per cent arrange gap insurance. Many lessors offer to arrange and claim on insurance policies on behalf of their customers because the exercise is generally viewed as time-consuming and therefore expensive; it can be more cost-effective to hand the process over to a dedicated third party.

All the parameters which impact upon the monthly rental rate are fixed at the contract's inception, though other services may be added to the agreement during the contract period. This ensures that the lessee has predictable outgoings and cash flow certainty for costs associated with vehicle hire and the range of services chosen by the user, while avoiding the risks inherent in vehicle ownership.

All capital allowances, subject to the annual £3000 limit, are claimed by the lessor, since it retains ownership of the vehicles until they are sold. The lessee deducts the monthly rentals from profits in the period to which the rentals relate; in other words, evenly over the full rental period. This deduction is subject to the same limitations under finance leases: a proportion of the rental for cars costing more than £12 000 is disallowed. It is therefore normal practice to invoice the vehicle hire portion of the monthly rental separately from any sums due for maintenance and services, otherwise the latter would also be subject to the disallowance formula.

The fleet user's ability to recover VAT on monthly contract hire invoices will also change from 1 August 1995. Where it has been possible to reclaim all the VAT levied on monthly contract bills, this will be restricted to 50 per cent on the funding element of the monthly cost unless it can be proven that the cars are used solely for business purposes. However, if the lessor utilises an appropriate contract structure which separates out funding and services, all the VAT can be recovered on charges for fleet management support services.

Since the tax and accounting treatments of contract hire are consistent, the assets embodied in the company fleet do not appear on the balance sheet, thus avoiding any potential gearing problems for the organisation. The arrangement also frees up other credit lines for alternative uses.

Another advantage of contract hire is the transfer of some or all of the administrative burden – as much as the lessee desires – to a third party specialist. The lessee benefits from the lessor's greater buying power and knowledge of the used car market, two key factors in determining the monthly rental, as well as the financial savings in fleet management derived from economies of scale. Some companies, however, may not view the abdication of responsibility for fleet administration as a key advantage, specifically if the fleet is of a size which justifies, in cost-effective terms, the employment of a full-time fleet manager and additional investment in the necessary support network.

While those opting for contract hire are shielded from the risks of ownership, they are also often prevented from benefiting from the rewards, such as lower than anticipated maintenance costs or an unexpected upturn in the residual value for a particular vehicle. There are early termination charges, though, in some instances, lessees can extend the contract beyond the original termination date at a discounted monthly rental rate to reflect the written-off depreciation; a practice which became more prevalent during the recent recession.

Contract purchase

Contract purchase is the most recent addition to the portfolio of options. It was introduced in response to the two limitations inherent in longer-standing alternatives: the pro-rata tax deduction disallowance on rentals for cars costing more than £12 000 and the double VAT burden on organisations unable to reclaim the tax on monthly payments. However, the introduction of the new VAT regulations will no doubt curb the viability of this acquisition method, not least because lessors' ability to reclaim VAT on cars' purchase price will bring more vehicles into the sub-£12,000 category. Moreover, since under a contract purchase agreement the lessor does not at any point own the vehicle (it is registered in the user's name), the lessor will be unable to reclaim the VAT on vehicle purchases, so

313

making the option less financially and fiscally attractive to customers compared with other acquisition methods. The core of the arrangement is either a hire purchase or conditional sale agreement – this may vary from lender to lender. Despite the similarity in name, contract purchase is never based on an operating lease, thus differing significantly from contract hire. However, like contract hire, and unlike the more basic financial structures on which it is based, a contract purchase agreement incorporates a menu of different support services from which the user can choose according to requirements.

The company using the vehicle agrees to its purchase through a series of monthly instalments, each comprising a proportion of the capital and an interest element. There is usually a final balloon payment, either less than or equivalent to the residual value. Economic ownership, for tax purposes, is transferred to the user on the date the contract is signed, as under a HP agreement.

Having gained legal title, the new owner can either keep the vehicle, sell it directly, commission the finance house as an agent for its sale, or sell the car back to the initial owner for a sum agreed at the contract's inception. The latter option relieves the user of carrying the residual value risk and is, therefore, the most common choice. It injects a key benefit of contract hire into what is essentially a purchase arrangement.

The tax treatment of contract purchase arrangements mirrors that of hire purchase. The assets must be shown on the user's balance sheet, but the user also gains access to the writing down allowances (subject to the £3000 a year restriction). For cars costing more than £12 000, a balancing charge or allowance is calculated upon disposal, which effects a full, if delayed, depreciation allowance. This contrasts with the tax treatment of contract hire for cars over the price threshold, where the user cannot offset all the monthly rental against profits and does not benefit from any form of balancing allowance on contract termination. Further, as long as the option-to-purchase fee written into the contract purchase arrangement is less than 1 per cent of the original cost of the car, the user can charge the interest element of each monthly instalment against taxable profit.

Meryl Cumber is a PR and communications consultant.

MANAGING THE FUEL COSTS

Keith Crichton

Whether a business is small or large, in the private or public sector, it probably owns or leases vehicles and bears the ensuing fuel and servicing costs. What role does the fuel card play?

More than half the diesel and petrol demand in the UK is for commercial (rather than private) use. Just take a look on the roads. There are trucks on the trunk roads, coaches cruising to the Continent, buses in busy cities, cars carrying sales reps, vans of various shapes and sizes, and the sirens of the emergency services. A fleet may comprise several thousand vehicles for service engineers in a blue-chip company or just one vehicle for a self-employed plumber. It may be the major operating expense for a haulage company or just one of several overheads that a business is trying to minimise in order to increase its competitiveness. The issue of improving fleet effectiveness is therefore relevant for most businesses. The solutions are manifold and depend on individual business circumstances. What role can card payments play?

Corporate charge card. On the face of it, if other business expenses such as hotel accommodation and air fares are purchased by a corporate charge card, then why not fuel? Whether a company uses American Express, Diners Club, or a corporate Mastercard or Visa card, this purchasing mechanism certainly gives access to a wide network of petrol stations.

There are, however, four main downsides, three of which come down to lack of control:

- First, such cards can be used to purchase anything – for example, sweets or cigarettes could be included in the transaction at a petrol station. These would not be itemised on the statement, which would simply indicate the location and the total value of all items purchased in the transaction.
- Second, there is no check that fuel is being purchased for the company vehicle rather than for the second vehicle of the household. The alternative – the fuel card – will overcome this by enabling cards to be specific to the vehicle, rather than the person, with the vehicle registration number being checked and entered at the point of sale. The registration number then appears against the transaction on the invoice.
- Third, there is no supplementary information on individual transactions. In contrast, when a fuel card is presented at a petrol station, the driver is prompted to give the vehicle's odometer reading. This subsequently appears on the customer's invoice, providing useful management information and input into miles-per-litre or cost-per-mile analyses.
- Finally, a corporate charge card does not enable a large fleet to secure any discounts off normal pump prices.

Garage accounts. This is still a common way of buying fuel, particularly for small fleets. Its main disadvantages are lack of network convenience, possible account-handling charges, and the administrative workload. A modern option which minimises the risk of manual errors is a local account card which is basically a fuel card limited to a single site.

Pay and reclaim. This simple system has the appeal to some businesses of putting the onus on the driver to justify and support his or her business mileage and fuel consumption by submitting monthly expense claims with receipts attached. (A fuel card relies on the driver crediting the company by accurately declaring private mileage and fuel consumption.) However, it is administratively burdensome for both the individual and the line manager; it does not provide management information for control purposes in a convenient form; and it limits a large fleet to buying at pump prices. Also, the payment of floats to individuals – which is associated with this mechanism – ties up valuable working capital.

Own bulk fuel tanks. Many businesses with commercial fleets that are parked in a depot (or depots) overnight have historically invested in their own fuel tanks. Then they order fuel at commercial prices from oil companies for delivery in bulk quantities by road tankers. The clear advantage of this mechanism is the lower price of fuel. However, in total cost terms this may be a more expensive option than an appropriately selected fuel card.

Any price advantage may be outweighed by the cost of investment in equipment and working capital; the operating costs of negotiation, ordering, maintenance, insurance and administration; physical and unexplained fuel losses; the costs of queuing and dead mileage (rather than buying en route); and, finally, the environmental risks, associated with storing fuel.

In effect, running a bulk fuel facility is the same as running a mini-service station. Economies of scale are critical in determining whether it is an economic proposition. Many companies are now either rationalising their fuel depots into smaller key networks of high-volume sites with modern equipment or even closing their bulk fuel facilities altogether on the basis that it is a distraction from their main business and a function which they should outsource via fuel cards.

The comparisons with alternative fuel purchasing mechanisms thus all point to the advantages of fuel cards. But that is just the beginning. Which is the best fuel card for a particular business? That depends on the following:

- *Network.* How large a network is required ? More important, what specific locations are needed to provide a convenient facility that allows drivers to refuel en route ? Is access to a European network needed?
- *Pricing.* What form of pricing is required? Options include pricing based on the pump price applicable to individual transactions, agency schedule (which tracks average pump prices) or commercial prices (plus handling fees). Is the fleet large enough to command discounts? Generally, the narrower the network selected (for example, just HGV-suitable sites), the lower the price. What trading terms are required? Card issuers will often offer a choice with corresponding discounts or surcharges.
- *Management information.* What level of management information is required? Will raw hard-copy transactional data contained on VAT-reclaimable invoices suffice? Or are further reports required that calculate miles-per-litre and cost-per-mile, or highlight suspect transactions where, for example, an odometer reading does not make sense? A preferred method may be to take the raw transactional data on a monthly floppy disc and input this into the company's own PC-based fleet management systems. Whatever method is selected, the management information from fuel cards provides a powerful tool for controlling costs.
- *Purchasing options.* What restrictions are required on allowable items to be purchased by the fuel card? Such restrictions are clearly marked on the cards and are encoded into the magnetic stripes so that genuine control exists at the point of sale. At one extreme, a fuel card may be limited to the purchase of diesel only. This may be widened at the customer's discretion to include all fuels and lubricants, car washes, other vehicle-related goods and services available at petrol stations, breakdown recovery, or even access to a comprehensive service and maintenance network of main dealers and specialist repairers. The latter itself is a major innovation that can save considerable adminis-

tration costs while still providing effective control (for example, repair authorisation) and access to a convenient network at competitive prices.

In summary, fuel cards are a simple and convenient way of improving fleet effectiveness. The surprising number of options now available on these cards can make step-changes in current business processes in fleet management.

Keith Crichton manages BP's sales of fuel cards and bulk fuels into commercial fleets in the UK. His international experience includes secondment to BP Australia as commercial transport and cards manager and graduation from the INSEAD MBA Programme in 1983.

The Complete Guide to Modern Management
Vols I and II

Edited by Robert Heller

(Vol I [1991-92]: HB, £25.00, 416pp, 234mm x 156mm, ISBN: 1-85251-105-2)
(Vol II: HB, £25.00, 448pp, 234mm x 156mm, ISBN: 1-85251-151-6)

A collection of studies by leading professionals, covering the entire range of vital management concerns, from strategy to logistics, in practical and concise style.

Subjects covered include global business, factory productivity, information technology, innovation, market research, total quality, human resource management - and many more.

Using these books is like taking the advice of top consultants - from whose ranks many of the contributors come. *The Complete Guide* is essential equipment for managers at all levels who want to know where management is heading in the 1990s.

ABOUT THE EDITOR
Robert Heller was the founding editor of *Management Today*, now Britain's leading monthly business magazine, and was also instrumental in the subsequent launches of *Campaign*, *Computing* and *Accountancy Age*. He has written many books, including *The Naked Manager*, first published in 1971, and *The Superchiefs* (also available from Management Books 2000).

'A dazzlingly good publication' *Sales and Marketing Management*

'It is like having at one's disposal advice from top experts, an hour of whose time would cost more than the price of the book' *Accounting World*